THE GRAYWOLF ANNUAL TEN:

CHANGING COMMUNITY

1993

Previous *Graywolf Annuals*
Edited by Scott Walker

One: Short Stories
Two: Short Stories by Women
Three: Essays, Memoirs & Reflections
Four: Short Stories by Men
Five: Multi-Cultural Literacy
(co-edited by Rick Simonson)
Six: Stories from the Rest of the World
Seven: Stories from the American Mosaic
Eight: The New Family
Nine: Stories from the New Europe

THE GRAYWOLF
ANNUAL TEN

CHANGING
COMMUNITY

Edited and with an Introduction by
Scott Walker

GRAYWOLF PRESS : SAINT PAUL

Publication of this volume is made possible in part by a grant
provided by the Minnesota State Arts Board through an appropriation
from the National Endowment for the Arts. Additional support
has been provided by the Andrew W. Mellon Foundation, the
Lila Wallace-Reader's Digest Fund, and other generous contributions
from foundations, corporations, and individuals. Graywolf Press
is a member agency of United Arts, Saint Paul. To these organizations
and individuals who make our work possible,
we offer heartfelt thanks.

ISBN 1-55597-202-0
ISSN 0743-7471

9 8 7 6 5 4 3 2
First Printing, 1993

Published by Graywolf Press, 2402 University Avenue, Suite 203,
Saint Paul, Minnesota 55114. All rights reserved.

Cover is an art quilt, titled "Frenzy,"
by Libby Lehman © 1990.

ACKNOWLEDGMENTS

The essays collected in this Graywolf Annual have appeared previously in publications as noted below. We gratefully acknowledge the
cooperation of editors, agents, and the authors for their permission to
reprint the essays here.

"The Companions of Duty" was first published in *Material for Thought*,
Issue #9. Copyright 1989 by Far West Editions.

Thomas Berry's "Bioregions: The Context for Reinhabiting the
Earth" is from *The Dream of the Earth* (Sierra Club Books, 1988).
Copyright 1988 by Thomas Berry.

Phil Catalfo's "America, Online" was first published in the *New Age
Journal* (January/February 1991). Copyright 1991 by Phil Catalfo.

James G. Cowan's "Aboriginal Solitude" was first published in *Parabola* (February 1992). Copyright 1992 by James G. Cowan.

Thomas Fleming's "A League of Our Own" was first published in
Chronicles (February 1993). Copyright 1993 by Thomas Fleming.

Jean Harris' "Finding the Gift in It" was first published in *Parabola*
(February 1992). Copyright 1992 by Jean Harris.

Stanley Hauerwas' "Discipleship as a Craft, Church as a Disciplined
Community" is from *After Christendom?* (Abingdon Press, 1991).
Copyright 1991 by Abingdon Press.

Václav Havel's "Politics, Morality, and Civility" is from *Summer Medita-
tions,* trans, Paul Wilson (Knopf, 1992). Copyright 1992 by Václav
Havel and Paul Wilson. Reprinted by permission of Alfred A.
Knopf, Inc.

Daniel Kemmis' "The Last Best Place: How Hardship and Limits
Build Community" was first published in *A Society to Match the Sce-
nery* (University of Colorado Press, 1991). Copyright 1991 by
Daniel Kemmis.

Jane Kramer's "Letter From Europe" was originally published in *The
New Yorker* (January 14, 1991). Copyright 1991 by Jane Kramer.

Lewis H. Lapham's "Who and What is American?" was first published
in *Harper's Magazine* (January 1992, vol. 284, #1700). Copyright
December, 1991 by Harper's Magazine. Reprinted by special permission.

CONTENTS

V. *Finding the American Tribe*

INTRODUCTION

Creating Community

"The trouble is everything is too big. There are too many people, for example, in the city I live in. In walking along the street, one passes scores of other people every minute; any response to them as human beings is impossible; they must be passed by as indifferently as ants pass each other in the corridors of the anthill. A style of behavior which refuses to recognize the human existence of the others has grown up of necessity. Just the scale on which people congregate in such a city breaks down human solidarity, alienates people from each other. There are so many people that there aren't any people; 7,000,000 becomes 0; too big."
— Dwight MacDonald (1946)

FORTY-SEVEN YEARS after Dwight MacDonald made that statement, we have passed beyond suffering "simple" alienation from a life once lived to acceptance of the condition of alienation as a way of life. Now we long not for what we've lost, but for a sense of community most of us have never experienced.

For thousands of years, humans have lived in small groups, for the days and months and years of each lifetime, secured by the bonds of absolute and proven methods of social discourse, and with very little contact with anything outside of the village or tribe. Our values, definitions of morality, and the structure of our societies are based on our experience of ourselves and others in community.

Nineteenth-century Europe's headlong rush toward industrialization, urbanization, and colonization permanently disrupted the dense weave of family, tribe, or village, and the deep rhythms of human lives resonant with those of the land. The twentieth century's technological miracles produced an incredibly shrinking world that has made us all one neighborhood, separated only by a phone call, a few hours' flight, or a tv screen. Even in the most far-flung areas of our neighborhood, people wear the same adver-t-shirts, the same running shoes, and hear the same stories told around the televised campfire.

In historical terms, this metamorphosis was sudden and cataclysmic. Its effects rippled through all aspects of culture, spurring profound political, religious, social, economic, and psychological changes.

Now, as a society, we are settled enough into those changes to begin to notice their effects. We feel the loss of individual identity, a lack of connection to our families, neighbors, and society, and an unsettling discord between our experience of life and our time- and-community-forged values. Political and social structures are breaking down.

We are feeling, in other words, a need to re-create community. This can't be done by going historically backwards, back to the land, tribe, or village. In the same ways we have had to redefine what constitutes a family in this decidedly non–Ozzie-and-Harriet age, we are searching for new forms of community. Many of the major strands of contemporary political and social movements may be seen as part of a general search for individual and community identity.

Finding or creating one's community can be an adventure in orienteering, as dizzying as when we learn enough about astronomy to place ourselves in space: we walk across the lawn; the continents drift; the world turns; the earth revolves around the sun, and the sun revolves in the galaxy; the galaxy revolves, even as it hurtles through space; and there's no accounting for what the molecules in our bodies are doing.

We are no longer able to define community simply as "these people in this place." We're faced with a complex set of options. We can find community through geographic location, geologic affinity (people who love the mountains), ethnic or racial cultures, peer and interest groups, regional and bioregional associations, sexual preference, linguistic and religious affiliations, etc. At the same time that the mass market works to blur the distinctions between us and we are faced with enormous pressure to homogenize, we must struggle to satisfy our basic need for community. Orienting ourselves in community is dizzying: we walk across the lawn; we are of x race, y ethnic heritage, and z gender; we think of others who share our passionately held beliefs as part of our family; we are citizens of the one world, our watershed, region, and neighborhood. . . .

The Graywolf Annual 10: Changing Community brings together many essays and authors who are variously attempting to understand our need for community and the ways we struggle to find it. This volume may be regarded as a natural extension of previous *Annuals* that explored notions of ethnic identity, new definitions of the family, and rise of the new European communities.

As in previous *Annuals*, this is not meant to be a definitive answer to any of these issues, but rather a provocative and stimulating gathering of some of the main currents of this important issue. We're pleased to present such a fine group of writers in one volume and recommend their other works to all readers of this book.

As the editor of record of this and most other Graywolf *Annuals*, I want to make note of the tenth anniversary of the publication of these volumes. Graywolf Press is a group of people—authors, workers, readers, bookstore clerks, reviewers—who care deeply about the work they do. We've always regarded ourselves as part of the family of the book, but have begun to see ourselves as part of a *community* of the written word. Ours is a community of people who believe in the use of clear, concise, and beautiful language and thought, in order to discuss important issues of the day. Graywolf Press – this entity and organization – has itself become more and more of a community, and I would like to take this opportunity to thank the staff and interns who make this good work possible.

I am greatly indebted to many members of the Graywolf community – and especially to Chris Faatz, whose curiosity, wide reading, and quick photocopying added immeasurably to this volume. Like most other *Annual*s, this collection is the product of a collective effort of understanding.

SCOTT WALKER
APRIL 1993

I.

THE

INDIVIDUAL

AND THE

VILLAGE

ELIEZER SHORE

The Soul of the Community

SEVERAL TIMES IN MY LIFE I have tried to escape the everyday world. In mountain huts, on ocean bluffs, in the still predawn hours, I sought a truth that I could not find among friends. Yet there was always something missing, something incomplete that kept calling me back.

Several times in life I have tried to enter the world – with community projects, group discussions, the routines of family and workplace. But I was always pulled back. Something was missing, an inner point was not being addressed.

Most true spiritual seekers, at some time in their journey, must struggle with the dilemma posed by these two opposites. While personalities differ, tending some towards solitude, others to community, most of us waver uneasily between the two, constantly searching for the proper balance in which we might best serve God. In the midst of joyous community celebration, a small voice can make itself heard, whispering in the pause between speeches, reminding us that there is something more. And in a quiet forest glen a peculiar loneliness echoes through the woods, calling us back to the world, to share ourselves with others.

The greatness of community is that it provides man with a context for his life. Before we can know God, we must come to know ourselves. Without a sense of identity, a person cannot be whole; it is community that provides man with his name. The social relationships, the responsibilities, the larger values, all help us know who we are. In an ideal community, a person's place would be so clearly defined as to make him indispensable. This engenders a sort of horizontal growth, as our lives touch and are touched by many others, and it fosters in us a greater compassion and awareness of the human condition. In Judaism, we find the ultimate curse to be that of exile, the dispersion of community, the loss of one's place.

On the other hand, solitude speaks to the part of us that has no name, that wants to break free of the limitations imposed upon us by the thoughts and expectations of others. Solitude holds the promise of such complete and utter commitment to God – pure vertical growth – that one completely transcends the mundane concerns of this world and moves into a realm of pure spirit. There, everything is good, everything is holy, and God alone is real. "Abraham was one," say the verse (Ezekiel 33:24). Like our father Abraham, a person who wants only God must learn to be one and alone.

The validity of both these positions, and the pull they exert on our lives, stems from the fact that solitude and community are two necessary components in the metaphysical makeup of man – based upon the interplay of body and soul. Community is a function of the body, because the body has needs that can only be met by the community. Judaism understands that physical needs, of course, and even emotional needs, are products of man's corporeality. The body, as a composite entity, intrinsically relates to the "body of the community," with its integration and interrelation of all parts. In Chassidic writings, the community is often referred to in physical terms. The head of the community is its leaders; the heart, its prophets and dreamers; the hands, its workers, the legs and feet, its financial supporters. Every single element is necessary, for if even one is missing, it causes a defect in the entire communal body.

Solitude, however, is the domain of the soul. Kabbalah understands the soul to be a portion of God, Himself, and so it shares in His total and unique Oneness and Transcendence. The soul does not need this world and God must force it to remain in the body, for it cannot bear limitation. Chassidic writings often compare the soul to a flame, burning with a constant love and awe of God, seeking at every moment to rise upward and be reabsorbed in its source. "The soul of man is a candle of God, searching out all the chambers of the heart" (Proverbs 20:27). It is precisely in solitude that soul feels most at home, in a setting closest to its own essential nature.

Solitude has always been an important aspect of Jewish spirituality. Inherent in the Biblical image of the Patriarchs as shepherds is the idea that these men were contemplatives seeking a truth beyond the false gods of society. Throughout Jewish history, and especially in the lives of the great mystics, solitude has played an important role. The great sixteenth-century Kabbalist, Rabbi Yitzhok Luria, spent twelve years in a hut on the Nile contemplating the mysteries of the *Zohar*, the Kabbalistic Book of Splendor. The Baal Shem Tov, founder of the Chassidic movement, developed his philosophy during his years of solitude in the Carpathian Mountains. His great-grandson, the famous Rabbi Nachman of Braslov, went so far as to say that one hour of solitude a day is a religious obligation as important as the formal daily prayers.

Nonetheless, even the great mystics eventually forewent their solitary endeavors to reunite with the community — the holy community of Kabbalists in Safed in Northern Israel led by Rabbi Luria, the communal Chassidic movement of the Baal Shem Tov — because the path of Judaism, while recognizing the need for solitude, clearly emphasizes the primacy of community as a vehicle for the revelation of God.

From its very inception as a nation – the deliverance from Egypt and the group revelation of God at Mount Sinai – community has been the focus and backbone of the Jewish nation. The Torah, including both the Bible and the Talmud, is by and large a testament of communal spirituality. In this, it is something of a holy constitution, whose main concern is to reveal God's presence in the mundane aspects of life. It speaks of business and finance, agriculture, family relations, and national holidays. In personal ritual observance as well, community is central. Prayer must be offered in a quorum of ten, Torah study is traditionally conducted with a partner. Life's major transition points, such as circumcision, entry into adulthood, and marriage are, above all, seen as milestones in one's deepening commitment to the community.

This emphasis on community in no way denies the validity of solitude, rather it seeks to engage the contemplative in an even higher purpose, namely, that of bringing the entire community into an enlightened relationship with God. It is the purpose of all the *mitzvot*, the Biblical commandments, to draw down God, who is utterly holy and removed (the Hebrew word *Kedushah* – Holiness – means "separateness"), into the world, so that from within the world itself, a new revelation of the unity of the Creator should emerge.

So important is community that Kabbalistic writings consider *Knesset Yisroel*, the body of the People of Israel, as synonymous with the Shekinah, the Divine Presence on earth. For they are both understood to share the same purpose, that of revealing God in the world, being "a light to the nations," in the words of the prophet. The Shekinah is the feminine element of creation, for it receives God's light, nurtures it, and reveals it in the world. Thus the union of

God and the Shekinah, of the transcendent and the immanent, is not a static act. It is constantly bringing to birth a new and ever increasing awareness of God. Every single act, performed according to the laws of the Torah, brings about a greater revelation of God in the world, a greater unity between the Soul of the creation and the physical. Every act becomes a prayer. And as the *Zohar* states, "prayer without intention is like a body without a soul."

This, then, is the role of mankind: to lift back up to God that which is furthest away. It is the reason why the soul leaves its pristine abode to come down into the body, why God descends to create a world, and why the contemplative must eventually leave his retreat and unite with humanity. The contemplative is to the community what the soul is to the body. He gives it life, inspiration, and leads its members to a higher level. Then, if he finds that he must retreat once again to his solitary path, it is because the final rectification has not yet been accomplished. He retreats, to draw from the source of inspiration, and he returns again to water the garden of souls. This back and forth movement will continue until peace if finally made between body and soul, and God's presence so fills the earth that there is no place empty of Him. "When will the Messiah come?" asks the Talmud. "When all the souls have come out in the body." Then there will be no need for solitude, for the whole world will reveal His glory. The duality of God and the world will no longer exist. And the words of the prophet will be fulfilled: "On that day God will be One, and His Name One" (Zechariah 14:9).

NOTE

Biblical quotations are the author's own translations from the Hebrew.

VÁCLAV HAVEL

Politics, Morality, and Civility

As ridiculous or quixotic as it may sound these days, one thing seems certain to me: that it is my responsibility to emphasize, again and again, the moral origin of all genuine politics, to stress the significance of moral values and standards in all spheres of social life, including economics, and to explain that if we don't try, within ourselves, to discover or rediscover or cultivate what I call "higher responsibility," things will turn out very badly indeed for our country.

The return of freedom to a society that was morally unhinged has produced something it clearly had to produce, and something we therefore might have expected, but which has turned out to be far more serious than anyone could have predicted: an enormous and dazzling explosion of every imaginable human vice. A wide range of questionable or at least morally ambiguous human tendencies, subtly encouraged over the years and, at the same time, subtly pressed to serve the daily operation of the totalitarian system, have suddenly been liberated, as it were, from their straitjacket and given freedom at last. The authoritarian regime imposed a certain order—if that is the right expression for it—on these vices (and in doing so "legitimized" them, in a sense). This order has now been shattered, but a new order that would limit rather than exploit these vices, an order based on freely accepted responsibility to and for the whole of society, has not yet been built—nor could it have been, for such an order takes years to develop and cultivate.

Thus we are witnesses to a bizarre state of affairs: society has freed itself, true, but in some ways it behaves worse than when it was in chains. Criminality has grown rapidly, and the familiar sewage that in times of historical reversal always wells up from the nether regions of the collective psyche has overflowed into the mass media, especially the gutter press. But there are other, more serious and dangerous symptoms: hatred among nationalities, suspicion, racism, even signs of Fascism; politicking, an unrestrained, unheeding struggle for purely particular interests, unadulterated ambition, fanaticism of every conceivable kind, new and unprecedented varieties of robbery, the rise of different mafias; and a prevailing lack of tolerance, understanding, taste, moderation, and reason. There is a new attraction to ideologies, too—as if Marxism had left behind it a great, disturbing void that had to be filled at any cost.

It is enough to look around our political scene (whose lack of civility is merely a reflection of the more general crisis of civility). In the months leading up to the June 1992 election, almost every political activity, including debates over extremely important legislation in Parliament, has taken place in the shadow of a pre-election campaign, of an extravagant hunger for power and a willingness to gain the favour of a confused electorate by offering a colourful range of attractive nonsense. Mutual accusations, denunciations, and slander among political opponents know no bounds. One politician will undermine another's work only because they belong to different political parties. Partisan considerations still visibly take precedence over pragmatic attempts to arrive at reasonable and useful solutions to problems. Analysis is pushed out of the press by scandal-mongering. Supporting the government in a good cause is practically shameful; kicking it in the shins, on the other hand, is praiseworthy. Sniping at politicians who declare their support for another political group is a matter of course. Anyone can accuse anyone else of intrigue or in-competence, or of having a shady past and shady intentions.

Demagogy is rife, and even something as important as the natural longing of a people for autonomy is exploited in power plays, as rivals compete in lying to the public. Many members of the party elite, the so-called *nomenklatura* who, until very recently, were faking concern about social justice and the working class, have cast aside their masks and, al-most overnight, openly become speculators and thieves. Many a once-feared Communist is now an unscrupulous capitalist, shamelessly and unequivocally laughing in the face of the same worker whose interests he once allegedly defended.

Citizens are becoming more and more disgusted with all this, and their disgust is understandably directed against the democratic government they themselves elected. Mak-ing the most of this situation, some characters with suspi-cious backgrounds have been gaining popular favour with ideas such as, for instance, the need to throw the entire gov-ernment into the Vltava River.

And yet, if a handful of friends and I were able to bang our heads against the wall for years by speaking the truth about Communist totalitarianism while surrounded by an ocean of apathy, there is no reason why I shouldn't go on banging my head against the wall by speaking *ad nauseam,* despite the condescending smiles, about responsibility and morality in the face of our present social marasmus. There is no reason to think that this struggle is a lost cause. The only lost cause is one we give up on before we enter the struggle.

Time and time again I have been persuaded that a huge potential of goodwill is slumbering within our society. It's just that it's incoherent, suppressed, confused, crippled and perplexed – as though it does not know what to rely on, where to begin, where or how to find meaningful outlets.

In such a state of affairs, politicians have a duty to awaken this slumbering potential, to offer it direction and ease its passage, to encourage it and give it room, or simply hope. They say a nation gets the politicians it deserves. In some senses this is true: politicians are indeed a mirror of their society, and a kind of embodiment of its potential. At the same time – paradoxically – the opposite is also true: society is a mirror of its politicians. It is largely up to the politicians which social forces they choose to liberate and which they choose to suppress, whether they rely on the good in each citizen or on the bad. The former regime systematically mobilized the worst human qualities, like selfishness, envy, and hatred. That regime was far more than just something we deserved; it was also responsible for what we became. Those who find themselves in politics therefore bear a heightened responsibility for the moral state of society, and it is their responsibility to seek out the best in that society, and to develop and strengthen it.

By the way, even the politicians who often anger me with their shortsightedness and their malice are not, for the most part, evil-minded. They are, rather, inexperienced, easily infected with the particularisms of the time, easily manipulated by suggested trends and prevailing customs; often they are simply caught up, unwillingly, in the swirl of bad politics, and find themselves unable to extricate themselves because they are afraid of the risks this would entail.

Some say I'm a naive dreamer who is always trying to combine the incompatible: politics and morality. I know this song well; I've heard it sung all my life. In the 1980s, a certain Czech philosopher who lived in California published a series of articles in which he subjected the "anti-political politics" of Charter 77 – and, in particular, the way I explained that notion in my essays – to crushing criticism. Trapped in his own Marxist fallacies, he believed that as a scholar he had scientifically comprehended the entire history of the world. He saw it as a history of violent revolutions and vicious power struggles. The idea that the world might actually be changed by the force of truth, the power of a truthful word, the strength of a free spirit, conscience, and responsibility – with no guns, no lust for power, no political wheeling and dealing – was quite beyond the horizon of his understanding. Naturally, if you understand decency as a mere "superstructure" of the forces of production, then you can never understand political power in terms of decency.

Because his doctrine had taught him that the bourgeoisie would never voluntarily surrender its leading role, and that it must be swept into the dustbin of history through armed revolution, this philosopher assumed that there was no other way to sweep away the Communist government either. Yet it turned out to be possible. Moreover, it turned out to be the only way to do it. Not only that, but it was the only way that made sense, since violence, as we know, breeds more violence. This is why most revolutions degenerate into dictatorships that devour their young, giving rise to new revolutionaries who prepare for new violence, unaware that they are digging their own graves and pushing society back onto the deadly merry-go-round of revolution and counterrevolution.

Communism was overthrown by life, by thought, by human dignity. Our recent history has confirmed that the Czech-Californian professor was wrong. Likewise, those who still claim that politics is chiefly the manipulation of power and public opinion, and that morality has no place in it, are just as wrong. Political intrigue is not really politics, and, although you can get away with superficial politics for a time, it does not bring much hope of lasting success. Through intrigue one may easily become prime minister, but that will be the extent of one's success; one can hardly improve the world that way.

I am happy to leave political intrigue to others; I will not compete with them, certainly not by using their weapons.

Genuine politics — politics worthy of the name, and the only politics I am willing to devote myself to — is simply a matter of serving those around us: serving the community, and serving those who will come after us. Its deepest roots are moral because it is a responsibility, expressed through action, to and for the whole, a responsibility that is what it is — a "higher" responsibility — only because it has a meta-physical grounding: that is, it grows out of a conscious or subconscious certainty that our death ends nothing, be-cause everything is forever being recorded and evaluated somewhere else, somewhere "above us," in what I have called "the memory of Being" — an integral aspect of the se-cret order of the cosmos, of nature, and of life, which believ-ers call God and to whose judgement everything is subject. Genuine conscience and genuine responsibility are always, in the end, explicable only as an expression of the silent as-sumption that we are observed "from above," that every-thing is visible, nothing is forgotten, and so earthly time has no power to wipe away the sharp disappointments of earthly failure: our spirit knows that it is not the only entity aware of these failures.

What can I do, as president, not only to remain faithful to that notion of politics, but also to bring it to at least partial fruition? (After all, the former is unthinkable without the latter. Not to put at least some of my ideas into practice could have only two consequences: either I would eventually be swept from office or I would become a tolerated eccentric, sounding off to an unheeding audience – not only a less dignified alternative, but a highly dishonest one as well, because it would mean another form of resignation, both of myself and of my ideals.)

As in everything else, I must start with myself. That is: in all circumstances try to be decent, just, tolerant, and understanding, and at the same time try to resist corruption and deception. In other words, I must do my utmost to act in harmony with my conscience and my better self. For instance, I am frequently advised to be more "tactical," not to say everything right away, to dissimulate gently, not to fear wooing someone more than my nature commands, or to distance myself from someone against my real will in the matter. In the interests of strengthening my hand, I am advised at times to assent to someone's ambition for power, to flatter someone merely because it pleases him, or to reject someone even though it goes against my convictions, because he does not enjoy favour with others.

I constantly hear another kind of advice, as well: I should be tougher, more decisive, more authoritative. For a good cause, I shouldn't be afraid to pound the table occasionally, to shout at people, to try to rouse a little fear and trembling. Yet, if I wish to remain faithful to myself and my notion of politics, I mustn't listen to advice like this – not just in the interests of my personal mental health (which could be seen as a private, selfish desire), but chiefly in the interests of what most concerns me: the simple fact that directness can never be established by indirection, or truth through lies, or the democratic spirit through authoritarian directives. Of course, I don't know whether directness, truth, and the democratic spirit will succeed. But I do know how *not* to succeed, which is by choosing means that contradict the ends. As we know from history, that is the best way to eliminate the very ends we set out to achieve.

In other words, if there is to be any chance at all of success, there is only one way to strive for decency, reason, responsibility, sincerity, civility, and tolerance, and that is decently, reasonably, responsibly, sincerely, civilly, and tolerantly. I'm aware that, in everyday politics, this is not seen as the most practical way of going about it. But I have one advantage: among my many bad qualities there is one that happens to be missing – a longing or a love for power. Not being bound by that, I am essentially freer than those who cling to their power or position, and this allows me to indulge in the luxury of behaving untactically.

I see the only way forward in that old, familiar injunction: "live in truth."

But how is this to be done, practically speaking, when one is president? I see three basic possibilities.

The first possibility: I must repeat certain things aloud over and over again. I don't like repeating myself, but in this case it's unavoidable. In my many public utterances, I feel I must emphasize and explain repeatedly the moral dimensions of all social life, and point out that morality is, in fact, hidden in everything. And this is true: whenever I encounter a problem in my work and try to get to the bottom of it, I always discover some moral aspect, be it apathy, unwillingness to recognize personal error or guilt, reluctance to give up certain positions and the advantages flowing from them, envy, an excess of self-assurance, or whatever.

I feel that the dormant goodwill in people needs to be stirred. People need to hear that it makes sense to behave decently or to help others, to place common interests above their own, to respect the elementary rules of human coexistence. They want to be told about this publicly. They want to know that those "at the top" are on their side. They feel strengthened, confirmed, hopeful. Goodwill longs to be recognized and cultivated. For it to develop and have an impact it must hear that the world does not ridicule it.

Frequently, regular listeners to my radio talks to the nation, "Conversations from Lány," ask to hear what might be called "philosophical" or "ethical" reflections. I occasionally omit them for fear of repeating myself too often, but people always ask for them again. I try never to give people practical advice about how to deal with the evil around them, nor could I even if I wanted to—and yet people want to hear that decency and courage make sense, that something must be risked in the struggle against dirty tricks. They want to know they are not alone, forgotten, written off.

The second possibility: I can try to create around me, in the world of so-called high politics, a positive climate, a climate of generosity, tolerance, openness, broadmindedness, and a kind of elementary companionship and mutual trust. In this sphere I am far from being the decisive factor. But I can have a psychological influence.

The third possibility: There is a significant area in which I do have direct political influence in my position as president. I am required to make certain political decisions. In this, I can and must bring my concept of politics to bear, and inject into it my political ideals, my longing for justice, decency, and civility, my notion of what, for present purposes, I will call "the moral state." Whether I am successful or not is for others to judge, of course, but the results will always be uneven, since, like everyone else, I am a fallible human being.

Journalists, and in particular foreign correspondents, often ask me how the idea of "living in truth," the idea of "anti-political politics," or the idea of politics subordinate to conscience can, in practice, be carried out. They are curious to know whether, finding myself in high office, I have not had to revise much of what I once wrote as an independent critic of politics and politicians. Have I not been compelled to lower my former "dissident" expectations of politics, by which they mean the standards I derived from the "dissident experience," which are therefore scarcely applicable outside that sphere?

There may be some who won't believe me, but in my second term as president in a land full of problems that presidents in stable countries never even dream of, I can safely say that I have not been compelled to recant anything of what I wrote earlier, or to change my mind about anything. It may seem incredible, but it is so: not only have I not had to change my mind, but my opinions have been confirmed.

Despite the political distress I face every day, I am still deeply convinced that politics is not essentially a disreputable business; and to the extent that it is, it is only disreputable people who make it so. I would concede that it can, more than other spheres of human activity, tempt one to disreputable practices, and that it therefore places higher demands on people. But it is simply not true that a politician must lie or intrigue. That is utter nonsense, spread about by people who—for whatever reasons—wish to discourage others from taking an interest in public affairs.

Of course, in politics, as elsewhere in life, it is impossible and pointless to say everything, all at once, to just anyone. But that does not mean having to lie. All you need is tact, the proper instincts, and good taste. One surprising experience from "high politics" is this: I have discovered that good taste is more useful here than a post-graduate degree in political science. It is largely a matter of form: knowing how long to speak, when to begin and when to finish; how to say something politely that your opposite number may not want to hear; how to say, always, what is most significant at a given moment, and not to speak of what is not important or relevant; how to insist on your own position without offending; how to create the kind of friendly atmosphere that makes complex negotiations easier; how to keep a conversation going without prying or being aloof; how to balance serious political themes with lighter, more relaxing topics; how to plan your official journeys judiciously and to know when it is more appropriate not to go somewhere, when to be open and when reticent and to what degree.

But more than that, it means having a certain instinct for the time, the atmosphere of the time, the mood of people, the nature of their worries, their frame of mind – that too can perhaps be more useful than sociological surveys. An education in political science, law, economics, history, and culture is an invaluable asset to any politician, but I have been persuaded, again and again, that it is not the most essential asset. Qualities like fellow-feeling, the ability to talk to others, insight, the capacity to grasp quickly not only problems but also human character, the ability to make contact, a sense of moderation: all these are immensely more important in politics. I am not saying, heaven forbid, that I myself am endowed with these qualities; not at all! These are merely my observations.

To sum up: if your heart is in the right place and you have good taste, not only will you pass muster in politics, you are destined for it. If you are modest and do not lust after power, not only are you suited to politics, you absolutely belong there. The *sine qua non* of a politician is not the ability to lie; he need only be sensitive and know when, what, to whom, and how to say what he has to say. It is not true that a person of principle does not belong in politics; it is enough for his principles to be leavened with patience, deliberation, a sense of proportion, and an understanding of others. It is not true that only the unfeeling cynic, the vain, the brash, and the vulgar can succeed in politics; such people, it is true, are drawn to politics, but, in the end, decorum and good taste will always count for more.

My experience and observations confirm that politics as the practice of morality is possible. I do not deny, however, that it is not always easy to go that route, nor have I every claimed that it was.

From my political ideals, it should be clear enough that what I would like to accentuate in every possible way in my practice of politics is culture. Culture in the widest possible sense of the word, including everything from what might be called the culture of everyday life – of "civility" – to what we know as high culture, including the arts and sciences.

I don't mean that the state should heavily subsidize culture as a particular area of human endeavour, nor do I at all share the indignant fear of many artists that the period we are going through now is ruining culture and will eventually destroy it. Most of our artists have, unwittingly, grown accustomed to the unending generosity of the socialist state. It subsidized a number of cultural institutions and offices, heedless of whether a film cost one million or ten million crowns, or whether anyone ever went to see it. It didn't matter how many idle actors the theatres had on their payrolls; the main thing was that everyone was on one, and thus on the take. The Communist state knew, better than the Czech-Californian philosopher, where the greatest danger to it lay: in the realm of the intellect and the spirit. It knew who first had to be pacified through irrational largesse. That the state was less and less successful at doing so is another matter, which merely confirms how right it was to be afraid; for, despite all the bribes and prizes and titles thrown their way, the artists were among the first to rebel.

This nostalgic complaint by artists who fondly remember

their "social security" under socialism therefore leaves me unmoved. Culture must, in part at least, learn how to make its own way. It should be partially funded through tax write-offs, and through foundations, development funds, and the like – which, by the way, are the forms that best suit its plurality and its freedom. The more varied the sources of funding for the arts and sciences, the greater variety and competition there will be in the arts and scholarly research. The state should – in ways that are rational, open to scrutiny, and well thought out – support only those aspects of culture that are fundamental to our national identity and the civilized traditions of our land, and that can't be conserved through market mechanisms alone. I am thinking of heritage sites (there can't be a hotel in every castle or château to pay for its upkeep, nor can the old aristocracy be expected to return and provide for their upkeep merely to preserve family honour), libraries, museums, public archives, and such institutions, which today are in an appalling state of disrepair (as though the previous "regime of forgetting" deliberately set out to destroy these important witnesses to our past). Likewise, it is hard to imagine that the Church, or the churches, in the foreseeable future, will have the means to restore all the chapels, cathedrals, monasteries, and ecclesiastical buildings that have fallen into ruin over the forty years of Communism. They are part of the cultural wealth of the entire country, not just the pride of the Church.

I mention all this only by way of introduction, for the sake of exactness. My main point is something else. I consider it immensely important that we concern ourselves with culture not just as one among many human activities, but in the broadest sense – the "culture of everything," the general level of public manners. By that I mean chiefly the kind of relations that exist among people, between the powerful and the weak, the healthy and the sick, the young and the elderly, adults and children, businesspeople and customers,

men and women, teachers and students, officers and soldiers, policemen and citizens, and so on.

More than that, I am also thinking of the quality of
people's relationships to nature, to animals, to the atmosphere, to the landscape, to towns, to gardens, to their
homes – the culture of housing and architecture, of public
catering, of big business and small shops; the culture of
work and advertising; the culture of fashion, behaviour,
and entertainment.

And there is even more: all this would be hard to imagine
without a legal, political, and administrative culture, without the culture of relationships between the state and the
citizen. Before the war, in all these areas, we were on the
same level as the prosperous western democracies of the
day, if not higher. To assess our present condition, it's
enough to cross into Western Europe. I know that this cata-
strophic decline in the general cultural level, the level of
public manners, is related to the decline in our economy,
and is even, to a large degree, a direct consequence of it.
Still, it frightens me more than economic decline does. It is
more visible; it impinges on one more "physically," as it
were. I can well imagine that, as a citizen, it would bother me
more if the pub I went to were a place where the customers
spat on the floor and the staff behaved boorishly towards
me than it would if I could no longer afford to go there every day and order the most expensive meal on the menu.
Likewise, it would bother me less not to be able to afford a
family house than it would not to see nice houses anywhere.

Perhaps what I'm trying to say is clear: however important it may be to get our economy back on its feet, it is far
from being the only task facing us. It is no less important to
do everything possible to improve the general cultural level
of everyday life. As the economy develops, this will happen
anyway. But we cannot depend on that alone. We must initiate a large-scale program for raising general cultural stan-

dards. And it is not true that we have to wait until we are rich to do this; we can begin at once, without a crown in our pockets. No one can persuade me that it takes a better-paid nurse to behave more considerately to a patient, that only an expensive house can be pleasing, that only a wealthy merchant can be courteous to his customers and display a handsome sign outside, that only a prosperous farmer can treat his livestock well. I would go even farther, and say that, in many respects, improving the civility of everyday life can accelerate economic development—from the culture of supply and demand, of trading and enterprise, right down to the culture of values and lifestyle.

I want to do everything I can to contribute, in a specific way, to a program for raising the general level of civility, or at least do everything I can to express my personal interest in such an improvement, whether I do so as president or not. I feel this is both an integral part and a logical consequence of my notion of politics as the practice of morality and the application of a "higher responsibility." After all, is there anything that citizens—and this is doubly true of politicians—should be more concerned about, ultimately, than trying to make life more pleasant, more interesting, more varied, and more bearable?

If I talk here about my political—or, more precisely, my civil—program, about my notion of the kind of politics and values and ideals I wish to struggle for, this is not to say that I am entertaining the naive hope that this struggle may one day be over. A heaven on earth in which people all love each other and everyone is hard-working, well-mannered, and virtuous, in which the land flourishes and everything is sweetness and light, working harmoniously to the satisfaction of God: this will never be. On the contrary, the world has had the worst experiences with utopian thinkers who promised all that. Evil will remain with us, no one will ever eliminate human suffering, the political arena will always attract irresponsible and ambitious adventurers and charlatans. And man will not stop destroying the world. In this regard, I have no illusions.

Neither I nor anyone else will ever win this war once and for all. At the very most, we can win a battle or two – and not even that is certain. Yet I still think it makes sense to wage this war persistently. It has been waged for centuries, and it will continue to be waged – we hope – for centuries to come. This must be done on principle, because it is the right thing to do. Or, if you like, because God wants it that way. It is an eternal, never-ending struggle waged not just by good people (among whom I count myself, more or less) against evil people, by honourable people against dishonourable people, by people who think about the world and eternity against people who think only of themselves and the moment. It takes place inside everyone. It is what makes a person a person, and life, life.

So anyone who claims that I am a dreamer who expects to transform hell into heaven is wrong. I have few illusions. But I feel a responsibility to work towards the things I consider good and right. I don't know whether I'll be able to change certain things for the better, or not at all. Both outcomes are possible. There is only one thing I will not concede: that it might be meaningless to strive in a good cause.

We are building our country anew. Fate has thrust me into a position in which I have a somewhat greater influence on that process than most of my fellow citizens do. It is appropriate, therefore, that I admit to my notions about what kind of country it should be, and articulate the vision that guides me – or rather, the vision that flows naturally from politics as I understand it.

Perhaps we can all agree that we want a state based on rule

of law, one that is democratic (that is, with a pluralistic political system), peaceful, and with a prospering market economy. Some insist that this state should also be socially just.
Others sense in the phrase a hangover from socialism and
argue against it. They object to the notion of "social justice"
as vague, claiming that it can mean anything at all, and that a
functioning market economy can never guarantee any genuine social justice. They point out that people have, and always will have, different degrees of industriousness, talent,
and, last but not least, luck. Obviously, social justice in the
sense of social equality is something the market system cannot, by its very nature, deliver. Moreover, to compel the
marketplace to do so would be deeply immoral. (Our experience of socialism has provided us with more than enough
examples of why this is so.)

I do not see, however, why a democratic state, armed with
a legislature and the power to draw up a budget, cannot
strive for a certain fairness in, for example, pension policies
or tax policies, or support to the unemployed, or salaries to
public employees, or assistance to the elderly living alone,
people who have health problems, or those who, for various
reasons, find themselves at the bottom of society. Every civilized state attempts, in different ways and with different degrees of success, to come up with reasonable policies in these
areas, and not even the most ardent supporters of the market economy have anything against it in principle. In the
end, then, it is a conflict not of beliefs, but rather of termi-
nology.

I am repeating these basic, self-evident, and rather general facts for the sake of completeness and order. But I
would like to say more about other aspects of the state that
may be somewhat less obvious and are certainly much less
talked about, but are no less important — because they qual-
ify and make possible everything that is considered self-
evident.

I am convinced that we will never build a democratic state

based on rule of law if we do not at the same time build a state that is—regardless of how unscientific this may sound to the ears of a political scientist—humane, moral, intellectual and spiritual, and cultural. The best laws and the best-conceived democratic mechanisms will not in themselves guarantee legality or freedom or human rights—anything, in short, for which they were intended—if they are not underpinned by certain human and social values. What good, for instance, would a law be if no one respected it, no one defended it, and no one tried responsibly to follow it? It would be nothing but a scrap of paper. What use would elections be in which the voter's only choice was between a greater and a lesser scoundrel? What use would a wide variety of political parties be if not one of them had the general interest of society at heart?

No state—that is, no constitutional, legal, and political system—is anything in and of itself, outside historical time and social space. It is not the clever technical invention of a team of experts, like a computer or a telephone. Every state, on the contrary, grows out of specific intellectual, spiritual, and cultural traditions that breathe substance into it and give it meaning.

So we are back to the same point: without commonly shared and widely entrenched moral values and obligations, neither the law, nor democratic government, nor even the market economy will function properly. They are all marvellous products of the human spirit, mechanisms that can, in turn, serve the spirit magnificently—assuming that the human spirit wants these mechanisms to serve it, respects them, believes in them, guarantees them, understands their meaning, and is willing, if necessary, to fight for them or make sacrifices for them.

Again I would use law as an illustration. The law is undoubtedly an instrument of justice, but it would be an utterly meaningless instrument if no one used it responsibly. From our own recent experience we all know too well what

can happen to even a decent law in the hands of an unscrupulous judge, and how easily unscrupulous people can use
democratic institutions to introduce dictatorship and terror. The law and other democratic institutions ensure little
if they are not backed up by the willingness and courage of
decent people to guard against their abuse. That these institutions can help us become more human is obvious; that is
why they were created, and why we are building them now.
But if they are to guarantee anything to us, it is we, first of
all, who must guarantee them.

In the somewhat chaotic provisional activity around the
technical aspects of building the state, it will do us no harm
occasionally to remind ourselves of the meaning of the state,
which is, and must remain, truly human – which means it
must be intellectual, spiritual, and moral.

How are we to go about building such a state? What does
such an ambition bind us to or offer us, in practical terms?

There is no simple set of instructions on how to proceed.
A moral and intellectual state cannot be established through
a constitution, or through law, or through directives, but
only through complex, long-term, and never-ending work
involving education and self-education. What is needed is
lively and responsible consideration of every political step,
every decision; a constant stress on moral deliberation and
moral judgement; continued self-examination and self-
analysis; an endless rethinking of our priorities. It is not, in
short, something we can simply declare or introduce. It is
a way of going about things, and it demands the courage
to breathe moral and spiritual motivation into everything,
to seek the human dimension in all things. Science, technology, expertise, and so-called professionalism are not
enough. Something more is necessary. For the sake of simplicity, it might be called spirit. Or feeling. Or conscience.

JOHN LEO

Community and Personal Duty

As a cursory reading of almost any newspaper will show, American politics is awash in rights talk. We have criminal rights, computer rights, animal rights, children's rights, victim rights, abortion rights, housing rights, privacy rights, the right to know the sex of a fetus, the right to own AK-47s for hunting purposes, the right not to be tested for AIDS and the right not to inform anyone we may be infected. Recently we have acquired the right to die, and, according to some rather imaginative theorists, a damaged fetus has "a right not to be born." During the Bret Easton Ellis flap, *Publishers Weekly* discovered "the right" of every author to have his book published. Mental patients used to have a right to treatment, but now that they have been dumped on the streets, they have an ACLU-protected right to no treatment and, therefore, the right to die unhelped in alleys. According to the ACLU, airline pilots have a right not to be randomly tested for alcohol, leaving passengers with an implied right to crash every now and then.

Defining and protecting rights is important in any political culture, but this culture has reached the point where the obsession with individual rights is making it hard for us to think socially, let alone restore the balance between individual and community rights, between personal rights and personal obligations. Rights talk has become so overwhelming that it distorts, co-opts or obliterates issues that are clearly social. ("Animal rights," for instance, is an example of an obligation decked out as a right: Sea slugs and cockroaches don't have "rights," but humans have a responsibility to treat the animal world and the environment with more care and respect.)

The good news is that the antibodies are starting to kick in. Amitai Etzioni, the George Washington University sociologist, predicts that communitarianism will be to the '90s what neoconservatism was to the '80s. Etzioni has just founded a magazine called *The Responsive Community: Rights and Responsibilities* to help chart a course between radical individualists, such as the ACLU and libertarians, and coercive conservative groups who want to use law to impose values and censorship. A Washington group, the American Alliance for Rights and Responsibilities, aggressively pushes a similar communitarian perspective. Partly because of William F. Buckley Jr.'s book *Gratitude,* the idea of national service is gaining important backing. The current issue of *Harper's* features a forum on how to balance the Bill of Rights with some sort of "Bill of Duties." In fact a spate of magazine articles and books, from both ends of the political spectrum, are sounding similar or related themes. In his brilliant book, *The Closest of Strangers,* Jim Sleeper, a liberal, shows how a one-sided harping on individual rights and the loss of a sense of civic obligation helped bring New York City to its knees.

The problem is this: America is more and more coming to look like a random collection of atomized individuals, bristling with rights and choices but with no connectedness or responsibility for one another. The crisis in the social order has many causes, but it clearly has something to do with the selfishness of the '80s and the institutionalizing of the "therapized" ethic of the Me Decade '70s, which freed clients by eliminating obligation (one of the mantras of pop therapy is "I'm not on earth to live up to your expectations, and you are not here to live up to mine."). More and more our laws as well as our customs are being shaped by this profoundly nonsocial ethic. Bruce Hafen, a law professor at Brigham Young University, writes: "We are witnessing a gradual decline in the legal and social significance of community interests."

What do communitarians want? Some argue for national service or for giving up minor freedoms for the common good. This might include partner notification in AIDS cases, drug and alcohol testing for pilots and antiloitering laws aimed at drug dealers and drawn tightly enough to pass a Supreme Court test. Some focus on programs needed to help the family function (day care, for instance) or on pushing schools to teach nonsectarian communal values such as honesty, self-discipline and responsibility for others.

One thing to note is that communitarianism is not the agenda of the right in new clothing, though it obviously has much in common with social conservatism. Here, for instance, is a communitarian perspective on plant closings: If a steel plant shuts down in Youngstown, why should the suddenly unemployed workers be left alone to pay the price for what is, predictably, the occasional result of our economic system? In Japan and in Western nations not infected by American hyperindividualism, society pays heavily to retrain or relocate workers, partly out of a sense of justice, partly to avoid the negative social effects of plant closings — chiefly alcoholism and severe family stress.

Community ethics have been used for so long to mask prejudice or to exclude minorities that communitarian thinking is likely to be suspect. But it is not simple majoritarianism. It does not exalt the group over the individual. It asks for social responsibility and laws based on connectedness. New York Mayor David Dinkins likes to refer to the city's racial and ethnic groups as "a gorgeous mosaic." A nice image, but as financier Felix Rohatyn replied, a mosaic needs some sort of glue to hold the pieces together.

KATHLEEN NORRIS

The Beautiful Places

> The Scarecrow sighed. "Of course I cannot understand it," he said. "If your heads were stuffed with straw like mine, you would probably all live in the beautiful places, and then Kansas would have no people at all. It is fortunate for Kansas that you have brains." — L. FRANK BAUM, *The Wizard of Oz*

THE HIGH PLAINS, the beginning of the desert West, often act as a crucible for those who inhabit them. Like Jacob's angel, the region requires that you wrestle with it before it bestows a blessing. This can mean driving through a snowstorm on icy roads, wondering whether you'll have to pull over and spend the night in your car, only to emerge under tag ends of clouds into a clear sky blazing with stars. Suddenly you know what you're seeing: the earth has turned to face the center of the galaxy, and many more stars are visible than the ones we usually see on our wing of the spiral.

Or a vivid double rainbow marches to the east, following the wild summer storm that nearly blew you off the road. The storm sky is gunmetal gray, but to the west the sky is peach streaked with crimson. The land and sky of the West often fill what Thoreau termed our "need to witness our limits transgressed." Nature, in Dakota, can indeed be an experience of the holy.

More Americans than ever, well over 70 percent, now live in urban areas and tend to see Plains land as empty. What they really mean is devoid of human presence. Most visitors

to Dakota travel on interstate highways that will take them
as quickly as possible through the region, past our larger cities to such attractions as the Badlands and the Black Hills.
Looking at the expanse of land in between, they may wonder why a person would choose to live in such a barren
place, let alone love it. But mostly they are bored: they turn
up the car stereo, count the miles to civilization, and look
away.

Dakota is a painful reminder of human limits, just as cities
and shopping malls are attempts to deny them. On a
crowded planet, this is a place inhabited by few, and by the
circumstance of inheritance, I am one of them. Nearly
twenty years ago I returned to the holy ground of my childhood summers; I moved from New York City to the house
my mother had grown up in, in an isolated town on the bor-
der between North and South Dakota.

More than any other place I lived as a child or young
adult – Virginia, Illinois, Hawaii, Vermont, New York –
this is my spiritual geography, the place where I've wrestled
my story out of the circumstances of landscape and inheritance. The word "geography" derives from the Greek
words for earth and writing, and writing about Dakota has
been my means of understanding that inheritance and re-
claiming what is holy in it. Of course Dakota has always been
such a matrix for its Native American inhabitants. But their
tradition is not mine, and in returning to the Great Plains,
where two generations of my family lived before me, I had
to build on my own traditions, those of the Christian West.

When a friend referred to the western Dakotas as the
Cappadocia of North America, I was handed an essential
connection between the spirituality of the landscape I inhabit and that of the fourth-century monastics who set up
shop in Cappadocia and the deserts of Egypt. Like those
monks, I made a countercultural choice to live in what the
rest of the world considers a barren waste. Like them, I had

to stay in this place, like a scarecrow in a field, and hope for the brains to see its beauty. My idea of what makes a place beautiful had to change, and it has. The city no longer appeals to me for the cultural experiences and possessions I might acquire there, but because its population is less homogeneous than Plains society. Its holiness is to be found in being open to humanity in all its diversity. And the western Plains now seem bountiful in their emptiness, offering solitude and room to grow.

I want to make it clear that my move did not take me "back to the land" in the conventional sense. I did not strike out on my own to make a go of it with "an acre and a cow," as a Hungarian friend naively imagined. As the homesteaders of the early twentieth century soon found out, it is not possible to survive on even 160 acres in western Dakota. My move was one that took me deep into the meaning of inheritance, as I had to try to fit myself into a complex network of long-established relationships.

My husband and I live in the small house in Lemmon, South Dakota, that my grandparents built in 1923. We moved there after they died because my mother, brother, and sisters, who live in Honolulu, did not want to hold an estate auction, the usual procedure when the beneficiaries of an inheritance on the Plains live far away. I offered to move there and manage the farm interests (land and a cattle herd) that my grandparents left us. David Dwyer, my husband, also a poet, is a New York City native who spent his childhood summers in the Adirondacks, and he had enough sense of adventure to agree to this. We expected to be in Dakota for just a few years.

It's hard to say why we stayed. A growing love of the prairie landscape and the quiet of a small town, inertia, and because as freelance writers, we found we had the survival skills suitable for a frontier. We put together a crazy quilt of jobs: I worked in the public library and as an artist-in-residence in schools in both Dakotas; I also did freelance writing and bookkeeping. David tended bar, wrote computer programs for a number of businesses in the region, and did freelance translation of French literature for several publishers. In 1979 we plunged into the cable television business with some friends, one of whom is an electronics expert. David learned how to climb poles and put up the hardware, and I kept the books. It was a good investment; after selling the company we found that we had bought ourselves a good three years to write. In addition, I still do bookkeeping for my family's farm business: the land is leased to people I've known all my life, people who have rented our land for two generations and also farm their own land and maintain their own cattle herds, an arrangement that is common in western Dakota.

In coming to terms with my inheritance, and pursuing my vocation as a writer, I have learned, as both farmers and writers have discovered before me, that it is not easy to remain on the Plains. Only one of North Dakota's best-known writers—Richard Critchfield, Louise Erdrich, Lois Hudson, and Larry Woiwode—currently lives in the state. And writing the truth about the Dakota experience can be a thankless task. I recently discovered that Lois Hudson's magnificent novel of the Dakota Dust Bowl, *The Bones of Plenty,* a book arguably better than *The Grapes of Wrath,* was unknown to teachers and librarians in a town not thirty miles from where the novel is set. The shame of it is that Hudson's book could have helped these people better understand their current situation, the economic crisis forcing many families off the land. Excerpts from *The Grapes of Wrath* were in a textbook used in the school, but students could keep them at a safe distance, part of that remote entity called "American literature" that has little relation to their lives.

The Plains are full of what a friend here calls "good tell-

ing stories," and while our sense of being forgotten by the
rest of the world makes it all the more important that we
preserve them and pass them on, instead we often neglect
them. Perversely, we do not even claim those stories which
have attracted national attention. Both John Neihardt and
Frederick Manfred have written about Hugh Glass, a
hunter and trapper mauled by a grizzly bear in 1823 at the
confluence of the Little Moreau and Grand rivers just south
of Lemmon. Left for dead by his companions, he crawled
and limped some two hundred miles southeast, to the trading post at Fort Kiowa on the Missouri River. Yet when
Manfred wanted to give a reading in Lemmon a few years
ago, the publicist was dismissed by a high school principal
who said, "Who's he? Why would our students be interested?" Manfred's audience of eighty—large for Lemmon—consisted mainly of the people who remembered
him from visits he'd made in the early 1950s while researching his novel *Lord Grizzly*.

Thus are the young disenfranchised while their elders
drown in details, "story" reduced to the social column of the
weekly newspaper that reports of family reunions, card parties, even shopping excursions to a neighboring town. But
real story is as hardy as grass, and it survives in Dakota in
oral form. Good storytelling is one thing rural whites and
Indians have in common. But Native Americans have
learned through harsh necessity that people who survive
encroachment by another culture need story to survive.
And a storytelling tradition is something Plains people
share with both ancient and contemporary monks: we learn
our ways of being and reinforce our values by telling tales
about each other.

One of my favorite monastic stories concerns two fourth-
century monks who "spent fifty years mocking their temp-
tations by saying 'After this winter, we will leave here.'
When the summer came, they said, 'After this summer, we

will go away from here.' They passed all their lives in this
way." These ancient monks sound remarkably like the
farmers I know in Dakota who live in what they laconically
refer to as "next-year country."

We hold on to hopes for next year every year in western
Dakota: hoping that droughts will end; hoping that our
crops won't be hailed out in the few rainstorms that come;
hoping that it won't be too windy on the day we harvest,
blowing away five bushels an acre; hoping (usually against
hope) that if we get a fair crop, we'll be able to get a fair price
for it. Sometimes survival is the only blessing that the terrifying angel of the Plains bestows. Still, there are those born
and raised here who can't imagine living anywhere else.
There are also those who are drawn here – teachers willing
to take the lowest salaries in the nation; clergy with theological degrees from Princeton, Cambridge, and Zurich who
want to serve small rural churches – who find that they cannot remain for long. Their professional mobility sets them
apart and becomes a liability in an isolated Plains community where outsiders are treated with an uneasy mix of hospitality and rejection.

"Extremes," John R. Milton suggests in his history of
South Dakota, is "perhaps the key word for Dakota . . . What
happens to extremes is that they come together, and the result is a kind of tension." I make no attempt in this book to
resolve the tensions and contradictions I find in the Dakotas
between hospitality and insularity, change and inertia, stability and instability, possibility and limitation, between
hope and despair, between open hearts and closed minds.

I suspect that these are the ordinary contradictions of human life, and that they are so visible in Dakota because we
are so few people living in a stark landscape. We are at the
point of transition between East and West in America, geographically and psychically isolated from either coast, and
unlike either the Midwest or the desert West. South Dakota

has been dubbed both the Sunshine State and the Blizzard State, and both designations have a basis in fact. Without a strong identity we become a mythic void; "the Great Desolation," as novelist Ole Rolvaag wrote early in this century, or "The American Outback," as *Newsweek* designated us a few years ago.

Geographical and cultural identity is confused even within the Dakotas. The eastern regions of both states have more in common with each other than with the area west of the Missouri, colloquially called the "West River." Although I commonly use the term "Dakota" to refer to both Dakotas, most of my experience is centered in this western region, and it seems to me that especially in western Dakota we live in tension between myth and truth. Are we cowboys or farmers? Are we fiercely independent frontier types or community builders? One myth that haunts us is that the small town is a stable place. The land around us was divided neatly in 160-acre rectangular sections, following the Homestead Act of 1863 (creating many section-line roads with 90-degree turns). But our human geography has never been as orderly. The western Dakota communities settled by whites are, and always have been, remarkably unstable. The Dakotas have always been a place to be *from;* some 80 percent of homesteaders left within the first twenty years of settlement, and our boom-and-bust agricultural and oil industry economy has kept people moving in and out (mostly out) ever since. Many small-town schools and pulpits operate with revolving doors, adding to the instability.

When I look at the losses we've sustained in western Dakota since 1980 (about one fifth of the population in Perkins County, where I live, and a full third in neighboring Corson County) and at the human cost in terms of anger, distrust, and grief, it is the prairie descendants of the ancient desert monastics, the monks and nuns of Benedictine communities in the Dakotas, who inspire me to hope. One of the vows a Benedictine makes is *stability:* commitment to a particular community, a particular place. If this vow is countercultural by contemporary American standards, it is countercultural in the way that life on the Plains often calls us to be. Benedictines represent continuity in the boom-and-bust cycles of the Plains; they incarnate, and can articulate, the reasons people want to stay.

Terrence Kardong, a monk at an abbey in Dakota founded roughly a thousand years after their European motherhouse, has termed the Great Plains "a school for humility," humility being one goal of Benedictine life. He writes, "in this eccentric environment...certainly one is made aware that things are not entirely in control." In fact, he says, the Plains offer constant reminders that "we are quite powerless over circumstance." His abbey, like many Great Plains communities with an agricultural base, had a direct experience of powerlessness, going bankrupt in the 1920s. Then, and at several other times in the community's history, the monks were urged to move to a more urban environment.

Kardong writes, "We may be crazy, but we are not necessarily stupid.... We built these buildings ourselves. We've cultivated these fields since the turn of the century. We watched from our dining room window the mirage of the Killdeer Mountains rise and fall on the horizon. We collected a library full of local history books and they belong here, not in Princeton. Fifty of our brothers lie down the hill in our cemetery. We have become as indigenous as the cottonwood trees.... If you take us somewhere else, we lose our character, our history – maybe our soul."

A monk does not speak lightly of the soul, and Kardong finds in the Plains the stimulus to develop an inner geography. "A monk isn't supposed to need all kinds of flashy surroundings. We're supposed to have a beautiful inner landscape. Watching a storm pass from horizon to horizon fills your soul with reverence. It makes your soul expand to fill the sky."

Monks are accustomed to taking the long view, another countercultural stance in our fast-paced, anything-for-a-buck society which has corrupted even the culture of farming into "agribusiness." Kardong and many other writers of the desert West, including myself, are really speaking of values when they find beauty in this land no one wants. He writes: "We who are permanently camped here see things you don't see at 55 m.p.h.... We see white-faced calves basking in the spring grass like lilies of the field. We see a chinook wind in January make rivulets run. We see dust-devils and lots of little things. We are grateful."

The so-called emptiness of the Plains is full of such miraculous "little things." The way native grasses spring back from a drought, greening before your eyes; the way a snowy owl sits on a fencepost, or a golden eagle hunts, wings outstretched over grassland that seems to go on forever. Pelicans rise noisily from a lake; an antelope stands stock-still, its tattooed neck like a message in unbreakable code; columbines, their long stems beaten down by hail, bloom in the mud, their whimsical and delicate flowers intact. One might see a herd of white-tailed deer jumping a fence; fox cubs wrestling at the door of their lair; cock pheasants stepping out of a medieval tapestry into windrowed hay; cattle bunched in the southeast corner of a pasture, anticipating a storm in the approaching thunderheads. And above all, one notices the quiet, the near-absence of human noise.

My spiritual geography is a study in contrasts. The three places with which I have the deepest affinity are Hawaii, where I spent my adolescent years; New York City, where I worked after college; and western South Dakota. Like many Americans of their generation, my parents left their small-town roots in the 1930s and moved often. Except for the family home in Honolulu—its yard rich with fruits and flowers (pomegranate, tangerine, lime, mango, plumeria, hibiscus, lehua, ginger, and bird-of-paradise)—and my maternal grandparents' house in a remote village in western Dakota—its modest and hard-won garden offering columbine, daisies and mint—all my childhood places are gone.

When my husband and I moved nearly twenty years ago from New York to that house in South Dakota, only one wise friend in Manhattan understood the inner logic of the journey. Others, appalled, looked up Lemmon, South Dakota (named for George Lemmon, a cattleman and wheeler-dealer of the early 1900s, and home of the Petrified Wood Park—the world's largest—a gloriously eccentric example of American folk art) in their atlases and shook their heads. How could I leave the artists' and writers' community in which I worked, the diverse and stimulating environment of a great city, for such barrenness? Had I lost my mind? But I was young, still in my twenties, an apprentice poet certain of the rightness of returning to the place where I suspected I would find my stories. As it turns out, the Plains have been essential not only for my growth as a writer, they have formed me spiritually. I would even say they have made me a human being.

St. Hilary, a fourth-century bishop (and patron saint against snake bites) once wrote, "Everything that seems empty is full of the angels of God." The magnificent sky above the Plains sometimes seems to sing this truth; angels seem possible in the wind-filled expanse. A few years ago a small boy named Andy who had recently moved to the Plains from Pennsylvania told me he knew an angel named Andy Le Beau. He spelled out the name for me and I asked him if the angel had visited him here. "Don't you know?" he said in the incredulous tone children adopt when adults seem stupefyingly ignorant. "Don't you know?" he said, his voice rising. "*This* is where angels drown."

Andy no more knew that he was on a prehistoric sea bed than he knew what *le beau* means in French, but some ancient wisdom in him had sensed great danger here; a terrifying but beautiful landscape in which we are at the mercy of the unexpected, and even angels proceed at their own risk.

II.

THE

DISAPPEARANCE

OF THE

NATION-STATE

PETER LASLETT

Europe's Happy Families?

Humpty Dumpty sat on a wall
Humpty Dumpty had a great fall
All the King's horses and all the King's men
Could not put Humpty together again.

THE METAPHOR IS AS FOLLOWS: the traditional family model, present in European countries for as many centuries as we can go back, with important differences from place to place, has been irrevocably shattered, fractured beyond restoration. There is no point in trying to return to it, and in any case no power on earth could restore it.

The definition of Europe in familial terms presents formidable and complicated problems, and there is certainly no family model which effectively includes all the countries of the European continent or the European Community. There is, however, a set of European family tendencies which are particularly well marked in the northern and north-western areas and present, if in sometimes extensively modified forms, in the southern areas. It is to this set of tendencies that my generalisations will refer.

Observations at the Cambridge Group for the History of Population and Social Structure go to show that family change has always been slow in pace, and that there is a tendency towards reversion to the median after change has taken place. Fast-paced, fundamental change is rare, and I cannot myself recall examples of it before the present period in any of our files. It did not happen in England or North West Europe during the Industrial Revolution. Familial change of the demographic kind, in birth speeds, death rates, proportions marrying and so on, has been very common of course, going on continuously at varying rates, though again within limits and apparently also with a tendency towards reversion to the median. Familial structure could in fact be said to be designed to accommodate changes of this kind, even to keep them within limits. To pursue our chosen illustration, these systems allow of Humpty Dumpty swaying to and fro and shifting his seat on the wall, but are intended to stop him falling off.

Families in contemporary European countries are marked:

1. by their exceedingly small size, and the huge proportion of solitary persons.

2. by the very pronounced lack of children, the small size of groups of children when present, and the large numbers of family groups without children, children with only one parent, children procreated outside the established institutional rules.

3. by the fact that reproduction takes place to quite an extent while the parents themselves are still in the socialisation stage of the life-course, not yet full members of the society.

4. by the fact that sexual relationships can be, and almost universally are, entirely separated from reproductive relationships, so that courtship has ceased to be of much importance, and marriage is decidedly not the universal background for sexual expression, for procreative activity, or even for the upbringing of offspring. Marriage-like associations between partners of the same sex are also to be observed.

5. by the fact that the spouse-bond is markedly insecure, divorce is a common outcome of marital careers, and high proportions of children suffer disruption of parental linkages, sometimes several of them.

6. by the fact that a high proportion of families have to rely for their support on the proceeds of employment away from the home of both parents, mother and father, leading to an episodic, improvised familial experience for children and other family members.

7. by the fact that family groups, or rather non-familial groups, of solitaries and couples without children, consist so very frequently of old persons, everyone being exceedingly long lived.

There are of course other characteristics of contemporary European families which mark them out as entirely exceptional, historically and geographically, but I hope I have said enough to justify my remarks about the fall of Humpty Dumpty. The traditional model of the family in European societies rested to such a degree on the conditions and regularities which these seven attributes have revised or made obsolete, that that model is not now recoverable. How extreme the differences are could be illustrated from any one of the seven features which have been named. We will take the seventh as a convenient example.

Over the 350 years of English social history before what is called the Secular Shift in Ageing began in the 1890s, the median proportion of persons over sixty fluctuated between 6 per cent and 10 per cent, the second an extreme value very rarely attained. Non-European societies of our own day have smaller proportions of those over sixty, 4 per cent or 5 per cent being fairly common. Expectation of life at birth in historical England varied a little more widely, between the outlying values of 28 and 42 years, the first of these figures being typical of the non-European world before the fall in mortality which began in those developing areas twenty years ago. If we contrast these standard figures for ageing, those which have obtained over all history before my lifetime and in all parts of the world, with those which obtain today in the United Kingdom, we find the following. Proportions over sixty are some 21 per cent, twice the highest value ever attained before 1900 and three times the expected historical value. Expectation of life at birth is about seventy-seven years for both genders combined, again well over twice the traditional level, the level assumed by the traditional model of European families.

These contrasts are so remarkable that it is difficult for us to recognise as yet what they imply. A society where people live for so much longer and where elderly people abound to such an extent, is quite simply a different society. It is also a society that has never existed anywhere before. The position of children is quite other than it used to be and is elsewhere, if only in respect of the extent to which they belong to generational linkages, elongating to three or four levels, to the great-grandparental level in fact. In traditional England and elsewhere in the contemporary world most children have had parents only, certainly from their tenth year onwards.

European families, like American families, historically simple or nuclear in structure, mostly lacking resident relatives (that is to say, are now even less likely to have resident kin), are smaller than ever before, and smaller than any we know about anywhere in the world. There are now unprecedented, unparalleled numbers of one-person households in all the European countries, and of households without children. Where children are present child-groups of more than three are exceedingly rare. Many children are only children, those whose socialisation is most likely to be disturbed. Proportions of children born outside marriage are very high indeed, higher over the whole arena of European countries than any previously recorded or otherwise known for populations of substantial size. Nearly one third of English babies are now born outside wedlock.

Amongst our European populations today age at sexual maturity is lower than it has ever been in human history and lower than in any undeveloped or developing country on which we have information. At the same time the age at which full membership of the society is accorded to the individual, a settled job at adequate pay, etc., has tended to go up. This has happened for several reasons of which the lengthening of the period of education is the most important. These two developments mean that the period of childhood now runs for nine years only, from the ages of three to twelve, as compared with thirteen years, between the ages of three and sixteen, assumed by the once accepted model of the family in European countries. Adolescence, however, the period between maturity and full acceptance as a responsible citizen, has been prolonged from twelve years old to twenty-one, or even twenty-four, as compared with sixteen to twenty-one, or even twenty-four, as compared with sixteen to twenty-one in earlier times. The consequences are that a very high proportion of individuals in the younger age groups is capable of full sexual life and the production of children well before social adulthood has arrived, along with the beginning of settled procreative association, usually marriage but increasingly consensual union.

When taken along with the fourth of the extraordinary family features on the list, that is the entirely efficient separation of sexual relationships from procreation by means of contraception, sterilisation and abortion, the last freely available in many, but by no means all, of the countries, the production of children in contemporary European families begins to look very exceptional indeed. As Europeans we tend to leave the bringing of children into the world to people early in the life-course; we spend the greater part of our very lengthy period in the married state, sometimes with a succession of partners, without considering the possibility of further births, and halfway through that period the responsibility even for the nurturing of our own children has passed us by. No other families have ever been like this. A recent tendency for average age at child-bearing to rise, makes little difference to the overall contrast.

The over-riding issue for the historian contemplating

these extraordinary developments is the following. How far do rapid familial changes since the 1950s have to be put down to the general process of overall social transformation in Europe associated with demographic, economic and industrial development? How far on the other hand have they to be classed as historically contingent, a question of decision, attitude and action? – deliberate 'revolution'.

These are exceedingly difficult questions to answer, but a good deal has to be attributed to structural rather than contingent change. The demographic transition from a regime of high birth and death rates to low is inevitably accompanied by drastic reduction in numbers of births to most mothers and a drastic fall in the size of groups of children. A sharp rise in the proportion of all children who are first children is also ineluctable, as well as a multiplication of older persons and the lengthening of life for everybody. The enormous rise in living standards and medical care is equally inevitably accompanied by a fall in the age of sexual maturity. When the crucial part that education has to play in the development process is taken into account, the foreshortening of childhood is necessarily associated with the elongation of adolescence and the presence of large numbers of persons in that condition capable of full sexual activity and procreation. The arrival of a position where women's work is wanted in the economy and where both spouses have to earn, where in fact both of them feel that they have the right to earn, may also be an unavoidable consequence of prolonged and intense economic development.

Then there is the pressure on European and other rich industrial countries to accept immigration from poorer areas of the world. How far immigration can be described as an inevitable, though distant, effect of development is uncertain. Its influence on European family life is very conspicuous, even if it involves small numbers. For it has introduced other models, other traditions of sexual, procreative and familial behaviour and attitudes alongside and within the generally unified family life of a once universally Christian Europe, with its fairly strict if not entirely uniform and universally respected codes of familial and procreative practice. Relativism has inevitably gained ground in the familial arena and direct imitation cannot be excluded.

It would not be entirely inaccurate to describe the sexual and procreative practices current amongst European youth as versions of the Caribbean, for example. In Great Britain pop music and pop culture, much of it closely associated with our Caribbean immigrants, have been an effective force in changing the relevant attitudes. Pop culture, we must remember, has also demonstrated its effectiveness as a dissolvent amongst the youth of Central and Eastern Europe in their engagement with the political regimes against which they have campaigned so successfully.

The adoption of radicalism and pop culture along with the imitation of people with different familial mores imported from abroad surely have to be regarded as deliberate actions, and in this way can be correctly classed as revolutionary.

Let me remind you of how the student movement began in Paris in the early months of 1968, a crucial period for changes in divorce, contraception, consensual unions, births outside marriage, and so on. The original event, so I was told when I took up residence in Paris to teach at the Sorbonne for the months of May and June 1968, occurred at a ceremony for the opening of a swimming pool at the already restive campus of Nanterre, on the day when the French Minister of Education and a galaxy of official and academic dignitaries gathered round the water. The loud, harsh voice of Danny le Roux, Danny the Red, rang out:

We don't want a swimming pool! We want sexual freedom!

As we listen to that imperative demand after twenty-four years, let us remember that this generation of students *en lutte* are the parents of the young persons of today, whose treatment of each other and of their own children is what has to concern us here.

The events that we are hastily running over, the events as distinct from pre-disposing structural influences, took place amongst the young and those of student age primarily. Their elders were concerned of course; they had been responsible for the upbringing of these children, and many still sheltered them in their homes. But it did not seem that much in the way of resistance was put up by the parents or elders, at least resistance which had any effect, either in Paris or elsewhere in Europe in those months and years of what the historians seem bound to entitle 'the sexual revolution.' This abdication of entrenched attitudes and institutions was and is evident in quite other areas of social activity and social authority. It is striking how easily these authorities, secular and spiritual, even in the Catholic European countries, accepted contraception, cohabitation and divorce.

Here we reach tendencies that go back a century or more and which make it possible to describe the events of the 1950s–80s as the culmination of a long-term movement of change. Secularisation and the rejection of religious belief had begun with the Enlightenment 200 years before the student movement in the late 1960s, and became compulsory doctrines for many European populations under authoritarian socialism, which initially rejected the family too, as an unacceptable bourgeois institution.

Perhaps the most surprising thing is how little, as it transpired, the traditional familial model in European countries hung together, how changing sexual and procreative practices have not necessarily involved the decline of solidarity within family groups, or of the strength of kinship bonds, or of the intense love of spouse for spouse, parent for child and child for parent, of grown children for old and failing fathers and mothers, even uncles, aunts and grandparents. The persisting power of kinship links in the maintenance of the dependent old is a perpetual surprise to those who observe it. The immemorial cult of innocence amongst women, celebrated *ad infinitum* in European poetry, prose, drama and the plastic arts, quite apart from the Christian religion, may have seemed to have vanished overnight. But family life and family values most decidedly survive, if in an increasingly modulated form. Anyone who doubts this should attend to the images used by marketeers to sell consumption goods to Europeans.

It remains to be seen of course whether family life of this kind will continue in spite of the persistence of anti-familial ideological changes and the further fall in fertility which is widely prophesied. It will be particularly important to observe how far the increased numbers of the dependent elderly are looked after by the children of spouses who have been divorced and by children who were irregularly born. But the proliferation of kinship connections because of the rise in the number of spouses a person may have, may turn out to be an unexpected source of support for those in need of it.

The collectivity and its agents, secular and spiritual, have taken responsibility for children and for the casualties of demographic change, such as the elderly, and of economic vicissitudes as well, for as long as European political organisation has existed. In recognising how very, very different the family now is in the European states from what is was or is elsewhere, and how vulnerable are our children, an extraordinarily demanding challenge is being faced.

JANE KRAMER

Letter from Europe

London

My FRIEND TOMMY, who is Persian and Punjabi by origin, Pakistani by birth, British by nationality, and by choice and, perhaps, destiny a graduate student of post-colonial politics in a radical department of a redbrick English university, has given up drinking and reading Salman Rushdie. He likes to say that he is "by politics a Muslim," though it is hard to know exactly what being a Muslim in Britain means, two weeks after Salman Rushdie embraced Islam—and two years after Rushdie's novel *The Satanic Verses* was burned in the Yorkshire cities of Bolton and Bradford by Muslim workers trying to believe that the imagined heresies of one complicated, worldly, and fantastical book stood, somehow, for the real humiliations of an immigrant lifetime. The Bradford Muslims come mainly from two villages in Pakistan called Mirpur and Campbellpur. They were peasants in Pakistan. Their life was primitive even by the local standards. They practiced a fervent, syncretic, folk Islam that evoked the mystical presence of the saints and the Prophet—something most orthodox Arab Muslims, the "Knightsbridge Muslims," would find heretical in itself—and it is unlikely, even now, that many of them could read

The Satanic Verses if they bought it, even if it were published in Urdu. They have as little (or as much) in common with those Knightsbridge Muslims, from the oil states, as they do with Bombay cosmopolitans like Salman Rushdie, or with the student I call Tommy and his friends, who met in the cafeteria at the School of Oriental and African Studies, on Malet Street, across from Dillon's Book Store, to talk about postmodernism and post-colonialism and post-structuralism and the multi-cultural experience, or with the Yemeni millworkers who live in Leicester, or the Bengali cooks who live in the London borough of Tower Hamlets, or even Pakistanis who happen to come from other towns. Nothing in the past bound the Muslims here. Not faith. Not race or politics or the common experience of loneliness, ignorance, prejudice, or rejection. It was *The Satanic Verses* that marked them. They were a community waiting to be raised, and the book turned them into a constituency waiting to be exploited. They were the stuff of a moral majority – people otherwise ignored.

There are, by most estimates, anywhere from a million to a million and a half Muslims in the United Kingdom – certainly a million and a half if you include, with the South Asians and the Arabs, the black Muslims from Africa and from the old West Indian colonies and the "white Muslims," with amalgamated names like Daud Musa Pidcock, who belong to a party called the Islamic Party of Great Britain, and who are by and large converts. Half the two million Asians in Britain are Muslims. (The English call everybody from the Indian subcontinent "Asian," whereas they call the Chinese, say, "Chinese" and the Koreans "Koreans.") They have their roots in the Raj, in what is now India, Pakistan, and Bangladesh, but many of them were born here, and by the end of the century the great majority of them will have been born here. Their population has doubled in the past twenty years – Pakistani and Bangladeshi women have the highest birth rate of any women in the country – and in towns like Bradford they account for fifteen or twenty per cent of the population.

To the anxious, xenophobic English, who have trouble distinguishing between foreigners to begin with, let alone between foreigners from the same Punjabi province, they can seem like half the population. They are, as one of Tommy's friends at the School of Oriental and African Studies put it, "bottom-line different." They would be different in the salons of Karachi and Bombay, and not just on the BBC nightly news shouting "Kill Rushdie!" and "Salman Rushdie must die!" To the extent that they remain different, the trouble that everyone calls "the Rushdie affair" – the trouble that began here with the publication of *The Satanic Verses* and the Bradford book burning and inspired the Ayatollah Ruhollah Khomeini to put a price on Salman Rushdie's head – is really about them, and about their rights in England and their rights *to* England. It is about being an immigrant in a country where identity has always been something settled, something particular – a country that never thought of itself as a place for, or even with, immigrants. It is about whether that country can transform itself to accommodate immigrants now, or should transform itself, or, indeed, will survive in a fractal "postmodern" world without transforming. It is about the civilization of hosts in conflict with the demands of strangers, about the unforeseen, inevitable implosion that has marked the end of the colonial adventure and turned Europe into a looking-glass world in which the frontier has relocated in the heart of the metropole, and strange, wild, incomprehensible Eastern people do indeed drop out of the sky and into Western life and assumptions, like Saladin Chamcha and Gibreel Farishta, Salman Rushdie's extravagant, exuberant heroes.

The historian Eric Hobsbawm said about the Rushdie affair that the trouble with the English is "we have no confusion as to who we are: the English are English, and anybody who isn't, isn't." He said the real reason the English won't let anyone assimilate is that it never occurs to them that assimilation is possible – a conviction they share, curiously, with the Muslim fundamentalists they criticize. English colonials were never educated to *be* English. To be English, they would have had to sail to England and breathe the air and read the history on English benches and in English libraries, and that was something reserved for a handful of rich men's sons, and for the math prodigies from Calcutta or Madras who were plucked out of village schools and sent to Cambridge, and eventually joined the faculty as token geniuses. There were rich Indian parliamentarians in England long before there was an Indian community – and, indeed, they were sent to England to represent their friends in India, and not the problems of whatever constituency was cajoled or bribed to put them in Westminster. A hundred years ago, a Parsi lawyer named Dadabhai Naoroji stood for Parliament as a Liberal (under the patronage of the Marquis of Ripon, who had bought him a constituency in Finsbury) and won, and then a Parsi lawyer named Mancherjee Bhownaggree stood as a Tory for Bethnal Green, and thirty years after that a Parsi named Shapurji Saklatvala stood for North Battersea, and won, first for Labour and two years later as a Communist. But Asian workers were not recruited in any numbers until the end of the Second World War, and most of those workers were in England anyway – Indian ships' stokers who had been stranded in Liverpool or Hull by the war and had made their way to Leeds and Bradford and the other mill towns, replacing as they went the young Welsh and Scottish millworkers killed in the fighting.

The Asians were known then as "the decent browns" – which meant mainly that they were cheap, tractable browns and did not complain and, in fact, had no one to complain to, being excluded from the Trades Union Congress by

English, Scottish, Welsh, and Irish workers who were barely on speaking terms among themselves. The Asians went
anywhere there were jobs for them—there are Pakistani
villages today on the outermost islands of the Outer
Hebrides—and they kept to themselves, and as long as Britain needed people to do the work no one else wanted they
were, in a manner of speaking, welcome. They made themselves useful. They set up little corner shops, where everyone in the family worked around the clock selling groceries,
and the English got used to having a place that was always
open, even nights and Sundays, when English shops are
closed—a place where they could buy milk or beer or a bag
of chips, or spicy, greasy exotic snacks with names like
papadums and chapattis. In those days, the English approved of the Asians they saw working at the corner shops.
They approved of the Asians' children. The children were
thought to be diligent, obedient, compliant, quiet—not
problem children, which is how the English thought of the
West Indian kids who cut school and smoked dope and got
in fights and preferred Bob Marley to Ringo Starr, and who
seemed to have no interest in getting jobs and doing well or,
indeed, in doing anything at all besides going to the nearest
dole office of the Department of Health and Social Security
once a week to collect their unemployment. The Asians
made few claims, at first, on the social services. They
worked all day and then went home to their neighborhoods
and shut their doors. They rarely disturbed the bland tran-
quillity of English habit. They were maybe a little too keen,
and it was generally agreed that they did not know how to
treat their women, but in good times they provided a kind of
background charm. They called to mind the rich incongrui-
ties of empire—Mr. Singh pumping gas in his turban, Mr.
Patel lighting joss sticks in his takeaway shop, Mr. Ali in the
tube station on his way to Friday prayers. In bad times, they
were a convenient scourge.
    At first, the Asians were able to enter freely, as old colo-

nials and, by extension, British subjects. They had British passports—eventually "New Commonwealth" passports, which was the official way of saying "colored"—and the right to keep them as the empire dissolved. They came at first, like the North Africans in France, with the intention of getting rich and going home, but it was only a matter of time before the British started legislating against them. In 1968, under pressure from Enoch Powell's "rivers of blood" nationalists, on the right, and from Arthur Scargill's xenophobic trade unionists, on the left, Harold Wilson's second Labour Government wrote a Commonwealth Immigrants Act, restricting the entry rights of Commonwealth subjects whose parents or grandparents were not subjects of the United Kingdom. It worked, perversely, to make the immigrants stay; the immigrants stopped commuting and took out residence papers and sent to India and Pakistan for their families, and in the end there were more Asians in Britain than before.

For a while, the Asians did a lively business in marriages. Men who would ordinarily have entered the country on their old British passports wrote to marriage brokers in Leicester or London, and the brokers put them in touch with British-Asian families with unmarried daughters, and, for a price, a match was made, and the happy husband immigrated as the new member of a British family. The British replied, in 1980, with what they called a "primary purpose" rule, which in effect allowed the immigration officers at the airport to turn back any immigrant whose marriage was not, to the officers' minds, "its own primary purpose." At first, the rule was meant to stop women marrying to bring in men, but in 1983 three women brought a case challenging the rule before the European Court of Human Rights, and the court ruled that it was sexist, and the British replied to *that* by extending the rule to stop men marrying to bring in women. By then, anyway, the issue was not immigration.

The British talked about immigration and immigrants and about an "immigrant problem," but the real problem was the fact that thousands of brown-skinned British-born British subjects were growing up and marrying and producing more brown-skinned British-born British subjects, and those subjects raised disturbing questions about what being British meant. By 1983, forty per cent of the Asians here were born here – about half in London and most of the rest to families in the old industrial northern towns. They were known, whatever their origin, as the Pakis. It was not a salutary term. The English said "Paki" the way they said "wog" or "nigger." They went to the Paki's for their groceries, and they went Paki-bashing for amusement. Paki-bashing got to be so popular as a pastime among English skinheads that it entered the language as a synonym for "beating up foreigners."

The Asian kids made easy targets. They were often small. They were often gentle. They did not like fighting, the way (the English said) the black kids in Brent or Brixton liked fighting. They did not stake out territory to defend. Eric Hobsbawm says that twenty years earlier they would have been Marxists – they would have turned to something political to explain or even articulate their despair. Instead, they practiced an eccentric, evasive conformity that sometimes passed for assimilation. They said Muslim prayers and burned Hindu joss and watched Australian sitcoms and smoked American cigarettes and drank English lager. The boys fancied blue-eyed Irish girls and Rasta clubs. The girls wore jeans and practiced purdah. The parents wondered why children like theirs, with three or four South Asian languages, were always held back at school because their English was poor. A lot of the parents wanted to assimilate. They wanted to conform, to fit in, to disappear into an Englishness that would cover for their strange faith and stubborn customs – that may be why they practiced servility and discretion and hard work and whatever other English virtues the English allowed them – but their children were involved in another kind of Englishness, which exposed the children and challenged the parents and their fragile status. The children were insulted by the English, but they loved the intoxicating liberty of British culture. They were more concerned with discrimination in the disco than in the courts or the classroom or the local housing office. Their problem was not survival but identity.

It is easy to see how the various parties to the Salman Rushdie affair – the local Muslim politicos and the foreign power brokers – could engage those made-in-Britain Asian children to their own advantage. It is easy to see how the question of who those children were could be turned into the question of what kind of Muslims they were – of how much they hated Salman Rushdie and his novel. For them, being *something* – being Asian, injured, protesting; being brothers in an Islamic nation of a billion people – was much more interesting than being "not English," being not cool, being not assimilated, being not accepted. It made them a force in British politics, and, indeed, in Iranian politics, and in Indian and Pakistani and even Saudi politics. Rejecting Rushdie, they were a symbol. They were on the front page of every paper in the world, and they were irresistible to the Saudi and Iranian rulers fighting for newsprint legitimacy among the far-flung faithful. They were solicited in the mosques of Bradford and Tower Hamlets. They were offered money for protest marches. Muslim nationalists from the Jamaat-i-Islami in Pakistan used them to challenge Benazir Bhutto, and Muslim politicians from the Janata Party in India used them to challenge Rajiv Gandhi – to force rivals to ban *The Satanic Verses* or, better, defend *The Satanic Verses* and see their governments fall. They used the

Muslims in England so that Muslims at home would keep on rioting, and policemen would keep on shooting them, and pious people would be horrified. It was quicker and more efficient—and it cost less—to export the Rushdie affair to England for the exposure than to leave the Islamic Revolution to creaking Third World parliamentary processes or bought votes or stuffed ballot boxes. One burned book in Bradford provided militant Islam with more prime time on Western television than the deaths of six Muslims demonstrating against the book in Islamabad or the injuries of a hundred Muslims demonstrating against it in Kashmir. And the result for Britain was that the immigrants it once had kept from assimilating started demanding *not* to assimilate—started demanding separate status, demanding that British laws and what the British like to call their Enlightenment values be suspended or changed to conform to the Islamic law the immigrants had left behind on the subcontinent. They started demanding the right to invoke their own theocratic sanctions against the freedoms of a secular state in which they had requested, and received, citizenship. They demanded, in effect, the right to create a theocracy within that state—saying that as long as they were in England, England was a Muslim country. They were disgruntled, defensive, and, suddenly, with the Rushdie affair, notorious, and it is hard to imagine how they could have been persuaded to ignore the quick symbols of community that they discovered—avoiding *The Satanic Verses* was surely as easy a way to "be" Muslim as avoiding gin or pork—and take up the grinding, anonymous business of confronting prejudice or poverty in their daily lives. Marx was in England when he decided that religion was the opiate of the people, and, while many Englishmen have pointed out that the opiate of the people was in fact opium (Anthony Burgess once wrote that laudanum had "reconciled, with a Sunday of dreams, the British proletariat to its damnable fate"), the old Marxists here believe that militant, immigrant Islam is the new opiate of a new British proletariat. They see the Islamic revival as a tactic, putting the immigrants beyond the reach of a "proper" politics. They say that it stands between the immigrants and their freedom, a mirror image of the system that exploits and excludes them now.

The Satanic Verses was published on September 26, 1988, and banned in India on October 5th, and it was apparently Muslim activists in India, working through the Islamic Foundation of Leicester (a British Muslim foundation financed by Saudis and controlled to some degree by Pakistanis from the Jamaat-i-Islami), who first suggested that British Muslims try to get the book banned, too. Salman Rushdie was an enfant terrible in India, a local boy who had gone to Oxford and got to be famous in the West and spent his time with other famous people—and the book was bound to be controversial, and everybody in India who read books knew it. Rushdie's two other South Asia novels, *Shame* and *Midnight's Children,* were notorious in India and Pakistan for what could be called their political blasphemies against (among others) Indira Gandhi, General Zia ul-Haq, and Benazir Bhutto. It was hard to imagine that the same people who had banned those books would ignore *The Satanic Verses,* especially when the first important Asian review, in the *Times of India,* had made a great deal of how provocative the book was and how fierce the Muslim reaction was going to be. (Rushdie's friends assumed that the review was planted by enemies, but his enemies insisted that it was planted by friends, for the publicity.) There was fighting in Kashmir at the time, and the tension between Hindus and Muslims was even worse than usual. Less than a year earlier, the publication of a short story about a Muslim deaf-mute—it was called "Muhammad the Idiot"—was the occasion for a riot that lasted three days and ended with seventeen people dead and parts of the country in a state of emergency.

There is still a lot of what used to be called "the colonial mentality" in India and Pakistan. People believe (despite their best efforts not to believe) that nothing important happens that does not happen in Great Britain, and enough of them have contacts in Britain, and phones and faxes and Xeroxes to feed those contacts with local news, to make sure it happens here. Malise Ruthven, a British Islamicist who wrote a book about Rushdie called "A Satanic Affair," calls it "the Raj in reverse." His particular theory is that people from the Jamaat-i-Islami were in fact orchestrating the spread of the affair in England, but the evidence is that it would have spread anyway, and spread fast. A few weeks after the Muslims in India got in touch with the Muslims in Leicester, a delegation of British Muslims went to Oxford to call on the director of the Oxford Center for Mission Studies, Bishop Michael Nazir-Ali (who is the son of a Shiite Muslim who was converted to the Church of England), to ask for Church support. Another delegation called on the Home Secretary, Geoffrey Howe (who complained later to the BBC that *The Satanic Verses* was "extremely critical, and rude about us," and said that he had not liked it any better than the Muslims liked it). A third delegation petitioned Rushdie's publisher, Peter Mayer, at Viking-Penguin, to withdraw the book from bookstores. The Queen was approached. The Prime Minister was contacted. A weekly magazine called *Impact International,* which I have heard described as "the unofficial organ of Islam in England," put out a Salman Rushdie issue. Ali Mughram al-Ghamdi, the director of the London Central Mosque, was instructed to name a United Kingdom Action Committee on Islamic Affairs, which in theory was going to represent the British Council of Mosques and all the other British Muslim groups in a campaign to ban *The Satanic Verses.*

Banning books is not something the British do. They maintain the traditions of a soapbox corner in Hyde Park and a parliamentary mudsling in which members shout insults at the Prime Minister, and it is unlikely that they would ever have been moved by petitions to ban a novel by one of their most important writers. It should have been clear, early on, to the people who organized the protests that there was no chance *The Satanic Verses* would be banned here. It was banned in India and Pakistan and South Africa and twenty other countries where it was considered dangerous to hard-won social or political arrangements, but not even Iran banned *The Satanic Verses*. (The anthropologist Michael Fischer, who wrote an impressive scholarly account of the Rushdie affair called "Bombay Talkies, the Word and the World," pointed out that both *Midnight's Children* and *Shame* were published in Iran, and that *Shame* won the state prize for the best translation of a novel into Persian.) There was a mildly negative review in the literary supplement of *Kayhan,* the country's biggest daily paper, and after that no one outside the Koranic center in Qum paid much attention to *The Satanic Verses* until a group of Qum mullahs read a selection of twenty pages to the Ayatollah, and the Ayatollah issued his *fatwa* – a *fatwa* is a kind of Koranic brief, or edict – sentencing Salman Rushdie to death for writing "in opposition to Islam, the Prophet, and the Koran," and the Iranians moved, so to speak, to take over the anti-Rushdie monopoly. The selection included a passage about a crazy imam hiding in a Kensington flat, and, according to British diplomats who heard about the reading, "it was designed to send the old boy incandescent." Khomeini was eighty-eight, and failing, and his mullahs were determined to offer him a cause with which – at far less risk than with a hostage crisis and for far less money than with an eight-year war – he could revive his flagging authority as a leader and his angry battle against a corrupt West and a corrupted Islam.

For a while, there was talk of a Saudi *fatwa*. The Saudis claimed that Khomeini had acted without what could be called theological due process. They said that Rushdie was guilty but had not been sentenced "correctly." They put about the idea that, while the *fatwa* against him was appropriate, it was invalid for having been issued without a proper trial – that is, a trial held according to the Sharia, or Islamic law, before an Islamic court, with Rushdie present. This gave the Saudis the chance to demand Rushdie's extradition "into Islam" – into a country under Islamic law. The obvious choice for them was Saudi Arabia.

The status of the *fatwa* was much discussed in academic circles in England. Arguments about the non-lieu of the *fatwa* became the scholars' equivalent of the arguments about political authority over Muslim immigrants in general. In the spring of 1989, Saudi ulema were said to be preparing a trial for Rushdie. Islamic scholars were writing briefs and wording the charges to be presented to (presumably) the judges in Mecca. Their claim that, whatever the Iranians said, Salman Rushdie could not be sentenced in absentia but had to be tried "in Islam by Islam" made a fine point, and was not much comfort or help to Salman Rushdie, hiding for his life, moving fifty or sixty times, never getting to see his child. In the end, it excited the white Islamicists much more than it did the Pakistani workers in Bradford or the Indian workers in Brent or the Bengali workers in East London, and the Saudis forgot about it, or seemed to forget about it, or, at least, stopped talking about it in meetings of the World Islamic League and the other Muslim organizations they dominated. The *fatwa* was Khomeini's. It gave him his last prominence. British Muslim workers repeated the words that Rushdie must die, and were frightened or delighted by the way they sounded, but they said of Khomeini that here at last was a bloke who had said "Fuck all!" to the Brits and made the Brits tremble. It is probably safe to say that making the Brits tremble is something every immigrant in Britain has dreamed of doing. In the end, the idea surely interests them as much as Salman Rushdie interests them, or even *The Satanic Verses* interests them. Most Asians were unmoved, and even surprised, when the English tried to persuade them to read the book before condemning it. They said it had never occurred to them to read it. The men in some British mosques appointed "representatives" to read it for them, and apparently some of the Muslim students—including my friend Tommy's sister, who is getting a doctorate—went to the bookstore, chose ten or fifteen pages at random, read *them*, and decided about the novel that way.

Michael Fischer says it would be interesting to see how many British Muslims would be able to identify the Satanic verses—"They are high flying birds, Their intercession is to be hoped for"—which Muhammad, deceived by Satan, either did or did not record as the word of God, and which are said to promote three goddesses of the Ka'ba to the intercessionary status of archangels, when the received truth is that angels are male. Professor Fischer is a Rushdie fan as well as a scholar of Islam, and he points out that Rushdie's story about Muhammad and his dream and the high-flying ladies (among other stories that were said to insult the Prophet) is a famous story in Hadith literature, and that learned Muslims have been arguing about it for hundreds of years, and, in fact, that "Rushdie's speculations in his novel... are no different than the debates in the long history of Islamic scholarship, which often too have drawn on humor, parables, analogies, and other devices of entertainment." But the immigrants here were less interested in what *The Satanic Verses* said than in what it was—a book that bore the imprimatur of the white world in which it had appeared, and which had received it warmly. Bhikhu Parekh, who teaches political theory at Hull and used to be active in the Commission for Racial Equality, wrote a piece for the *Indepen* ini a few days after the *fatwa* was issued, and talked at length about the "suspicion and alienation" between the immigrant communities here and their intellectuals. He said that "the large masses of Asians have long felt that those Asians who write, make films and television programmes or engage in instant punditry about them do not understand their innermost hopes and fears, and that they earn a handsome living and white acclaim by selling tired stereotypes and biased stories," and that many Asians think of them as being as racist as the English. The older immigrants had their Koranic education back in Pakistan, in villages like Campbellpur and Mirpur—it was the only education they had, and it was often the only literacy they had. The mullahs and ulema they have now are usually the same teachers they had at home—village savants and self-made schoolmasters who would have nothing in common with the Koranic scholars in centers like Cairo who spend a lifetime arguing fine points of the same passage, or with the Sufi poets in Fez and Damascus, or with the students at Qum, on their long apprenticeship in Islamic literature and history, or with the professors at Princeton and Oxford who fill the chairs that a rich Iranian named Seyyed Ali Golestaneh endows for the study of Shiite mysticism. Their ulema guide them, like village priests, down paths as narrow and defended as the back paths—the women's walks—they build behind the council flats in their new English neighborhoods. The fact that there is a tradition of religious satire in Islam, or an "ironist" school of interpretation of the Suras and the Hadith, is not something that concerns them, and they would probably be as reluctant to acknowledge it as they are to acknowledge that a lot of educated Muslims think *The Satanic Verses* is a good book. The literary theorist Homi Bhabha says that the immigrants have taken *The Satanic Verses* outside the realm of fiction and "into the realm of intention"—and that the important question is therefore not whether the book is insulting to Islam but who *sees* it as insulting to Islam, and what this means to what Professor Bhabha calls "the project of modernity." He says the immigrants are simply expressing what postmodernists like him have been saying all along: that there is no "master narrative" for reality anymore; there is only what Rushdie once called "the *bricolage* of experience"—a kind of eternal argument in which the terms of the cultural exchange are always changing, always in the process of being undermined and reconstituted and undermined again. Homi Bhabha says that the only certainty now is the one certainty that fundamentalism resists—the certainty that there are no final vocabularies, and no communities that are "structured for all time," whether they are the great rationalist communities of the Enlightenment or the *umma* of orthodox Islam.

The English used to believe they had a "multi-cultural society." It was a way of saying that they preferred their immigrants, and especially their Asian immigrants, to keep their quaint customs and their religious enthusiasms to themselves. The English talked about assimilation as something Americans practiced, something peculiar to Americans, having to do with the American dream of a melting pot. They said that assimilation happened in America because being an immigrant, or having been an immigrant, or having had parents or grandparents who were immigrants, was an experience that all Americans but the Native Americans shared, and was part of the common definition of "American," as powerful in the end as any of the differences that kept Americans apart. But assimilation had nothing to do with England. If being English meant anything, it meant *not* being an immigrant. It meant being white, and Anglo-Saxon, and looking English and acting English and having a

very particular English history, which was rooted in place
and in common assumptions and expectations and illusions
about the world. It was not something you thickened or en-
riched, like stock, with new ingredients from somebody
else's garden, which is why the shock of the Rushdie affair in
England had less to do with the English discovering their
"immigrant problem" – everybody knew there was an immigrant problem – than with the English discovering that
they were still so unprepared for their immigrant problem.
It had to do with people realizing that, despite decades of
immigration and legislation about immigration and violence against immigrants, there had been no real debate
about the kind of society the British were going to make, or
even wanted to make, once immigrants were a fact of British
life. British-Asian writers like Salman Rushdie and Hanif
Kureishi were describing that life in books and films, and
British-Asian scholars like Homi Bhabha were theorizing
about it in learned journals, and British-Asian students like
Tommy were attending seminars called "Life After Colo-
nialism" and "Post-Colonial Man." But the politicians ignored it. They pursued the Asian vote (and the West Indian
vote) as if it were the old English vote cast and counted in
another color, never asking themselves how they would respond to crises or resolve conflicts that had nothing to do
with English values or English sentiments.

By the time *The Satanic Verses* was published, there were
six "ethnic" seats in the House of Commons – six seats from
constituencies where the Asian-and-black minority was a
majority and controlled the vote – and Roy Hattersley, the
Home Secretary in the Labour Shadow Cabinet and a member from one of those constituencies, in Birmingham, says
that they were "wedded to labour like steel." (Asians vote
Labour three times as often as they vote Tory.) There were
ten seats where immigrant voters held the margin, and neither Labour nor the Tories could win an election without

them. There were three black members. The most powerful
was a British Ghanaian barrister named Paul Boateng,
whose Brent constituency represented the highest concen-
tration of blacks and Asians in the country—and who had
his eye on 1992, and European unity, and was determined
to survive the subject of Salman Rushdie and stake his
claims in a "black Europe" of sixteen million immigrant
workers. There was one Asian member, the first since
Shapurji Saklatvala retired his North Battersea seat, in
1929. His name was Keith Vaz. He was not a Muslim; he was
a Christian from Goa, with a predominantly white constituency, and, unlike Boateng—who had made his reputation
working for minority rights—he seems to have had no interest in Muslims until he saw his main chance in the Salman
Rushdie affair, and marched with the Bradford book burn-
ers, and started talking about Islam as "a religion for the
nineteen-nineties." By then, Bradford had had an Asian
mayor. Southall, the first of the big Asian neighborhoods in
London, had been organized for ten years. (The British National Front, which is a neo-Fascist party, had tried to hold a
meeting in the Southall town hall, and the Southall Asians
demonstrated, and the riot police arrived and arrested
three hundred Asians—and after that they organized.) The
Commission for Racial Equality had opened eighty-four
"racial-equality councils" around the country, and there
were at least as many Asian youth-movement groups
funded by mosque councils. People were producing studies
with names like "Black and White Britain," and were docu-
menting cases of discrimination: what it meant, say, when a
local council stopped building the three- or four-bedroom
flats that an extended Asian family, with three generations
in residence, needed to survive; what it meant when a bright
child was streamed into a trade-school apprenticeship because his English wasn't strong enough for the academic
track; what, indeed, it meant when a fourteen-year-old

Asian boy was shot from a car by three white boys on a ram-
page, and the boys explained themselves by saying, "So
what, it's only a Paki," and the local police said that it was not
a racist incident.

My friend Tommy collects what he sometimes calls "discrimination statistics." He says, for instance, that for years
there were only ten or twenty Asians and blacks among
eight thousand London firemen; it was understood that
Asians were small and didn't meet the physical requirements, and that blacks were big but didn't meet the "mental
requirements." For years, there were no blacks or Asians at
the Palace, in the Queen's Household Division of the Grena-
dier and Cold Stream Guards; it was understood that they
wouldn't have matched the white soldiers. In 1988, there
was an Education Reform Act to emphasize "Christian curriculum" and British history, and Tommy says that thousands of parents – most particularly white parents – applied
to take their children out of local schools and put them in
schools that were better, or more congenial. In 1989, there
was only one Asian family on the television soap "East-
enders," and Tommy says that they went to the pub so often
they might as well have been English. In 1990, Norman
Tebbit, who used to be the Tory Party chairman, suggested
that the way to solve the immigration problem was to ask everyone who wanted to enter England whose cricket team he
would support if it came to a choice between England and
the country he was leaving.

It is difficult to think of Tommy as an immigration problem. He lives with a group of other students, including a
Catholic and a Jew and a couple of young women who are
"into feminism," and he likes to dress in black, like a biker,
and occasionally puts a coat of black polish on his finger-
nails. In Bradford, the "new" Islam appealed to young
people who were perhaps intolerably confused – people
who could not accept what Homi Bhabha has called the "in-

commensurability" of the immigrant experience. But Tommy and his friends are London children, disciples of Bhabha and Ernesto Laclau and quite comfortable with incommensurability, as well as with the "dialogic principle of culture" and the "project of modernity" and the "eternal argument," and they can spin fascinating theories about their own despair. The fact that many of them are embracing Muslim custom by way of denouncing Salman Rushdie (or what they think of as Salman Rushdie) is as striking as the fact that familiar, peaceable, dependable Yorkshire Muslims—the "decent browns" and their compliant children—are burning books and rioting and working themselves up into a commitment to murder. Tommy has come to believe that the understanding between the British and their "browns" has always been superficial, and always self-deceiving, on both sides.

The idea of community is something very different for Muslims than for Europeans. Community means "community of faith," and cannot be separated from politics or law. It makes no difference that orthodox Muslims describe it by talking about *umma* and Tommy describes it by talking about Adorno and Horkheimer and the theory of negative dialectics. Tommy says that he never thought much about community before, but during the Rushdie affair he began to think about it all the time. It was not so much that the book troubled him; it was British astonishment that the book *might* trouble him. He saw, he says, that there was something very exclusive beneath the rubric of Britishness. He and his friends, at their cafeteria lunches, began to wonder if the only choice they had in England was between becoming completely assimilated and becoming completely marginal. They wondered if the Rushdie affair was really a kind of attrition, the cost of a crisis that had started ten years earlier when Mrs. Thatcher, standing for her first term, said she could understand how English people were feeling "swamped" by foreigners, and respectable politicians began telling Muslims to learn to behave like Englishmen or go home. Tommy and his friends had thought of themselves as normal London students – in other words, left-wing students – but Tommy says that the left had no answer to the Rushdie affair, that the old left leaders like Michael Foot were mouthing the clichés of an aging liberalism and the new left leaders were talking about Salman Rushdie's paperback while the British Asians were talking about pain. In a way, they blamed the Rushdies they knew for the fact that Asian workers were moving into a defiant orthodoxy instead of what Tommy calls a defiant identity. They looked at the celebrities of the British-Asian left – Rushdie and Kurcishi and the playwright Farrukh Dhondy, and Tariq Ali, who had been a student leader in 1968 and had moved, as Tommy put it, from Trotsky to Labour to a producer's office at Channel 4 – and were disturbed by the high comedy those Asians made of the immigrants' experience. Being young, they took (or mistook) seriousness for respect. A lot of young Asian women started wearing headscarves to the library. They started saying that the few British-Asian feminists were dupes of a white, male plot to "control fecundity." They talked about their scarves "freeing them from the 'male gaze'." Tommy, as I said, stopped drinking. He went to the same London parties and saw the same sophisticated London people, and he says that whenever those people asked him why he wasn't drinking and he told them he was "being political," they treated him like one of the mad mullahs on the evening news – they treated him like a Muslim.

Tommy says that he wondered, growing up, why anyone in England was a Muslim, since people tended to treat Islam as something shameful, on the order of a sexual disease. He says that as a boy the closest he came to answering the question "Who am I?" was watching old movie epics like "El Cid" and "Khartoum" and trying to ignore Charlton Heston and identifying with the bad guys – and discovering that he was no longer "not there," and wondering if Sioux and Apache children watching cowboy-and-Indian movies felt the same way. In the end, though, he identified with Charlton Heston, and sometimes he hated himself for it. He says he would ask himself – even now he asks himself – "What does it matter, after fourteen hundred years, if Muhammad was a wog, or a vampire, or even if Muhammad was *wrong*? Does that mean we don't exist? Does that mean we have produced nothing of value?"

There is an extremely active Council of Mosques in Bradford – which is one reason Bradford got to be known as the British Muslim capital during the Rushdie affair. Muslims organized there about ten years ago; they forced out a local principal – who had attacked a "multi-cultural education" program that was providing *halal* meat twice a week to Bradford schoolchildren and making other concessions to foreign customs which the principal said were undermining "British traditions of understatement, civilized discourse and respect for reason." The principal, whose name was Ray Honeyford, had made his case for British traditions in the *Salisbury Review,* a radical right-wing quarterly devoted to "the consciousness of nationhood." He included a description of the "hysterical political temperament of the Indian subcontinent," and wrote off Pakistan as criminal, corrupt, and despotic. It was a fairly accurate description of General Zia's Pakistan, but it was not – as Hanif Kureishi pointed out in a piece he wrote about Bradford for *Granta* – "merely an alternative view on matters of education," and it reminded the Bradford Muslims that their principal had once described a parent, in the *Times Educational Supplement,* as having an accent "like that of Peter Sellers' Indian doctor on an off day."

The Bradford Muslims brought a case against Honeyford. It went to Britain's High Court and then to Britain's Appeals Court, and by the time it was settled, in 1985 (Honeyford "retired" early, with a hundred and sixty thousand pounds, the biggest redundancy settlement in the history of the country), he had such a reputation on the right that Mrs. Thatcher invited him to Downing Street to give his views on education policy. By then, too, the Bradford Muslims were organized. Their Council of Mosques had seventy thousand pounds in Bradford Council funds and represented twenty-two of the twenty-six mosques in the city. They had their Muslim mayor. They had a resident scholar named Shabbir Akhtar, who had come to Bradford with a Canadian doctorate, set himself up as a theologian, and proposed to the locals what Salman Rushdie's friend the writer Michael Ignatieff describes as "a rationalist's defense of fundamentalism." And they had as chairman of their Council of Mosques a supermarket manager named Sher Azam, who was an avid promoter of Bradford and himself, and wanted to use the Council as a kind of theological chamber of commerce. Sher Azam says that he heard about the Indian reaction to *The Satanic Verses* when friends in Blackburn sent him clippings about the book from Indian magazines. He asked the Bradford ulema to read excerpts from the book in Urdu, and they apparently did – and pronounced it blasphemous – because late in 1988 Azam and Akhtar and the rest of the board of the Council of Mosques demanded an injunction against it. When their suit failed, they were distressed enough, and shrewd enough, to see to it that the Bradford protests got more attention than any of the other protests that were taking place in England. Muslims in Bolton had burned *The Satanic Verses* early in December of 1988 and had suffered the humiliation of being totally ignored. The Bradford Muslims called the papers. They hired a British lawyer to advise them. They made a videotape of their book burning and sold the rights to use it.

(They still charge what amounts to twenty-seven hundred dollars to anyone who wants to use the footage.) They ended up in the local press, and then in the national press, and by the end of the week half the world knew that the Bradford Muslims had burned *The Satanic Verses*. They came to think of themselves as symbols of Muslim Britain. They supplied a lot of the "crazies" in the debates about Salman Rushdie on British television. They were interviewed, interrogated, scrutinized, and analyzed. They became experts in literary theory, Islamic theology, and the British blasphemy law. Celebrities from the evening news followed them home from their garages and their corner shops and respectfully solicited their views on whether it was right or wrong to murder Salman Rushdie or to disestablish the Church of England.

Bradford is a bleak place, like every other mill town that has seen its mills close and its wealth vanish and Burgess's laudanum proletariat turn into a new kind of lumpen-proletariat—a population on the dole. A quarter of the people are unemployed—more if you count the Asians alone—and there is literally nothing for them in Bradford: nothing to do, nothing to build from or build for. Investment in England moved south during Margaret Thatcher's eleven years to the extent that people describe England now the way they used to describe Italy, as two countries—a prosperous South England, and a godforsaken North England whose hopelessness and abandonment evoke the *miseria* of the Mezzogiorno, with its empty fields and alienated people. When strangers complain that the Bradford Muslims are unassimilated, they tend to forget that this is not only because of British snobbery or Muslim intransigence. In Bradford, there is very little to assimilate *into*—very little that could be called, positively, a British way of life. I have heard the culture of the north described as "the culture of loss." Its institutions are the pub, the council house, and the empty shopping mall where boys collect at night, under the neon lights, to rev their motorcycles and head for trouble.

It is not hard to exploit grievances in towns like Bradford. There are not many claims on anyone's identity. From the point of view of the Bradford Asians, *The Satanic Verses* was a book by a writer who didn't have to live in Bradford and, by all accounts, didn't want to live in Bradford – a writer who rejected them. Salman Rushdie was an easy grievance to invent, and an easy grievance to communicate. The Bradford Asians resented Asians like him. Many of them saw Rushdie's sophisticated English life as a comment on their own bleak English life and Rushdie's success as a comment on their own failure. The kind of success they could accept in other immigrants was something closer to their own experience. It was the kind of success the local mullah had when he got on the evening news and everybody saw him exhorting against the Great Satan, or the kind of success a Muslim merchant had when he cornered the local market in, say, radio cabs or groceries and all the English in the neighborhood had to depend on him in order to get along. It was the kind of success that was enviable, perhaps, but never threatening, never judgmental, the way Salman Rushdie's success was somehow threatening and judgmental. Rushdie's success raised questions of class and confidence and advantage which were bitter enough at home. In a place like Bradford, those questions were intolerable.

Half the Muslims in Great Britain live in London, and their experience has always been different from the experience of Muslims in the mill towns. For one thing, discrimination is something they share with the Sikhs and Hindus here, not to mention the West Indians, and, indeed, a couple of million English and Irish workers who are also excluded from the pleasures of Central London life, by tube schedules and closing hours and other expressions of a deep, common conviction that the English working classes need to be home and in bed by eleven at night or England will suffer and decline from their fatigue. The fact that people enjoying London are apt to be rich white people who can afford to live in town—and to frequent clubs that serve after the pubs close, and to own cars or hire taxis to take them home—is not an injustice directed specifically at Muslims. Muslims used to be considered the most integrated of the Asian immigrants—"most integrated" being a London code for "least noticeable." You could spot a Sikh, for example, because Sikhs had long beards and wrapped their hair in turbans, and their wives wore baggy white cotton tunics and their children little white topknots. You could spot a Hindu, because his wife wore saris and had a red smudge on her forehead and sometimes a diamond stud on the side of her nose, above the right nostril. But Muslims were "discreet," people in London said—if you didn't count the Arabs, of course, and if you ignored the dark skin and the black hair. Most of the Asian Muslims dressed like Englishmen. And while most of their wives obeyed the Koranic injunction to "dress modestly and cover the hair," and assumed the various forms of what the Asians call purdah and the Arabs *hijab,* the men so rarely went anywhere with their wives that no one outside their neighborhoods knew whether those wives were cloaked in chadors or draped fashionably in gauzy silk *dupattas,* like Benazir Bhutto. Then, too, the Asian Muslims were spread over many neighborhoods. A Bengali living in Brick Lane or Tower Hamlets or one of the other East London boroughs rarely saw a Pakistani from Brent or Southall, and almost never saw an Arab from Knightsbridge or Kensington. They went to their own mosques, and listened to ulema in their own languages, and, whereas most of the Hindus spoke Hindi and most of the

Sikhs spoke Punjabi, the Muslims came from all over and spoke their own languages, and it would have been difficult for an Iranian from Plaistow to understand a word of the conversation a mile away in Spitalfields, at the mosque at the corner of Hessel Street and Brick Lane.

Not all that many British Muslims are Shiites, like the Iranians – people say about fifteen per cent, which is roughly the percentage of Shiites in Pakistan and, in fact, of Shiites in Islam. *Shia* comes from the Arabic *shi'at Ali,* or "taking the part of Ali," and refers to the followers of the Prophet's nephew (and son-in-law) Ali, who was the Fourth Caliph, and of Ali's son Husayn, who fought and was beheaded in a war over caliphal succession. Most Muslims are Sunni – *sunni* comes from the Arabic for something "firmly rooted," and refers to the followers of the Prophet's father-in-law, Abu Bakr, who was the First Caliph. Before the Rushdie affair, not many Englishmen could distinguish a Shiite immigrant from a Sunni immigrant. But there is a tradition of martyrdom in Shiism, and the Shiites the English saw on television, beating themselves with chains, were enacting the rituals of an ecstatic tradition, mourning the death of Husayn, whom they consider the "first martyr." The closest that most Englishmen came to Muslim immigrants and their faith and customs was chatting with the Paki in the corner shop or with the waiter in the local curry house. The Muslims *they* knew best were the Arabs, who were foreigners but rarely immigrants (and so were not included in the "Black and White Britain" breakdowns), and were by far the smallest – only ten per cent of the Muslims here – and the richest of the Muslim communities. The Arabs could afford to live in "white" London, in the smart neighborhoods, and to shop in white London, in the smart shops, where the ordinary Muslims could not, and Tommy says they had contempt for the immigrants. They thought that Islam belonged to them.

The Arabs have been spending their oil money here for thirty years, but mainly it was the Saudis who spent any of it on the immigrants. Londoners got used to the sight of Kuwaiti or Abu Dhabian harems shopping together in Harrods, and filing into fleets of limousines at the Dorchester's front door, but the money invested in influence, and not just spread in affluence, was spent by the Saudi king and his princes in pursuit of the far-flung faithful – the Islamic diaspora, Muslim historians in the West call it. The Saudi royalty wanted the immigrants' favor. The Saudi royal family – the Wahhabis – wanted the immigrants to support them or, at least, not oppose them in their claim to the holy places, and to the oil around the holy places, and to the enormous income both produced. They built the immigrants' mosques and paid the immigrants' mullahs and ulema, and sometimes they even sat on the immigrants' mosque councils. Their money was carefully placed to fix the influence of the Wahhabis, who ruled at the indulgence of the West, among those people in the West who actually were Muslims, like them. The British Muslims watched enough television and saw enough movies to think of Saudis, if they thought of them at all, as pudgy despots who murdered their princesses for indiscretion but frequented women at the safe remove of Cap d'Antibes or Lake Geneva.

King Fahd himself was unpopular, even as despots go. He had hoped to settle his credibility with the faithful by becoming, officially, the Keeper of the Holy Places – it was a title he invented in the summer of 1987, when Iranians on a hajj began rioting in Mecca, and the Saudi police opened fire, and four hundred pilgrims were killed. But with the Iranians demanding "the liberation of the holy places," accusing Fahd of profiteering at the holy places and running them like carnivals and never taking care of them properly (last summer, the air supply failed in a pedestrian tunnel from Mecca to a tent city called Mina, and more than four-teen hundred pilgrims died), Fahd decided to be Keeper of the Holy People, too, even if those people were Pakistanis selling beer at a Brent pub or Bengalis running numbers from a Spitalfields newsstand.

The Saudis always worked through the mosques here. In 1978, they paid for the London Central Mosque—which Muslims call the Regent's Park Mosque, because it sits at the edge of the park, on land they got from the British after the British used land in Cairo for a Church of England cathe-dral, and which is one of the biggest mosques in the country, with room for five thousand men at prayer (but not much room for women, the Muslim women say) and five different holiday congregations. The Saudis installed as head of the mosque a civilized and scholarly Egyptian by the name of Zaki Badawi (who responded to Khomeini's *fatwa* against Rushdie by inviting Rushdie to live at his house), and when Dr. Badawi proved to be too liberal for their purposes they replaced him with Ali Mugram al-Ghamdi, a Saudi geogra-pher with no theological credentials, whom they judged, correctly, to be more compliant. It isn't surprising that the people who got to spend the Wahhabis' money were close to them in their thinking—people who shared their dislike of other Sunni rulers, like Benazir Bhutto, who to their minds were secular and worldly, as much as they shared their fear of Shiites like Khomeini, who traditionally undermined their influence. The Saudis' most notorious client was the British rock star Cat Stevens (he is Yusuf Islam now, and tells everyone that Salman Rushdie must "die for his crimes"), who got five million dollars from a Saudi mufti to found a Muslim school, in Brent, where music, sports, and Darwin were forbidden. Stevens borrows the Regent's Park Mosque on Thursday afternoons for a fundamentalist in-struction group he runs called the Islamic Circle.

Bishop Nazir-Ali says that to understand the politics of

Muslims abroad you have to accept that Muslims are not only under the obligation of jihad but also, by extension, under the obligation of vigilance against each other. Islam does not recognize the right of Muslims to break the faith. For Muslims, there is no such thing as an "assimilated Muslim" or a "lapsed Muslim" or a Muslim agnostic or a Muslim atheist or a Muslim who is converted, like the Bishop's father. There are only blasphemers, heretics, and apostates. The Pakistani fundamentalist Sayyid Abu al-Ala Mawdudi, who founded the Jamaat-i-Islami in 1941, used to preach that "for the entire human race, there is only one way of life which is Right in the eyes of God and that is al-Islam." He once compared Islam to a one-way door, because you can enter Islam easily but can never leave it. (This is why some Muslims refused to accept Rushdie's argument that he had not blasphemed because he was not a Muslim anymore, and why they refuse now to accept his "conversion.") Jihad can be interpreted as anything from missionizing to fighting, and Bishop Nazir-Ali says it is not the commitment to jihad but the interpretation and exercise of jihad that differs with the orthodoxy and intentions of the leaders involved.

The interests of the Saudis in England had to do with a very pragmatic notion of jihad: the Saudis assumed that the recovery of a million citizens of the Islamic diaspora from apostatic longings would in the end underline the legitimacy of their dynasty and their claims to the Arabian peninsula. Those interests were by definition international. There is not a Muslim leader of any power who has not entertained the possibility that his own particular nationalism is in fact Islamic internationalism – that his proper subjects are not only the people he rules now but the peoples of a "Muslim nation" constituted by faith and spread wherever there are Muslims living. The Saudis used to finance a propagandist in Britain named Kalim Siddiqi, who spent their money on what he sometimes called "rewriting Muslim politics" and sometimes "disengaging from the West at the intellectual level." Siddiqi, who has a degree from University College, London, and worked briefly at *The Guardian*, br ˙.e with his backers in 1978 (Dr. Badawi says there was an argument about money), and a year later he discovered the Iranian revolution and became a professional zealot in the Iranian cause. He is known to every Englishman with a television set. He has been urging the immigrants to murder Rushdie ever since the *fatwa* was issued — he was nearly charged with incitement to murder, and English liberals like to point out that in a country like France he would have been stripped of citizenship and deported, whereas in England he was protected by the same laws that protect Salman Rushdie — and last month, after Britain and Iran had established relations for the fourth time since the revolution, he left for Tehran to try to persuade Hashemi Rafsanjani, the Iranian President, not to give in and lift the *fatwa* now.

Dr. Siddiqi wants the British to create (among other things) what he calls a "non-territorial" Parliament for British Muslims, who will presumably use it to write their own laws and administer their own justice. He has convinced a good many of those Muslims that British Islam is indeed its own state, a kind of portable nation, and that in cases of conflict with the British state, Islam and its laws take precedence. Siddiqi works out of an office next to his house in Slough called the Muslim Institute, which is registered as a charitable trust and is something on the order of a one-man think tank — and which I have often heard described as a conduit for Iranian money entering England. There is nothing unusual, per se, about British think tanks' getting money from foreign governments, or representing foreign governments or other foreign interests — especially since there are no lobbies here, and no legal provision for lobbying. (Dr. Badawi got money from Libya for a think tank he calls the Muslim College after the Saudis fired him from the

Regent's Park Mosque.) British universities often accept money on proviso, and one way Iranians have lobbied, in effect, has been by endowing chairs and institutes and research centers and planting their own people in them. Islamic studies have always been political here, and, by and large, so have the Islamacists. They used to go straight from Oxbridge in the Colonial Office, and now they go straight from Oxbridge to the Foreign Office, and the ones who stay in college have a keen interest in influencing policy. The Muslim leadership in England is rife with feuds and rivalries, and everyone involved in Muslim politics tries to use the feuders – to court them or to buy them or simply to provide them with a base and make them comfortable.

Still, it is debatable whether the Iranians would have got involved in the Rushdie affair if the Saudis hadn't tried to exploit it. Some Iranians believe that the mullahs' decision to support a *fatwa* against Rushdie had very little to do with Rushdie *or* his book. They think the decision was made in anticipation of Khomeini's death, and had to do with the religious politics in Qum – which were the politics of succession, and of the temper of the succession – and was a victory for the "purist" faction and for the idea that their revolution continue. The British had already recalled their diplomats twice from Iran – first in 1980, when a group of Iranian terrorists seized the Iranian Embassy in London and murdered two hostages, and then in 1987, when an Iranian from the consulate in Manchester was arrested for stealing five pairs of socks and a plastic pocketbook from a local department store and the Iranians retaliated by abducting the British deputy head of mission in Tehran and accusing him of a series of capital crimes that ran from drug trafficking to "speculating in gold for the purposes of undermining the Iranian economy in wartime." (The diplomats were exchanged.)

The third mission that was sent arrived in Tehran in December, 1988, two months after *The Satanic Verses* was published. It lasted through the plane crash at Lockerbie – when two hundred and seventy Americans, flying home for Christmas, were killed by a bomb – and through the Bradford book burning, and was finally recalled six days after the *fatwa*, as were the heads of all the other European Community missions. The *fatwa* was in its second year (and Khomeni had died) by the time the British tried again. By then, the Special Branch – which is the national-security branch of the British police – had informers in most of the three hundred and eighty-two mosques in Britain. The Foreign Office had circulated a secret two-volume report on Muslim political activity written by one of its Islamicists and called (with no evident irony) "Islam Observed." An Iranian terrorist had blown himself up in a hotel room near Paddington Station, handling a bomb that was meant to blow up Rushdie. And the government had deported more than twenty Iranians, nine of them students, as foreign agents. Some of the students were known to have been organizing in the mosques in East London and Plaistow. There were reports of plots and cells in other "well-defined pockets of activity," though not much agreement on which pockets of activity they were.

A few days after the Bradford book burning, Salman Rushdie had with some confidence talked to Jonathan Randal, of the Washington *Post,* about "a very carefully orchestrated campaign . . . run by a number of extremists centered on the Regent's Park Mosque," and funded largely by Saudi and Iranian interests, but that particular campaign had to do with discrediting Rushdie, not with murdering him – with getting his book banned and Rushdie himself prosecuted for blasphemy under British law. It had to do with exposing what Homi Bhabha calls "the liberal fundamentalists" – meaning intellectuals like himself who tend to accept that writers inhabit a special social space, and have their own, almost priestly privileges, and are accountable to a "truth" not available to ordinary men and women. But once the *fatwa* was issued and the Ayatollah offered a bounty on Rushdie's head – it started as a million and a half dollars, but people contributed and now it is closer to five million – it was clear that professionals were going to try to enter the country in various disguises, and that the Muslims who are known in England as the "crazies" were going to have a field day, and that ordinary British Asians with heroic fantasies would discover the heady pleasures of plots and clandestinity.

One thing that British Islamicists seem to have understood about the Rushdie affair is that, however small the Shiite population here, there is what could be called a "hidden Shiism" among the Sunnis from the subcontinent – an impulse to martyrdom, a fervor that attaches itself easily to figures like Khomeini, a native populism that made it easy for Sunni workers from Pakistan and Bangladesh to hang Khomeini's picture on their sitting-room walls or march on Parliament to support his *fatwa*. Some Islamicists have compared the Shiite revival in Islam to liberation theology in Latin America, because in both cases the leaders of a mass religious movement have been able to mobilize masses of poor people, and to give them a sense of power, and, in the end, to threaten all the old hierarchies, religious and political.

In theory, Sunnis and Shiites are still fighting the wars of caliphal succession. If you ask a Sunni from Southall what he thinks of Shiism, he will probably say some of the same terrible things he says about Salman Rushdie (who comes from a Sunni family), but insofar as he is poor and is feeling put down and put upon in England he will respond to a Shiite like Khomeini, who says that Islam is the revolution that will free him. Immigrant communities are vulnerable to fundamentalism. In France, where there are three million

North African Muslims (immigrants and their children and grandchildren), the Muslim Brotherhood is installed, like religious police, in every immigrant neighborhood. What makes England different is that in England the immigrants are a prize being contested by any number of groups like the Muslim Brotherhood, each with its loyalties, and as long as they *are* contested they are more important to the political arrangements thousands of miles away in the Gulf or in India or Pakistan than they are in England, working on their own behalf.

It is not so clear what Khomeini stood to gain then, or what Rafsanjani or the new Ayatollah, Ali Khamenei, stands to gain now, from one dead writer. Rushdie is a *cause célèbre* only as long as he is alive to *be* a *cause célèbre*. He is not much use otherwise to any faction — and this may be why policemen who have followed the Rushdie affair tend to think that the real danger to Rushdie now, two years into the *fatwa* and two weeks into Rushdie's public "reconciliation" with Islam, lies with some angry and obscure Pakistani worker or with a mullah from one of the local mosques, somebody no one suspects, or has ever heard of, rather than with an Iranian secret agent or a professional terrorist. Rushdie has been a bandwagon for those mullahs. They never had the status among immigrants that they have now. Certainly young Pakistanis never took them very seriously, or listened to them very seriously, until Rushdie taught them the uses of hyperbole, and they learned that in England the most important muslim is the Muslim who commands the most attention. Their hyperbole was catching. For a while, their leaders got caught in a kind of one-upmanship of indignation. Ali Mugram al-Ghamdi called *The Satanic Verses* "the most offensive, filthy and abusive book ever written by any hostile enemy of Islam." Sayyed Abdul Quddus, the joint secretary of the Bradford Council of Mosques (and the man who set the match to *The Satanic Verses*), said, "Rushdie has tortured Islam and has to pay the penalty for it. He deserves hanging." Iqbal Sakranie, an accountant on the United Kingdom Action Committee on Islamic Affairs, said, "Death, perhaps, is a bit too easy for him . . . his mind must be tormented for the rest of his life unless he asks forgiveness of Almighty Allah."

Kalim Siddiqi, who was considered the most telegenic of the anti-Rushdie people because of his chubby, professorial looks and his old cardigans and rumpled tweeds, outdid them all by saying he had "circumstantial evidence" concerning the publication of *The Satanic Verses* and could prove that the book was part of a Western conspiracy against Islam which had been worked out during the Crusades and was still in force. Last week, he said that the "sad fact" was that Rushdie "could never be forgiven."

The British blasphemy law was incorporated into common law in the seventeenth century, after the Restoration. It was meant to protect the Church of England, as the state church, carrying the authority of the Crown, from what was called "seditious calumny." In effect, it was meant to protect the most important institution of the Crown—the one that conferred on England's kings a God-given right to rule—from dissidence. It had to do with an established church, and it is doubtful whether the law could be interpreted or extended, even now, to cover the disestablished Christian churches—the Methodists and the Presbyterians and the other chapel congregations—let alone Judaism or Islam, or, for that matter, Hinduism or Buddhism or Zoroastrianism or any of the other religions that British immigrants practice. (No one invokes the blasphemy law when, say, people call Kali a "pagan goddess.") But it used to be vigorously applied in Church of England circles, as a simple and convenient way of disciplining enemies and rivals. The most famous victim of the blasphemy law was the eighteenth-century Cambridge theologian Thomas Woolston, who was prosecuted for denying the literal truth of the Christian miracles – he had suggested that the Gospels were allegories – and was convicted, and spent the rest of his life in prison. The law is understandably out of fashion now. It was invoked once in the nineteen-twenties, and no one used it again until 1977, when a right-wing activist named Mary Whitehouse (who now sits in the House of Lords) brought suit against a magazine called *Gay News* for publishing a poem that involved Jesus as a homosexual love object. (Eric Hobsbawm says that to understand the Rushdie affair you have to think of what would happen in Poland, or in Ireland, if someone tried publishing that poem.) Most people tempted to invoke the blasphemy law were diverted by counsel to more conventional expressions of distress – the libel laws or the Public Order Act or the law against publishing racist abuse or the law against offending public decency. The public-decency law was invoked in 1987 when a sculptor exhibited a mannequin's head with freeze-dried fetuses for earrings, and that same year the Royal Court had to stop production of a play called "Perdition," about Hungarian Zionists collaborating during the war, which Immanuel Jakobovits, Britain's chief rabbi, considered anti-Semitic.

Immanuel Jakobovits was a defender of the blasphemy law. Like many of the Church of England clerics, he wanted to see the blasphemy law extended to "protect" all the faiths in Britain – including, it can be presumed, his own. He is an Orthodox Jew and, by reputation, an authoritarian character, and he was much criticized by liberal Jews for his interventions in the Rushdie affair – he said he agreed with his Muslim friends that *The Satanic Verses* was blasphemous and should be banned. Liberal English Jews, like English liberals in general, would prefer finally to separate the church and the state, and abolish the blasphemy law as a form of censorship. The blasphemy law is different from other British laws involving freedom of speech and freedom of expression, because intent is irrelevant in cases of blasphemy. The only "liberals" who want to extend that law rather than revoke it are liberals in the Anglican clergy, who are usually quite fierce about defending civil liberties, but who want what Tommy calls "a more global articulation of religion in the post-colonial discourse." Bishop Nazir-Ali, who is one of those liberal clergymen, explains it by saying, "It's not the theological aspect of the Rushdie affair but the social consequence that interests me."

Liberal priests and bishops like Nazir-Ali are often accused of being "wet." The Anglo-Catholics and evangelicals, who are the majority of the faithful but often the minority of the clergy, claim that the Church of England is full of wets, and are eager to expose them as meddlesome, muddleheaded, and sentimental, and the Salman Rushdie affair has been the best chance they had since the Bishop of Durham took up Thomas Woolston's argument about whether Christ's bones could really be said to have gone to Heaven three days after the Crucifixion and tried to relate it to the politics of England's unemployed coal miners. Anglo-Catholics are rarely wet. They regard the causes their liberal colleagues are always taking up as symptoms of the same sloppy ecumenicalism that reduced the Mass in most Church of England churches to comfortable ritual chat and took the mystery out of the holy sacraments and opened the door to women priests and gay marriages. Anglo-Catholics believe in the supremacy of the Church of England. They think of the blasphemy law as having to do exclusively with them, and the idea of extending it to any other church strikes them as fairly blasphemous itself. Oddly, it is Anglican evangelicals – the Church of England's own fundamentalists – who talk most often about abolishing the blasphemy law. The words they use about blasphemy and the Rushdie

affair are words like "affirmation" and "conversion." Pat-
rick Sookhdeo, the minister of two London churches—St.
Andrews Church, in Plaistow, and a Tamil-speaking evangelical congregation—is a convert to evangelical Christianity. He says that, as an evangelical ministering to twenty-
three nationalities in a neighborhood where forty per cent
of the population is Asian (and where the local mullah used
to preach every Friday for Rushdie's death, and one Iranian
has been deported as a terrorist), he has come to believe that
it is more important to write new laws that "affirm conversion and protect converts" and encourage what he calls "a
national identity as British" than to waste time arguing
about the blasphemy law and whom it covers and what blasphemy means. Evangelicals, of course, tend not to believe in
metaphorical truth or allegorical truth or in different vocabularies for divinity. They believe (like Dante, like the
mullahs who bewilder them now) in the revealed literal
truth of doctrine, and many of them consider the issue of
blasphemy against Islam to be a false issue, saying you cannot blaspheme against a false prophet—you can blaspheme
only against God-in-Christ as He appears in their version of
the Bible.

No one knows how long the Rushdie affair will last, or can
last. Rushdie came out of hiding this fall to film a television
interview for London Weekend Television, and in December he showed up at three London bookstores to sign copies
of his latest book, which is a children's fable called "Haroun
and the Sea of Stories," written for his son, Zafar—and on
Christmas Eve, in London, after some negotiation and in
the presence of six Muslims, he affirmed the tenets of the
faith and entered "into the body of Islam after a lifetime
spent outside it." He was also, of course, trying to enter the
world. There have not been any demonstrations against

him to equal the one in May, 1989, when fifty thousand British Muslims marched on Parliament to demand that *The Satanic Verses* be banned. The Saudis gave a million dollars to the people who organized that march – after the organizers let it be known that if the Saudis didn't pay the Iranians would – and it may be that both the Saudis *and* the Iranians, being preoccupied with Iraq, have lost interest in sponsoring British marches. The main organizer of the march – a Bengali businessman from the Brick Lane Mosque named Abdal Hussain Chowdhury – formed a committee called the Muslim Action Front to petition the High Court in London to try Salman Rushdie under the present blasphemy law. In June, 1989, the court agreed to a judicial review of a case against Rushdie, but last April the case was rejected – and, with it, any control the Saudis may have had over the course of the Rushdie affair in Britain. Two months later, Kalim Siddiqi, with Iranian backing, published his Muslim Manifesto for the introduction of Islamic justice in Britain. But by the end of the year Britain and Iran had exchanged their diplomats, and Hesham el-Essawy, an Egyptian from the Islamic Society for the Promotion of Religious Tolerance, had brought Rushdie together with the six Muslims, and Rushdie had affirmed that "there is no God but Allah, and that Muhammad is his last prophet" and agreed not to publish a paperback of *The Satanic Verses* (though not to withdraw the hardback from circulation). Rushdie's friends read his statement on Christmas morning in the paper. Some of them got angry – the playwright Arnold Wesker said that "the religious terrorists have won" – and some were relieved, and turned the page to see what else was going on in England, and if there was likely to be a war in the Persian Gulf. No one in Iran forgave Rushdie, or was in a position to forgive Rushdie, because the Ayatollah Khamenei quickly announced that the *fatwa* held and Rushdie had to die, "even if he repents, and becomes the most pious man of his time."

There used to be one category for all the immigrants in England who were not European, and that was "black." The Indians and Pakistanis had a subcategory of their own – "Asian" – but "black" was the official word, the word that told them that, as far as the English were concerned, everybody who was not English was the same black stranger. The categories changed after a sample census in 1989. There is now a category "black" that includes African immigrants and Afro-Caribbean immigrants and a potluck group called "others," but there is no general "Asian" category or subcategory – there is "Indian," "Pakistani," "Bengali," and so on through the various Asian immigrant groups. Bhikhu Parekh, who is fascinated by what he calls "this process of naming" and by what it says about the people who name and the people who get named (the way Rushdie is fascinated by the ironies and ambiguities of naming in *The Satanic Verses*), says that Asians see themselves by nationality and blacks by race, and that for an Asian the important thing is "nation" – political nation, Muslim nation – while for a black the important thing is his black skin.

Over the last few years, it was fashionable among British-Asian intellectuals to "be black." Young Asians called themselves "blacks." Young Asians called themselves "blacks." They said that by calling themselves "blacks" they exposed the official view of immigrants. Some of them used "black" ironically and some politically and some passionately but all of them used it to say something about black pride and British prejudice, and about being powerless in Britain. The feminists in Southall called themselves the Southall Black Sisters, and it didn't matter that the Sisters were run by a Jordanian woman and a Pakistani woman or that they had their headquarters and shelter in a neighborhood where eighty per cent of the population was Asian. The Asian artists and writers who wanted to support Rushdie called themselves Black Voices in Defense of Salman Rushdie. (It was at a time when it looked as if all the prominent pro-

Rushdie people were white liberals indulging what Professor Parekh describes as "a conviction that all religion is fundamentalist.") But blacks themselves were not much interested in Rushdie. Blacks in Britain worried less about British prejudice against Asians than about Asian prejudice against them, and Salman Rushdie never concerned them as much as, say, the Uganda Asian girl from Birmingham who was killed by her father a couple of years ago for getting pregnant by a black boyfriend. Many of the Asians were not that interested in Rushdie, either. It was mainly the Pakistanis who organized against him. The Muslims from India were never very active, and Bhikhu Parekh says that the Muslims from Bangladesh who were not East London Muslims rarely talked about Rushdie at all. As for the Sikhs and Hindus, their reaction to the Rushdie affair was usually to complain that Muslim fundamentalism was giving Asians a bad name.

Marc Jaffrey, a young counsellor at the racial-equality councils in Ealing and Southall, says that using "black" was meant to be a way for Asians to get to the heart of their own problem — to make people understand that the skinhead beating up the Paki was doing it not because the Paki was Muslim but because the Paki was foreign, and colored. Some people thought the Rushdie affair would serve the same purpose. Asians who supported Rushdie assumed that it would raise the consciousness of the "black" left to the real issues of rage and helplessness among immigrants, issues that were seldom raised by white people meeting in London to discuss free speech and English values. The problem was that no one agreed on what those real issues were. Paul Boateng said that the Rushdie affair was decadent and diversionary and "aberrant," and that it involved only "a few people in a few mosques with a few journalists" and had nothing to do with "the black discourse," which was about immigration policy and race relations and the shut-

ting of borders. Boateng had refused to join a black parliamentary caucus (the two other black members joined it, and
so did the Asian member, Keith Vaz), and he refused to
support the caucus's call for a ban on *The Satanic Verses*. But
students like Tommy said the black discourse was a smoke-
screen – it joined the argument in the old official terms of
race and racism.

Tommy has a theory about the Muslims who are in Europe now. He says that since the Middle Ages the Jew has
been the enemy within Europe, and the Muslim the enemy
without, and that now not only are Jews and Muslims fighting each other but they are both in and out of Europe at the
same time, complicating everything. He says that Europeans, in distress, have been narrowing their definition of
what being European means – narrowing it to something
white and Christian, if not in fact then in its characteristic attitudes – but that the barbarians are now *within* the gates.
They are part of the biggest migration of labor since the Ro-
man Empire, and nobody knows what to do with them except to send them home. Tommy thinks that the "mad mullah" has become a trope – the way the figure of shylock is a
trope – and he says that people are talking about the Koran
as if it were a document of conspiracy, a kind of Muslim
"Protocols of Zion." Rushdie has been quoting Dostoyevski,
saying that Dostoyevski, in prison, thirsted for faith and
found it, because "truth shines in misfortune." Tommy also
likes to quote Dostoyevski, who said that if you want to save
your people you have to love them.

Tommy says that about ten years ago there was a moment
when everybody talked about a Rainbow Coalition, which
was going to involve Asians and blacks and gays and feminists, and replace the "white, male, Labour Party power" on
the British left. There was a radical Greater London Council – Mrs. Thatcher took care of the Council by abolishing it
in 1986 – and the Council was handing out "empowerment

grants" of five thousand pounds to people in immigrant neighborhoods. The message then was "We're all black together." But the truth is that nobody felt black together, and the moment passed, and from Tommy's point of view the first "radical moment" since then was the moment the Bradford Muslims burned *The Satanic Verses*. I wonder how radical the Bradford Muslims feel now. They were not well served by the people who claim to lead them, and today they are told that Rushdie has made his peace not with them but with sophisticated Egyptians who are closer to his world than to anything remotely like theirs. Hating Rushdie did not solve any of their problems. It merely distracted them from their problems, perhaps for longer than they could afford to be distracted.

THOMAS FLEMING

A League of Our Own

NINETEEN NINETY-TWO WAS an opportunity for Americans to reflect on both their past and their future. In less than a month, we celebrated the birthday of Columbus and the transfer of power from the New Deal to the Big Chill, from the civics-class pieties of George Bush to the *Penthouse* improprieties of Bill Clinton.

I watched a good part of the campaign from an Italian vantage-point. I went to Italy primarily to speak about Columbus and the American tradition and to continue my very limited education in things Italian. At the end of the month, I was more confused than ever about Italian politics, but— as is always the case—I had learned something about my own country.

A year or so ago, a part-Italian friend took me to task for saying that Italy was in crisis. Without admitting I was right then, he now acknowledges the real sense of emergency that exists everywhere in Italy. At the end of the summer, the middle classes were practically up in arms against the government's handling of economic questions. Faced with mounting debt, the government ordered property-owners to pay a second round of real-estate taxes. All over Italy, people lined up to pay the impost and avoid the threatened penalties, only to discover that no one knew how much was owed, and, besides, the government had not printed up the tax forms.

The government wanted the extra money, in part, to pursue its futile plan to stabilize the lira on world markets. After hearing, day after day, that the lira would never be devalued, businessmen woke up one morning to read of the devaluation. Even opponents of the policy were outraged, and one businessman told me that the regime had forfeited any claim to be taken seriously.

The Italian economy is in ruins; none of the major parties inspires confidence even in loyal members; the Mafia is murdering every judge and prosecutor who stand in its way. In the midst of this crisis, the labor unions – pampered and coddled by the government – are once again threatening strikes that will shut down the entire country, just like in the good old days of the 1970s. I got up early one morning in Genoa to catch the train to Milan, and when I asked the desk clerk to call me a cab, she gave me a crude version of Hotspur's response to Owen Glendower's boast that he could summon spirits: "But will they come when you do call for them?" Somewhere in the monologue I picked out the most dreaded word in Italian vocabulary: *sciopero* (strike).

The unions have a right to be unhappy. After squandering vast sums of money on monetary stabilization, the government decided to balance the budget by cutting health benefits. The unions – part of the party-state that governs the country – went along, but when the most powerful union leader in Italy attempted to hold a rally, he was attacked by union members who have joined the Lega Nord, a coalition of localist movements in Northern Italy that preaches a doctrine of economic liberty and political decentralization.

The Lega has increased its share of the vote in every recent election and is now the dominant party in the rich industrial North. In response to the double taxation, Lega's leaders called for a tax protest; their answer to government-controlled unions is to form their own unions; and their solution – only half in jest – to the collapse of the lira is to coin their own money, the Lega.

The ruling coalition is terrified. Opinion polls in Monza and Varese, two wealthy cities in Lombardia, gave the Lega 35 percent or better in the next mayoral elections – high figures in a country with dozens of parties. The government responded to these polls by postponing the elections. Umberto Bossi's threat, reported in the *Corriera della sera* last September, could not have been plainer: "If the government will not reverse its decisions, a march on Rome could start from Milan to ask for the North's succession."

Bossi's hand was strengthened by a recent victory in Mantova, a city outside the center of the Lega's strength. For the first time in years the Socialists openly campaigned together with the former Communist Party leader, Achille Ochetto, in a popular front with the Greens for the sole purpose of defeating the Lega, but when the votes were counted the Lega Nord polled 34 percent, roughly double what the second-place Christian Democrats (DC) received.

A high-ranking official of the Lega asked me what I thought of the government's postponement of elections, and when I called it *"un piccolo colpo di stato,"* he smiled and expressed his agreement. The elections were rescheduled for December (the day after the election an Italian friend called to say *"La Lega ha stravinto"* – it won hands down). So far, the second march on Rome has not materialized, but it is possible to sense the trembling of the DC leadership even from one thousand miles away. Former head of state Francesco Cossiga, in an interview in London, performed an uncharacteristic act of truckling diplomacy: "I prefer to think of it as an excursion (*passeggiata*)," he commented, explaining that unions and parties always come to Rome for their meetings. The headline should have read: "NEW LIGHT SHED ON MUSSOLINI."

Perhaps more frightening than Bossi's original threat was his denial last October of any plans for a march. Conceding that if he did decide to march "the citizens would support us," he explained that it was only his "profound democratic conviction that prevented him from venturing upon solutions of this type."

I cannot think of a major American political figure since MacArthur who would let a little thing like democratic process stand in the way of his ambitions. If, for the time being, the head of the Lega Nord has rejected "solutions of this type," he began his electoral march on Rome several years ago. At the end of the 1980s, when the *leghisti* were boasting of getting 10 or 15 percent of the vote in local elections in Lombardia, the movement was considered a joke. Reviving the dialect and customs of their Lombard ancestors, the members of the Lega Lombarda struck most educated Italians as participants in a historical pageant representing Manzoni's *I promessi sposi*. Even two years ago, when the Lega's threat was confined to the North, Italians made fun of me for expressing an interest in a movement that was as irritating as it was quaint. They laughed when I tried to explain that whatever they might think of the style of the "Senatur" (Lombard for "senator"), his message of decentralized federalism and economic reform offered the only hope for Italy.

In general, the *leghisti* would like a new constitution along the lines of Swiss federalism. The country would be divided into three republics of the North, Center, and South, which would function like Swiss cantons and maintain considerable autonomy in political, cultural, and economic affairs. Although regional and local autonomy is part of Bossi's original conception, the Swiss flavor of the three republics owes something to Gianfranco Miglio, a senator and political scientist often described as the Lega's ideologue, even though he is technically independent.

Miglio has spent much of his professional life analyzing the deficiencies of the Italian constitution and proposing such remedies as a directly elected president and large autonomous regions. In his most recent book, *Come cambiare*, Miglio once again defends his idea of a federal system of macroregions and of a new *Unione italiana* that would give the peoples of Italy the rights of self-determination guaranteed by the Helsinki agreement.

Under a federal system, the historic regions of Italy—Lombardia, Toscana, Veneto, etc.—would be able to assert their cultural identities without interference from bureaucrats imported from other parts of the country. Traditionally, Italians have accepted the imposition of senior officials from outside as a guarantee of impartiality, a custom that echoes the institution of the *podesta* of the later Middle Ages. What disgusts many Northern Italians is the swarm of Southern bureaucrats, teachers, and policemen who have little or no sympathy with the customs and traditions of Lombardia or Piemonte.

One key to the Lega's growing popularity is its position on immigration. In reasserting the cultural identity of its regions, a federalized Italy would move to expel illegal aliens and tighten restrictions on immigrants. Despite the popularity of the Lega's stand on immigration, it—more than anything else—was responsible for much of the bad press.

The really explosive issue, though, is not foreign immigration, but domestic. Northern Italian hostility to Sicilians and other Southerners is proverbial. While much of the generalized resentment is unjustified—Sicilians take jobs that Lombards are unwilling to accept—it is also true that the Southerners have brought their way of life with them, which includes revenge killings, the drug trade, and their great criminal organizations, the Mafia, the Camorra, and the 'ndrangheta.

Italian crime syndicates are no joke. In America we might entertain the fantasy that the Genoveses or Gambinos are just like Vito Corleone, but their cousins in Italy—the real Corleone family, by the way—are lethal parasites upon the political and economic systems. Giorgio Bocca in La dis-UNITA d'Italia made plain for even the simplest readers what the situation is in the South: "connected" judges rigging acquittals and token sentences; appeals judges overturning convictions; sequestered gangsters returning to Palermo and Naples to resume their careers. Two honest judges in Palermo were compelled to meet in secret to prevent their colleagues from leaking information to friends in the Mafia. One of them was assassinated in 1983. More recently, the most famous anti-Mafia judge in Italy, Giovanni Falcone, was the victim of a car bomb powerful enough to have taken out a small village.

Everyone has always known that the Mafia was instrumental in delivering the Sicilian vote to the Christian Democrats. Americans can hardly point a finger at the Italians, since it was our own President, Franklin Roosevelt, who restored the Mafia after it had been effectively scotched, if not killed, by the Fascists. Ever since the war, the Mafia has been a political fact of life in much of the South, and if the Christian Democrats were going to succeed against the Communists, they could not afford to be selective about their allies. But who is the master and who the servant in this alliance? There have been persistent rumors that Salvo Lima, the DC's power-broker in Sicily and longtime friend of former party secretary Giulio Andreotti, was connected with the Cosa Nostra leader "Toto" Riina. Despite Andreotti's frequent denials, Lima has been named more than once by Mafia *pentiti* (informers) as their ambassador to the DC.

Several years ago, when Umberto Bossi declared that a vote for the DC was a vote for the Mafia, his critics cried "for shame," because he had slandered the greatest statesman in contemporary Italy, the fox who had by his own machinations kept Italy in the Western alliance and prevented a Communist-Socialist takeover. If the allegations are proved, they will do nothing to diminish Andreotti's accomplishments except to reveal him as one more great man who learned to value power for its own sake.

What really offends Northern Italians about the Mafia is the hold it appears to exercise over DC politicians and the ease with which it extorts millions out of government contracts. In the new Mafia, drugs and prostitution are small potatoes. The big-ticket items are highways, office buildings, and welfare fraud. I spent an afternoon touring a great city in the North accompanied by a Sicilian lady of great charm and erudition. Although she has spent her professional life in the North, she remains a Sicilian patriot, and as we drove by a great new building, she explained, "It makes me so proud. A Sicilian company got the contract. To get work done of this quality, they had to go all the way to Sicily."

It is, in fact, a magnificent building, and the contract may well have been on the level, but none of the natives I spoke with would even concede the possibility. (If the lady reads this, I hope she has forgotten her promise to come to America to kill me if I say anything bad about Sicily.) The Sicilians do have their own story to tell, of how they were conquered by Northerners who have been complaining ever since about the problem of the South, but it is time to give up those resentments and to acknowledge that a federal system will ultimately do as much for the South as it does for the North. As it is, by depending heavily on the largesse distributed by Rome, some Southern Italians have become like the Québecois in Canada: impotent and resentful. Autonomy would force them to address their own problems.

When I made this statement to a member of the Lega Liguria in Genoa, he was very skeptical. Federalism will work in the North, he insisted, because Northerners are capable of self-government, but only a strong central government can do anything about the Mafia. But Italy has a centralized government, and it appears to be under the Mafia's thumb.

The polemics of the leghe against Southerners caused few problems so long as they were strictly regional movements, but with the chance for national power in sight, Senator Bossi, it has been predicted, will have to tone down the rhetoric. Paul Piccone, in a special issue of *Telos* devoted to the leghe (Winter '91–'92), notes that "ethnicity was officially abandoned with the launching of the Northern League. . . . The radical decentralization and federalization of the present unitary state . . . should . . . allow the populations of both South and North to put their own houses in order." Piccone's analysis–and predictions–were borne out at the end of October, when Bossi suspended a local secretary in Trent for holding demonstrations telling Southerners to go home.

Although the power center of the Lega Nord continues to be Lombardia, its strength is growing in other regions: the Veneto, Emilia (where the Reds are deserting the Communist parties for the Lega), the Piedmont, and even Liguria. In the North as a whole, one recent poll gives the Lega 22 percent (which would be up from 10.3 in the last communal elections), just behind the DC's 23.4 percent (down from 33.4).

In broadening their base, the leghe may run the risk of losing their regional identities. In Liguria, for example, the emphasis is almost strictly on economic and political reform. I spoke with a Ligurian Leghista, a lawyer, who was faintly amused by the Lombard myths and symbols—the *carroccio,* the oath of Alberto da Guisanno, the songs in dialect—and cast the Lega Nord's program in terms that would appeal to students of Austrian economics: an end to corruption and welfare fraud, the deregulation and privatization of banking, commerce, and industry.

In fact, he described himself as *liberalista* in economics and against the current *industria dello stato,* which means intervention of politicians into all levels of business. It was such intervention that led to the great bribery scandal—the so-called *tangenti*—in which leading members of the Socialist Party have been implicated. In September, one of the most-beloved Socialist leaders shot himself, rather than face the music. The response of party chief Bettino Craxi has been to denounce the judges. Bets are being made on how long Craxi can remain the Socialist *capo dei capi,* and the smart money is selling short on Craxi and long on his chief critic, Claudio Martelli, the best friend of Italy's illegal immigrants. Despite his personal charm, Martelli's hip Third-Worldism may make Socialists long for the old-fashioned crook.

Of the Lega Lombarda's original program, decentralization remains an important issue, even in Liguria. The *communi,* I was told by my friend in the Lega Liguria, have lost the power to control taxation because of the "need" to drain resources toward the South. As a result it is impossible to have balanced local budgets, no matter which party is in power.

The North/South problem is really a difference in the *"modo di pensare"* (way of thinking). The Sicilians are not so much lazy as aristocratic and disdainful of manual work. This, combined with their refusal to see government in any but personal terms, has meant the persistence of feudalism, albeit in distorted forms. From one perspective, at least, this description makes the Sicilians seem much more attractive than the hardworking and responsible *borgesia* of the North, whose regional and local identities have been homogenized, my Genovese friend observed, by television.

A few days after leaving Genoa – my kind friend from the Lega had to drive me to the station because of the strike – I had the chance to speak with Dr. Elia Manara, a distinguished physician in Como and one of the Lega's newest senators. Since Dr. Manara, the Lega's point-man on health care, is unusually well informed on practical matters of economics and technology, he is a far cry from the sentimental regionalism of the early days. I asked him if the leagues were in danger of losing their regional identities. He explained that while maintaining their local attachments, the leagues were also discovering a common unity in a larger Northern ecosystem that Miglio and others call *Padania*. He derided the notion of the universal citizen and went on to reject Italian nationalism as a fascist idea. As a metaphor for the whole movement, he described Lombard provincialism as the locomotive of the autonomist train.

Manara regards himself as the very opposite of an ideologue. As a scientist, he is interested in the self-evident principles of human nature as they are revealed in history and experience. Federalism, he insisted, because it is rooted in human nature, is a theory for human survival. We talked of the original American system of federalism as a successful example to set beside Switzerland. I explained that, while our system had been undone by war, the federalist thinking of Jefferson, Madison, and Calhoun had new relevance in both Europe and the Americas.

But if the Italians have much to learn from our past, we can benefit from a study of Italy's present. In Genoa, because of an international convention of philatelists, I had to stay in an old hotel out in Sturla. Neither the hotel nor the neighborhood had much to recommend it, except for the view of the harbor from my balcony. It was from here that Garibaldi launched his invasion of Sicily and helped to inaugurate that process of centralization that every major Italian statesman—from Cavour to Mussolini to Andreotti—has followed. After World War II, various federalist provisions were written into the new constitutions, but few were implemented and those few were circumvented if not hamstrung, corrupted if not ignored. The result is the familiar spectacle of a corrupt conspiracy of a few thousand politicians micromanaging the lives of millions of people, most of whom could get along quite well with a minimum of intervention.

The current economic situation is so acute that many Italians, in and out of the leagues, are beginning to rethink the basic political mythology of the nation—the *Risorgimento,* Garibaldi, and Cavour. We are not quite so desperate, here in the United States, but who knows what thoughts we might entertain after four years of "Compagno Bill" in the White House.

Our own political mythology is built on the doctrine of equality, open borders at home, and the imposition of democracy abroad; the heroes of our myths are Presidents Lincoln, Wilson, and Roosevelt who made war for the sake of peace, suspended laws for the sake of the Constitution, and thought domestic tyranny was the best vehicle for exporting democracy. Some Italians are brave enough to confess the mistakes of the past and intelligent enough to long for the kind of government our own ancestors lived under. What about us?

POSTSCRIPT: Are Americans ready for something like a League of their own? None of the three candidates in the recent presidential election was willing to face the reality of life in America: the rioting and rampages perpetrated by an underclass that consists, for the most part, of unassimilated minorities. Pillaging, arson, and murder have taken place in Los Angeles and Miami, but since these criminals were fighting under the black flag of racial sensitivity, the leadership of this country refused to defend the innocent. In New York, a murderer was turned loose by a jury, because the killer was black and the victim Jewish. Shortly afterwards, Spike Lee turned out a hagiography of a pimp and a con-artist who evolved into a leading anti-white racist, and the only controversy over the film had to do with teenagers who sport the "X" symbol without reflecting deeply on its meaning. They do not need to reflect on Spike or Malcolm; they have already imbibed the symbol's meaning from Ice-T and Sister Souljah.

With widespread public approval, the outgoing President, eager to relive the thrill of the Gulf War, decided to send troops to Somalia. To judge from the columns, news programs, and call-in shows, Americans think this is a good idea, because they could not bear to see all those pictures of starving Somalians on network television. Rather than turn off the set and find a book to read, we go to war. What, in the meantime, is news, big news? News is when the addlepated female who owns controlling interest in the Cincinnati Reds is accused of telling race jokes in the office. This calls for investigations, denunciations in Congress, and demonstrations organized by such major-league racists as Al Sharpton and Jesse Jackson.

Apart from our collective soft head on matters of ethnic sensitivity, what is the connection between Marge Schott and the invasion of Somalia? We no longer know how to mind our own business, take care of our own neighborhoods, defend our own interests. We get our kicks from TV riots and African civil wars, and when the station signs off, we sleep a sleep untroubled by dreams of what we and our representative government are doing, in failing to protect us at home while sending armies abroad to lay down the peace. We created the problem in Somalia by inflicting the humanitarian aid that resulted in a population that cannot be sustained. At the same time, we are pursuing an immigration policy that even David Broder now realizes will turn the United States into Somalia. If human life is so precious, why don't we protect it in Detroit, in Miami, or in Cabrini Green?

If something like a League movement were to develop here in the States, urban mayors would not be calling upon the National Guard to restore order; it would be up to the cities and even the neighborhoods to defend themselves. We would have a national government, but it would be restricted to defending the national interest, not to giving away American lives to a debating society for the criminally insane – the United Nations.

There are only two alternatives for this continental empire that has never been a real nation: either we find the means to decentralize decision-making and restore authority to the old institutions of family and town and county (and even state), or else we lapse into a multifaceted civil war of blacks against Hispanics against whites against blacks against Jews. . . . It is too late for a man on horseback leading a militia of populist rednecks. There aren't enough rednecks to go around – besides, Bubba is too busy watching X-rated movies on his Japanese-made VCR. Bubba and his Midwestern counterparts might have just enough manhood left in them to stand up for themselves and their families, if they have no alternative, but they – or rather we – will have to be dragged, kicking and screaming, before we will take responsibility for ourselves.

The revolution cannot be made overnight, and the first step would be the creation of a movement devoted to the long-range goals of political devolution, privatization (ours is not a free enterprise system), protection of the national interest in matters of immigration, trade, and foreign policy, and the reassertion of our old cultural identities as a European and – dare we echo the Governor of Mississippi? – a Christian nation. If there is no movement or party willing to embrace a Leghist program, then one needs to be formed, and if that is impossible, my advice is to stockpile ammunition and invest in bullet-proof doors and shutters.

JUDITH ORTÍZ COFER

Silent Dancing

W*E HAVE A HOME MOVIE OF this party. Several times my mother and I have watched it together, and I have asked questions about the silent revelers coming in and out of focus. It is grainy and of short duration but a great visual aid to my first memory of life in Paterson at that time. And it is in color – the only complete scene in color I can recall from those years.*

We lived in Puerto Rico until my brother was born in 1954. Soon after, because of economic pressures on our growing family, my father joined the United States Navy. He was assigned to duty on a ship in Brooklyn Yard, New York City – a place of cement and steel that was to be his home base in the States until his retirement more than twenty years later. He left the Island first, tracking down his uncle who lived with his family across the Hudson River, in Paterson, New Jersey. There he found a tiny apartment in a huge apartment building that had once housed Jewish families and was just being transformed into a tenement by Puerto Ricans overflowing from New York City. In 1955 he sent for us. My mother was only twenty years old, I was not quite three, and my brother was a toddler when we arrived at El Building, as the place had been christened by its new residents.

My memories of life in Paterson during those first few years are in shades of gray. Maybe I was too young to absorb vivid colors and details, or to discriminate between the slate blue of the winter sky and the darker hues of the snow-bearing clouds, but the single color washes over the whole period. The building we lived in was gray, the streets were gray with slush the first few months of my life there, the coat my father had bought for me was dark in color and too big. It sat heavily on my thin frame.

I do remember the way the heater pipes banged and rattled, startling all of us out of sleep until we got so used to the sound that we automatically either shut it out or raised our voices above the racket. The hiss from the valve punctuated my sleep, which has always been fitful, like a nonhuman presence in the room—the dragon sleeping at the entrance of my childhood. But the pipes were a connection to all the other lives being lived around us. Having come from a house made for a single family back in Puerto Rico—my mother's extended-family home—it was curious to know that strangers lived under our floor and above our heads, and that the heater pipe went through everyone's apartment. (My first spanking in Paterson came as a result of playing tunes on the pipes in my room to see if there would be an answer.) My mother was as new to this concept of beehive life as I was, but had been given strict orders by my father to keep the doors locked, the noise down, ourselves to ourselves.

It seems that Father had learned some painful lessons about prejudice while searching for an apartment in Paterson. Not until years later did I hear how much resistance he had encountered with landlords who were panicking at the influx of Latinos into a neighborhood that had been Jewish for a couple of generations. But it was the American phenomenon of ethnic turnover that was changing the urban core of Paterson, and the human flood could not be held back with an accusing finger.

"You Cuban?" the man had asked my father, pointing a finger at his name tag on the navy uniform—even though my father had the fair skin and light brown hair of his northern Spanish family background and our name is as common in Puerto Rico as Johnson is in the United States.

"No," my father had answered, looking past the finger into his adversary's angry eyes. "I'm Puerto Rican."

"Same shit." And the door closed. My father could have passed as European, but we couldn't. My brother and I both have our mother's black hair and olive skin, and so we lived in El Building and visited our great-uncle and his fair children on the next block. It was their private joke that they were the German branch of the family. Not many years later that area too would be mainly Puerto Rican. It was as if the heart of the city map were being gradually colored in brown—*café con leche* brown. Our color.

The movie opens with a sweep of the living room. It is "typical" immigrant Puerto Rican decor for the time: the sofa and chairs are square and hard-looking, upholstered in bright colors (blue and yellow in this instance, and covered in the transparent plastic) that furniture salesmen then were adept at making women buy. The linoleum on the floor is light blue, and if it was subjected to the spike heels as it was in most places, there were dime-sized indentations all over it that cannot be seen in this movie. The room is full of people dressed in mainly two colors: dark suits for the men, red dresses for the women. I have asked my mother why most of the women are in red that night, and she shrugs, "I don't remember. Just a coincidence." She doesn't have my obsession for assigning symbolism to everything.

The three women in red sitting on the couch are my mother, my eighteen-year-old cousin, and her brother's girlfriend. The "novia" is just up from the Island, which is apparent in her body language. She sits up formally, and her dress is carefully pulled over her knees. She is a pretty girl but her posture makes her look insecure, lost in her full-skirted red dress which she has carefully tucked around her to make room for my gorgeous cousin, her future sister-in-law. My cousin has grown up in Paterson and is in her last year of high school. She doesn't have a trace of what Puerto Ricans call "la mancha" (literally, the stain: the mark of the new immigrant—something about the posture, the voice, or the humble demeanor making it obvious to everyone that that person has just arrived on the mainland, has not yet acquired the polished look of the city dweller). My cousin is wearing a tight red-sequined cocktail dress. Her brown hair has been lightened with peroxide around the bangs, and she is holding a cigarette very expertly between her fingers, bringing it up to her mouth in a sensuous arc of her arm as she talks animatedly with my mother, who has come up to sit between the two women, both only a few years younger than herself. My mother is somewhere halfway between the poles they represent in our culture.

It became my father's obsession to get out of the barrio, and thus we were never permitted to form bonds with the place or with the people who lived there. Yet the building was a comfort to my mother, who never got over yearning for *la isla*. She felt surrounded by her language: the walls were thin, and voices speaking and arguing in Spanish could be heard all day. *Salsas* blasted out of radios turned on early in the morning and left on for company. Women seemed to cook rice and beans perpetually—the strong aroma of red kidney beans boiling permeated the hallways.

Though Father preferred that we do our grocery shopping at the supermarket when he came home on weekend leaves, my mother insisted that she could cook only with products whose labels she could read, and so, during the week, I accompanied her and my little brother to La Bodega—a hole-in-the-wall grocery store across the street from El Building. There we squeezed down three narrow aisles jammed with various products. Goya and Libby's— those were the trademarks trusted by her Mamá, and so my mother bought cans of Goya beans, soups, and condiments. She bought little cans of Libby's fruit juices for us. And she bought Colgate toothpaste and Palmolive soap. (The final *e* is pronounced in both those products in Spanish, and for many years I believed that they were manufactured on the Island. I remember my surprise at first hearing a commercial on television for the toothpaste in which Colgate rhymed with "ate.") We would linger at La Bodega, for it was there that mother breathed best, taking in the familiar aromas of the foods she knew from Mamá's kitchen, and it was also there that she got to speak to the other women of El Building without violating outright Father's dictates against fraternizing with our neighbors.

But he did his best to make our "assimilation" painless. I can still see him carrying a Christmas tree up several flights of stairs to our apartment, leaving a trail of aromatic pine. He carried it formally, as if it were a flag in a parade. We were the only ones in El Building that I knew of who got presents on both Christmas Day and on *Dia de Reyes*, the day when the Three Kings brought gifts to Christ and to Hispanic children.

Our greatest luxury in El Building was having our own television set. It must have been a result of Father's guilty feelings over the isolation he had imposed on us, but we were one of the first families in the barrio to have one. My brother quickly became an avid watcher of Captain Kangaroo and Jungle Jim. I loved all the family series, and by the time I started first grade in school, I could have drawn a map of middle America as exemplified by the lives of characters in *Father Knows Best, The Donna Reed Show, Leave It to Beaver, My Three Sons,* and (my favorite) *Bachelor Father,* where John Forsythe treated his adopted teenage daughter like a princess because he was rich and had a Chinese houseboy to do everything for him. Compared to our neighbors in El Building, we were rich. My father's navy check provided us with financial security and a standard of living that the factory workers envied. The only thing his money could not buy us was a place to live away from the barrio – his greatest wish and Mother's greatest fear.

In the home movie the men are shown next, sitting around a card table set up in one corner of the living room, playing dominoes. The clack of the ivory pieces is a familiar sound. I heard it in many houses on the Island and in many apartments in Paterson. In Leave It to Beaver, *the Cleavers played bridge in every other episode; in my childhood, the men started every social occasion with a hotly debated round of dominoes. The women would sit around and watch, but they never participated in the games.*

Here and there you can see a small child. Children were always brought to parties and, whenever they got sleepy, put to bed in the host's bedrooms. Babysitting was a concept unrecognized by the Puerto Rican women I knew: a responsible mother did not leave her children with any stranger. And in a culture where children are not considered intrusive, there is no need to leave the children at home. We went where our mother went.

Of my preschool years I have only impressions: the sharp bite of the wind in December as we walked with our parents toward the brightly lit stores downtown, how I felt like a stuffed doll in my heavy coat, boots and mittens; how good it was to walk into the five-and-dime and sit at the counter drinking hot chocolate.

On Saturdays our whole family would walk downtown to shop at the big department stores on Broadway. Mother bought all our clothes at Penney's and Sears, and she liked to buy her dresses at the women's specialty shops like Lerner's and Diana's. At some point we would go into Woolworth's and sit at the soda fountain to eat.

We never ran into other Latinos at these stores or eating out, and it became clear to me only years later that the women from El Building shopped mainly at other places – stores owned either by other Puerto Ricans or by Jewish merchants who had philosophically accepted our presence in the city and decided to make us their good customers, if not neighbors and friends. These establishments were located not downtown but in the blocks around our street, and they were referred to generically as La Tienda, El Bazar, La Bodega, La Botánica. Everyone knew what was meant. These were the stores where your face did not turn a clerk to stone, where your money was as green as anyone else's.

On New Year's Eve we were dressed up like child models in the Sears catalogue – my brother in a miniature man's suit and bow tie, and I in black patent leather shoes and a frilly dress with several layers of crinolines underneath. My mother wore a bright red dress that night, I remember, and spike heels; her long black hair hung to her waist. Father, who usually wore his navy uniform during his short visits home, had put on a dark civilian suit for the occasion: we had been invited to his uncle's house for a big celebration. Everyone was excited because my mother's brother, Hernán – a bachelor who could indulge himself in such luxuries – had bought a movie camera which he would be trying out that night.

Even the home movie cannot fill in the sensory details such a gathering left imprinted in a child's brain. The thick sweetness of women's perfume mixing with the ever-present smells of food cooking in the kitchen: meat and plantain *pasteles*, the ubiquitous rice dish made special with pigeon peas – *gandules* – and seasoned with the precious *sofrito* sent up from the Island by somebody's mother or smuggled in by a recent traveler. *Sofrito* was one of the items that women hoarded, since it was hardly ever in stock at La Bodega. It was the flavor of Puerto Rico.

The men drank Palo Viejo rum and some of the younger ones got weepy. The first time I saw a grown man cry was at a New Year's Eve party. He had been reminded of his mother by the smells in the kitchen. But what I remember most were the boiled *pasteles* – plantain or yucca rectangles stuffed with corned beef or other meats, olives, and many other savory ingredients, all wrapped in banana leaves. Everyone had to fish one out with a fork. There was always a "trick" *pastel* – one without stuffing – and whoever got that one was the "New Year's Fool."

There was also the music. Long-playing albums were treated like precious china in these homes. Mexican recordings were popular, but the songs that brought tears to my mother's eyes were sung by the melancholic Daniel Santos, whose life as a drug addict was the stuff of legend. Felipe Rodríguez was a particular favorite of couples. He sang about faithless women and broken-hearted men. There is a snatch of a lyric that has stuck in my mind like a needle on a worn groove: *"De piedra ha de ser mí cama, de piedra la cabecera . . . la mujer que a mí me quiera . . . ha de quererme de veras. Ay, ay, corazón, ¿por qué no amas . . . ?"* I must have heard it a thousand times since the idea of a bed made of stone, and its connection to love, first troubled me with its disturbing images.

The five-minute home movie ends with people dancing in a circle. The creative filmmaker must have asked them to do that so that they could file past him. It is both comical and sad to watch silent dancing. Since there is no justification for the absurd movements that music provides for some of us, people appear frantic, their faces embarrassingly intense. It's as if you were watching sex. Yet for years, I've had dreams in the form of this home movie. In a recurring scene, familiar faces push themselves forward into my mind's eye, plastering their features into distorted close-ups. And I'm asking them: "Who is she? Who is the woman I don't recognize? Is she an aunt? Somebody's wife? Tell me who she is. Tell me who these people are."

"See the beauty mark on her cheek as big as a hill on the lunar landscape of her face – well, that runs in the family. The women on your father's side of the family wrinkle early; it's the price they pay for that fair skin. The young girl with the green stain on her wedding dress is *la novia* – just up from the Island. See, she lowers her eyes as she approaches the camera like she's supposed to. Decent girls never look you directly in the face. *Humilde,* humble, a girl should express humility in all her actions. She will make a good wife for your cousin. He should consider himself lucky to have met her only weeks after she arrived here. If he married her quickly, she will make him a good Puerto Rican-style wife; but if he waits too long, she will be corrupted by the city, just like your cousin there."

"She means me. I do what I want. This is not some primitive island I live on. Do they expect me to wear a black mantilla on my head and go to mass every day? Not me. I'm an American woman and I will do as I please. I can type faster than anyone in my senior class at Central High, and I'm going to be a secretary to a lawyer when I graduate. I can pass for an American girl anywhere – I've tried it – at least for Italian, anyway. I never speak Spanish in public. I hate these parties, but I wanted the dress. I look better than any of these *humildes* here. My life is going to be different. I have an American boyfriend. He is older and has a car. My parents don't know it, but I sneak out of the house late at night sometimes to be with him. If I marry him, even my name will be American. I hate rice and beans. It's what makes these women fat."

"Your *prima* is pregnant by that man she's been sneaking around with. Would I lie to you? I'm your great-uncle's common-law wife – the one he abandoned on the Island to marry your cousin's mother. I was not invited to this party, but I came anyway. I came to tell you that story about your cousin that you've always wanted to hear. Remember that comment your mother made to a neighbor that has always haunted you? The only thing you heard was your cousin's name and then you saw your mother pick up your doll from the couch and say: 'It was as big as this doll when they flushed it down the toilet.' This image has bothered you for years, hasn't it? You had nightmares about babies being flushed down the toilet, and you wondered why anyone would do such a horrible thing. You didn't dare ask your mother about it. She would only tell you that you had not heard her right and yell at you for listening to adult conversations. But later, when you were old enough to know about abortions, you suspected. I am here to tell you that you were right. Your cousin was growing an *Americanito* in her belly when this movie was made. Soon after she put something long and pointy into her pretty self, thinking maybe she could get rid of the problem before breakfast and still make it to her first class at the high school. Well, *niña,* her screams could be heard downtown. Your aunt, her Mamá, who had been a midwife on the Island, managed to pull the little thing out. Yes, they probably flushed it down the toilet, what else could they do with it – give it a Christian burial in a little white casket with blue bows and ribbons? Nobody wanted that baby – least of all the father, a teacher at her school with a house in West Paterson that he was filling with real children, and a wife who was a natural blond.

"Girl, the scandal sent your uncle back to the bottle. And guess where you cousin ended up? Irony of ironies. She was sent to a village in Puerto Rico to live with a relative on her mother's side: a place so far away from civilization that you have to ride a mule to reach it. A real change in scenery. She found a man there. Women like that cannot live without male company. But believe me, the men in Puerto Rico know how to put a saddle on a woman like her. *La Gringa,* they call her, ha, ha, ha. *La Gringa* is what she always wanted to be . . ."

The old woman's mouth becomes a cavernous black hole I fall into. And as I fall, I can feel the reverberations of her laughter. I hear the echoes of her last mocking words: *La Gringa, La Gringa!* And the conga line keeps moving silently past me. There is no music in my dream for the dancers.

When Odysseus visits Hades, asking to see the spirit of his mother, he makes an offering of sacrificial blood, but since all of the souls crave an audience with the living, he has to listen to many of them before he can ask questions. I, too, have to hear the dead and the forgotten speak in my dream. Those who are still part of my life remain silent, going around and around in their dance. The others keep pressing their faces forward to say things about the past.

My father's uncle is last in line. He is dying of alcoholism, shrunken and shriveled like a monkey. His face is a mass of wrinkles and broken arteries. As he comes closer, I realize that in his features I can see my whole family. If you were to stretch that rubbery flesh, you could find my father's face, and deep within *that* face — mine. I don't want to look into those eyes ringed in purple. In a few years he will retreat into silence, and take a long, long time to die. *Move back, Tío, I tell him. I don't want to hear what you have to say. Give the dancers room to move, soon it will be midnight. Who is the New Year's Fool this time?*

III.

DISCIPLINES

AND

DISCIPLESHIP

ANONYMOUS

The Companions of Duty

Les Compagnons du Devoir, until recently little known even in Europe, is a lay community for French artisans organized under a secret Rule at least six hundred years ago and still in existence. Its members aspire to rectify some of the deviations from which their consciences suffer and to become an example to the multitudes of other workers.

Each one spends his professional life subject to the ordinary conditions of existence as a carpenter, a mason, farmer, plumber, metal-worker, shoemaker, draper, milliner or whatever. Returning to the community in the evening, he adapts to a program of activities and rituals which establish his right place in the communal hierarchy and are specially devised for his training or mastership as a man.

Houses were established by the Order in the principal cities of France, including Lyons, the original capital of the Order, Paris, Nantes, Bordeaux, Marseilles, Avignon. In these houses, the young artisans lived and took their meals under the guidance and protection of a Mother, chosen for her exceptional character, assisted by a doctor, an employment officer and others. One of the practices, the Tour de France, made it an obligatory part of his training for everyone to spend some months at his trade in each of these cities.

Eventually, each worker has to give himself the final test – in an era when the world no longer gives it – of producing a worthy piece of work by hand. This "masterwork" becomes a means for meditating on the deep meaning of all human work, and after the test the Companion is regarded by his brothers as "Finished." The conscience of the Finished Man is opened and the awareness of its movement in him is added to what moves in him as he works at his trade. One movement does not stand in the way of the other. The two movements together integrate the Man's complete force. His trade becomes what it is meant to be, a natural service to society accomplished in full knowledge of its cause, Himself.

The *Compagnonnage* was reformed and revived in the first part of the nineteenth century and has survived the industrial revolution in France and the growth of the trade union movement, many of whose benefits it anticipated. It is tempting to imagine the appearance of a similar (and much needed) Order among the workers in America. But here a new revolution is already taking place, as "white collar" workers – clerks, draftsmen, laboratory assistants, etc., using their heads more than their hands – already greatly outnumber manufacturing employees. Managements of large corporations are concerned, from the point of view of functional efficiency, about the morale of these people, who perform repetitive jobs analogous to assembly-line operations. Many of the more resourceful ones compensate for their sedentary work by engaging in crafts and hobbies at home. But this is only a partial answer to the fundamental question. Will the modern Finished Man be able to learn to regard his own thoughts as external material to be worked on worthily as he sits at his desk?

The following essays, translated from the editorial articles in the monthly journal *Les Compagnons du Devoir* in Paris (published as *Le Compagnonnage* by Jean Bernard, Paris: Press Universitaires de France, 1972), deal with the whole question of what is work in the contemporary mass-production culture, and with the need to bring the idea of quality back into the minds of "blue collar" workers, especially through the mastery of traditional crafts.

The New Barbarian

Times are hard. Those coming will be harder still, but this is not what makes us apprehensive. We greatly fear that in the conceivable future men will be made to forget the little that remains to them of conscience and we will be on the verge of a barbarism the likes of which has never been witnessed — worse by far than that displayed by those blond-haired ancestors of ours who, dressed in bear skins, descended in hordes on the mighty decadence of Rome.

Certainly the new barbarian will not present himself in the guise of an inferior. Better organized and still better armed, he will without doubt have all the developments of science at his disposal and in such force that man, overwhelmed by this display, will all the more readily give up his freedom and even the memory of it.

Even now, the barbarian is in our midst taking root among us in the realm of the mind. It is not a matter of invasion by new races as before. The attack comes from the behavior of those beings growing ever more numerous with whom we daily rub shoulders, and whose concept of life runs counter to everything that makes life worth living. Today it is from within that the invasion takes place.

But what then separates us from these men? The answer is not simple, for the distinctions are many. We are especially struck by the new barbarians' lack of hope and by how little they love freedom.

Let us first examine the nature of hope itself, since this suffices to separate humanity into two categories. For we do not mean by hope what animates the masses, namely the struggle for simple social justice. What will become of the people when they have attained these goals? This revolt, with which we can sympathize to a degree, will change nothing. If hope ends here, it is not hope. Hope goes beyond justice.

What we call hope is this attraction to the future; it is this feeling deep inside each of us without which the whole of humanity falls into decay. It animates each of us, and because of it each of us brings to the community of man his portion of good will and being. When a man does good it is because he hopes. And this is true even if his effort is made with purely personal views in mind. It is only necessary that this effort be freely made.

To suppress hope and all that it creates of excellence in us deprives humanity of an outlook toward something beyond itself, of a direction vital to life. It is one of the hallmarks of the new barbarism not to recognize this hope. Instead it promises to give to the masses all kinds of material advantages and a patterned, prefabricated intellectual nourishment formulated and standardized.

As for freedom, that is lost in the measure that barbarism grows.

The myth of progress which so fascinates modern man accommodates itself perfectly to a lack of hope and the absence of freedom; do we not see already what the world attempts to offer to the crowd in exchange? The games and circuses of the ancient Romans, but more subtle, more diffuse and diluted, are here with us now pursuing man and tracking him down.

The Companions do not see how they can set themselves in direct opposition to this state of things no matter how we measure the road already traveled. What they can do, those who are resolutely free and faithful to hope, is to live their lives as Companions in spite of everything, to remain with those who will always have the taste of being complete and finished men.

Education

Deceived by the enormous and complicated machinery of instruction which no longer gives them confidence to live from within, in respect to their futures nor in relation to their fellow creatures, the young are isolated. They take refuge in refusal or some other disconcerting attitude in front of long-established habits and conventions proposed to them by their elders, or they remain depressed and dishonored in a life without character. Can we pretend that it is the fault of youth? Government efforts in the fields of education do not get to the depth of the problem. It is not at all enough that they work with highly evolved material means and innovative methods. Nothing will change the facts of the matter. In school one can learn, but one can only be truly educated through contacts with life.

The *Compagnonnage* is, for the worker, the school of life, a school in which the values and virtues of work are developed, a life in which the trade brings a substance which enriches the man, permits him to fulfill himself and to face all of his duties. It is not just one particular aspect of the life of the young worker which is studied, but everything is taken into account in order to make of him a complete man, endowed with a well-tempered character which cannot be drawn into the bitterness to which nearly all our contemporaries fall prey, and which cannot be blamed on difficult times since it flourishes even now in this "fat cat" era. Because the life in and surrounding the trades provides a normal and proper condition of life, it prompts and generates learning, and makes possible the development of conscience. It is then between these two domains – the man and the conditions of his life – that education takes place.

The Idea of Order

The idea of order comes from conscience. It is entirely different in nature from those structures, so often illusory, erected like houses of cards by falling powers hoping to remedy their woes.

Order reaches out to offer men what they lack in moments of need. It is always a breakdown in society which gives birth to order. Order which does not come from this need is only the fruit of men's fantasies and is short-lasting.

Those who consider themselves modern, and who are only of today, without a yesterday or tomorrow, will poorly understand the usefulness of order. They are oblivious to the fundamental scheme of things underlying society's movements. They do not see on so large a scale at all. Doubtless they think that the idea of order is finished; that there is no longer any need for it. They are mistaken. Never before has it been so necessary to make the conscience of man emerge again, so as to overcome the present difficulties and those no less serious which are in the making. For our existent institutions are not up to the task of leading us out of our agonizing age. Our institutions, by the measures they take, will only hasten the decay, and will strangle the movements of freedom to which we aspire. For it is the principal characteristic of order to be the refuge of freedom. And it is by this freedom in action (among brothers who are known to one another) that men can thus find again the original and permanent ideas which have been profoundly altered by modern society. It is by this freedom that order will be able, once its task is completed – when it has gathered the fruit of its task, protected and reformulated it – to reintegrate this essential thing into society.

What then is the essential thing that the *Compagnonnage* is dedicated to preserving? It is the conscience of the working man. Like all movements of conscience, it has two paths. One is purely interior, leading toward the liberation of the individual, toward personal progress and the conquest of self. To that is directed all the teaching of the *Compagnonnage*, its method of training, and its spirit of work. The other path is to the exterior; it renders the individual responsible for humanity, since our civilization, like all other civilizations, will be judged by the evidence of the works of its workers.

Let us therefore look for this contact with conscience. With this flame alive in each of us, to which our world actually denies oxygen, let us share in this rediscovery. What do we fear? Who can stand in fear of finding what is true and essential? For us, our field of experience is well known and we do not wish to go beyond it: it is the domain of work in the everyday sense, in its development at the core of the life of man, in its projection outside the individual. What an enormous factor work is, the practice of a trade! Man is involved with the business of his life at the minimum of a third of his time. If one calculates that the remaining time is spent in sleep, in an active physical life, in pastimes intelligent or not, one sees that the place of work is immense. How can such a factor of preparation and accomplishment be slighted? How can these human potentialities be restored?

Passivity

When one heard the mason singing on the scaffolding at the top of his voice or the painter whistling (that very curious ability of the lips which seemed to be beneficial to the operation of the paintbrush) it would have been hard to believe that some short decades later these men would be rendered mute and that a transistor radio ever-ready with quick tunes would replace the part that those men gave to the sounds of nature.

We have all had the occasion to sing while working. And

we know without any pretension that it can express an inner state, a moment of accord and unity with what one is and with what one is doing.

To work while singing expresses an action rich with a certain equilibrium. It does not destroy attention. To listen to a radio is not, properly speaking, "to listen" in the full meaning of the term; it is to be absent from oneself at the invitation of a noise. This makes me think of those households in which the radio is played and thus people do not listen to their lives. When one sings while working and when one stops singing, one reaches silence, and that silence is without doubt a moment available for thought. For the transistor people, there is no longer a silence of this kind and very little availability: they are absent from themselves. Of course they are absent from their work and always taken up by the outside. It is perhaps one of the explanations for passivity: to be passive is to be absent.

Not only does the worker rarely sing anymore while working, but he also writes less and less. The problem is the same in its essence. Of course we are not speaking of the avalanche of books, journals and diverse periodicals which submerge us on all sides. That is a little like the noise of the transistor. One can read like one can go to the cinema, in order to forget, not in order to think (in order to be passive, and not in order to be active) and the image is a powerful aid for this forgetting. This refusal of thought is a symptom of our time.

Progress

We maintain this: The only real progress is individual progress, brought about by one's own effort. Collective tendencies are all around us beckoning us toward a perfect mirage which has nothing to do with the undertaking of this personal effort. We are all too inclined to place ourselves above and beyond the other forms of life, whereas we are inside of them, as they are also in us, and we are answerable to them in all the fibers of our being, both physically and spiritually. We do not dominate them, we support them and they us. None of the great discoveries which mark the march of what we call progress has taken into account this inner property. We believe that a progress of such a nature in which quantity is the profit, and because of which quality becomes questionable, uncertain and without duration, does not take into account the idea of the complete development of man. It cannot therefore be true progress. For not only is the man intentionally forgotten, but everything turns against him and he comes away crushed by the experience.

The present-day tendency toward professional specialization causes us to lose sight of the real idea of the perfecting of human beings.

We do not repudiate progress, we do not set it up against the mind, nor the hand, and we do not abide by a system which opposes the machine and the hand as one might suppose. Furthermore, we think that the *Compagnonnage* must offer some solutions by throwing light on the situation and by continuing its research based on the results of the kind of work which allows thought and hand to work together, a research which will contribute to the humanization of work (a humanization which will not simply play into the hands of the materialists).

JEAN HARRIS

Finding the Gift in It

Solitude is a word one quickly associates with prison; community is not, though, depending upon the prison and the nature of those who fill it, today one can even find a modicum of community there. "The Hole" at Leavenworth in Kansas and the twenty-two-and-a-half-hour daily lockdowns at Marion Prison in Illinois are modern monuments to total solitude. Even simple human requirements like an occasional glimpse of the sky are missing. Each prisoner is alone, immersed in nothingness.

Solitude was the rock upon which the American prison system was founded, a system invented by the Quakers at the end of the eighteenth century as far more humane than the casual maiming of sinners or the administration of the death penalty, both of which had been common systems of punishment for more than twenty different crimes. It was thought by the Quakers that solitude, the chance to be alone with one's God and the Bible, would give wrong-doers ample opportunity to think on their crimes and repent, hence the name *penitentiary*.

For many the Bible was little company because they couldn't read, and God was often difficult to conjure up. Suicide or madness overtook some prisoners, and there wasn't a noticeable amount of repentance in the others. Equally destructive was the fact that prisoners learned nothing about fitting back into society if and when they were paroled.

In a few years the Quaker system was modified into what is called the Auburn system, named after the first big prison in New York State. A large part of each day was spent alone, but the solitude was broken by work assignments done in groups. The human need for human contact was acknowledged, but communication was still forbidden. "Up the river" was a very quiet place. The no-talking rules lasted well into the 1950s and 1960s, which is why in my early recollections of George Raft and Edward G. Robinson movies, prisoners were always devising clever pulleys and secret hiding places for written messages. Today at Bedford Hills Correctional Facility where I am imprisoned, no one suggests that we can't talk to one another, though guards are quick to call out, "Keep moving. Keep moving there," if two or three women stop in the work line to talk.

Here, women are locked from 10:00 P.M. to 6:30 A.M., and for the counts from 11:20 A.M. to 12:00 P.M., and 5:30 P.M. to 6:00 P.M. Additional lock-downs occur if someone is missing in the count or if a floor-wide or facility-wide cell search is in progress. If you are being punished for a prison transgression, you may be locked-down twenty-three hours a day for anywhere from a week to two months in a regular housing unit. If the transgression is more serious, you usually go to solitary in a separate building. Two years is the longest I'm aware of any woman being in solitary here, locked twenty-three hours per day.

I'm one of the lucky ones. Solitude is my friend. I can think when I'm alone. With people I'm more apt to react. The only isolation I have known in my lifetime I felt in the presence of others. In here I get my space where there is least of it, in my 6½-by-10-foot cell. I almost always ask for my doors to be locked several hours before the required lock-in time. Some other women do it too, each for her own particular reasons.

For Corinne, solitude means putting on another coat of fingernail polish, blowing it dry and going to sleep. She sleeps away the weekends. She sleeps whenever she isn't required to be up. Solitude is wasted on her, as gift or as punishment. She will never know what she wasted or what she missed. Or maybe she knows and is glad.

Ethel is another who asks the guard to lock her in by 7:30 P.M. at the latest. Her light goes out soon after the door closes. In the morning she is up and dressed and out of her cell by 6:30, when the doors open. She walks to the recreation room and sits on an old plastic chair just to the right of the entrance. There until 8:30, when the line for work leaves, she sits tall and straight, her knees tight together, her eyes straight ahead. The television set is only a few feet further to the left, but once it is on she barely glances its way. She carries her solitude with her as surely as a turtle carries its shell. What are the uses of solitude for her I cannot say. Whether she remembers, or plans for the future, or fine-tunes her resentments and regrets, no one knows. For her, solitude is part of the agony of living. People do not break its spell. She is a walking isolation booth.

Frances is another one who brought her solitude with her. Before she was paroled she would sit in her cell for hours knitting pretty dresses for her little girl. Occasionally when her door was open she would venture to it and hold up her work for me to admire. I didn't know until almost a year after I met her that her little girl was dead. Frances had killed her.

Prison for Nellie is her first experience at being alone in a room. She lived in an apartment with three to a room, shared a bed all her life, lined up to use the toilet and the stove. Now a grown woman, she sleeps with her cell light on, afraid of being alone in the dark.

For a few women the closed door means not solitude but claustrophobia. There is no time to enjoy or dread the uses of solitude. They are consumed by the closing in of four walls. Tracy slept on the floor for weeks after she arrived here, next to the door where she could slip a mirror under it and get a view up and down the empty corridor. It helped.

For some women, prison provides the closest thing to friends and companionship they have ever known. The street can be a lonely place and the street sent many of them here. They stay in the recreation room playing cards, watching television or just talking until the very last minute before 10:00 P.M. and then run screaming down the corridor like schoolchildren when the doors begin to close. Some call back and forth to one another long after they've been told to be quiet, trying to wring the last drop of companionship out of the day and to put off the moment when they have only themselves for company again.

Some women use their solitude as the Quakers would have had them do. They study their Bibles. On my floor on Sundays after the chapel services, eight of the women sit at a table in the recreation room and discuss the lesson of the day and re-read all the references to it, often many the minister or priest left out. Their Bibles are underlined from beginning to end, and the pages give evidence of many turnings. Of course there are humbugs among them too, lugging a Bible around to impress a parole officer or to make it easier to get to chapel and sit next to a girlfriend from another housing unit, but some are devoutly sincere, however new or old their conversion may be.

Some women here use their solitude much as I do, reading, writing, and thinking. A few college students study late into the night and worry that their chance to finish their degree will be cut off next year because of the shortage of funds and because people outside think a college education is a luxury prisoners don't deserve. Some with little education can still write letters home, letters to children, letters to lovers, letters to strangers, anyone who might write back. And some write books. "I'm writin' a book, Jean. You wouldn't believe what I've done in my lifetime." One woman had painstakingly filled an entire notebook with figures she thought looked like Japanese and asked me if I knew of a Japanese publisher. I told her I didn't but that if she translated her story into English maybe something could be done with it. "The story's the important thing," I told her. "Tell me about your story." "Oh," she shrugged, "it's not finished yet. I still got pages to fill." For her the writing of a book meant making endless designs on endless pieces of paper. Meaning had no meaning. The designs had filled in the empty spaces that solitude brings.

Many of us use up some of our solitude just being relieved to be away for a while from the obscenities that fill the air here all day long, and to be free from the arbitrary, often childish, even paranoid little rules that change constantly, serving only as ubiquitous reminders that virtually every move we make when not locked in a cell is controlled by others. One day we can wear colored blouses into the visiting room. Then we can wear only white ones, and some of the colored ones are sent home. Later it changes again; we can wear colored blouses in the visiting room, but the ones sent home cannot come back again. "Only new clothes can be sent into the facility and a price tag of not over $50 must be on every item." Cotton underpants sent by a family member are turned back at the gate. "No price tag. They might have cost more than $50."

"Dental floss is important to use at every brushing," the

prison dentist assures the women. She gives them dental floss. Suddenly, "No more dental floss. Dental floss is now contraband. If you are found with dental floss you will receive a Charge Sheet." For Charge Sheets you can be locked down, and your prison record is stained. The beat goes on. "You can. You can't. You must. You mustn't. Who said you could do that? Well from now on you can't." Reduced to an errant two-year-old, you find yourself wondering, "Will I ever be able to function outside again? Will I be able to cross a street by myself?" A certain amount of otherwise useful solitude is consumed in fearing or disdaining the trivia by which we all live.

Some may spent their solitude planning an escape. I have one acquaintance who quietly, very quietly – for her cell was near mine and I heard nothing – filed through one of the bars on her louvered prison window. She also made the mistake of telling someone her plan, and the someone traded the information for earlier release for herself. There may have been other escape attempts during my eleven-year stay, but news travels fast in prison and I haven't heard of another that was actually set in motion. Between seventy and eighty percent of women in prison have children. When the most important thing outside is your children, escape is not a viable option. When the most important thing outside is drugs, that's something else again. For the many dispossessed who come here, prison is the safest place they have ever lived. Why would they leave early?

In one of her letters, Katherine Mansfield wrote, "Like everything else in life, I mean all suffering . . . we have to find the gift in it. We can't afford to waste such an expenditure of feelings; we have to learn from it." I have that taped to my wall and try assiduously to remember it. Depending upon my mood and the degree of today's trivia, I meet with different degrees of success.

Perhaps it is in the hope of "finding the gift in it" that so many dreams are dreamed in prison solitude, of a new life where everything will be better than it was before: "You wait and see," often with no realistic plans for how to achieve the dream. Prison is a land of shattered dreams and wishful thinking. Sadly, a bootstrap approach to life is not noticeably prevalent in public utterances here. What private thoughts are, one can only surmise by the next day's questions. One of the women, a parole violator who was back for the second time, wrote this: "When I was in prison for four years I worked very hard to better myself. I got my GED. I learned typing and word-processing and took three semesters of college. I was a success in prison and a failure on the outside. Could I have set myself up to return here where I was successful?" Tough questions. Deep thoughts.

For the most part plans for a better tomorrow are conceived in the womb of guilt. Weighed in pounds, guilt is the heaviest product of a woman's prison solitude, at least if she has children. She may have neglected them on the outside. She may not have seen them for a long time before she came here. She may have lived from drug hit to drug hit, lost in the haze of heroin or crack. But once the drugs have left her system, the children fill it again. Plans for finding a house where they can all live together warm her cell. Many were good mothers on the outside, sometimes doing what they did to put food on the table. Arlene has three children in college. I asked her one day, "Are they angry with you for what you did?" "No," she said, "They've known all their lives I was out hustlin' for them." The need to see her children again, the ache because she can't, the worry over what's happening to them out there on the street—these leave a lonely cell cold and wet with tears. There's plenty of time for crying in prison cells. Who can say what river might have been born if all the tears of prison solitude had met somewhere?

T.S. Eliot described hell as a place where nothing connects. For many people in prison, life has had a way of being hell because nothing in it ever connected. They have never known community, shared compassion, shared caring. For many of them there is a total absence of community in here too, unless mutual loathing of their jailers and the system can be said to bind them together in community.

It is difficult to evaluate or judge the amount of community in this prison. Compared to what? To the growing Balkanization of the world outside? To the ever-rising crime rate, homelessness, illiteracy, the growing chasm between rich and poor, the lack of medical care for so many millions? Should a prisoner be expected to demonstrate more compassion, more concern for others, less racial hatred, more the long-term view, less the urge for instant gratification than her judges and jailers do? I think not.

Community is not what prison is about. Even too much togetherness is understandably suspect. "What are they talking about over there?" "'I don't want those two women in the same housing unit." "Ethel can't work in the school building while Candy is there." There is some togetherness allowed, well monitored. But togetherness and community are not the same.

In clear weather there is a period morning and afternoon when the yard is open, and if you don't have a work assignment and you aren't locked for some wrong-doing, you can join as many as 100 other women there. Most of the women spend the time alone or in twos. Maybe four play cards. Maybe seven or eight sit under one of the two trees. For the most part they're looking into space, whispering an occasional secret, thinking their own thoughts. One of the women has recently organized an exercise group in the yard, and sometimes as many as twenty or thirty women join in. That's a germ of community, I guess.

To help one another smacks of empowerment, which is the antithesis of prison policy. The system must have the power; the inmate must be rendered impotent. I'm told male inmates are far more apt to stand together to redress a grievance than women are. Women complain but endure. They rarely take a stand in here on anything that is not their particular problem. Thus joint action is a rarity. We are easier to divide and conquer.

Bedford women have won some important class action suits over the years, two in particular. One concerned the lack of stated policy and procedure for the meting out of punishment, the other concerned the quality of facility medical care. But those were the work of a few energetic activists, not an expression of true community. The community part came in dividing up the spoils.

The brightest genuine star in the firmament of prison community at Bedford is a group called ACE, which stands for AIDS Counseling and Education. In 1986 when the AIDS scare was still new both inside and outside of prison and the subject was clouded in ignorance, ostracism, secrecy, and denial, even the nurses were unwilling to touch an AIDS patient, who was twice pariah, as inmate, and as AIDS patient. Now twenty percent of New York inmates test positive for the AIDS virus, and it is the primary cause of our prison deaths.

The idea for ACE was conceived by a few inmates who care deeply about their peers. Their goal is to teach women how to reduce high risk behavior to save lives, to eliminate stigmatization of AIDS patients, to create a safer and more humane atmosphere for them, and to build bridges to the outside community so there will be support for them when they leave prison. It's a large order. As one of the ACE founders wrote, "Although we share life inside together which provides the potential for community, there is not an existing consciousness of community. That had to be struggled for to help in the fight against AIDS." It was an uphill struggle, and it took time.

At their first meeting, held with the permission of the superintendent, thirty-five women out of eight hundred showed up. Some had AIDS, some were afraid they had it, and some just wanted to know more about it. Almost at once an atmosphere of caring began to grow, and at that meeting for the first time at Bedford women stood up and said publicly, "I have AIDS." It was the beginning of a community of trusting and helping and learning.

An education program began for ACE members, organized by inmates, with doctors, nurses, and social workers from Montefiore Hospital coming weekly to give seminars. ACE members held memorial services for women who died of AIDS. They adopted the song "Sister" as their theme song: "Lean on me, I am your sister." More women began to join the group. Some volunteered to be on call at any hour to go to a sick woman to comfort her, bathe and massage her, and keep her company. And they were allowed to.

Then suddenly for six months the Administration stopped the program. I'm led to believe they feared that so much community was a threat to security. Prisoners were being mobilized for a common purpose. It wouldn't do. The program floundered and the women who had had such high hopes for it were left frustrated and angry. But as the AIDS problem grew worse and the prison staff was overtaxed, the Administration relented, called ACE members back and told them they could become active again. Not only was the work they did important, the sense of community it inspired couldn't be replicated by the professional staff.

My community in prison is made up of the young mothers and their infants who live here in the prison nursery. New York State is the only state in the union in which infants born while the mother is incarcerated may stay with her for one year and up to an additional six months more if the mother will be paroled within that time. Teaching young mothers, often still in their teens, about the needs of their babies, the vital importance of the first few years of life, and the role a good mother plays in those years is my main activity away from my cell. It has involved much learning as well as teaching, and it doesn't stop at the prison gates. Work with children, two or twenty or two hundred, inevitably leads one's observations and readings and concerns to a global scale, to the community of children all over the world, and that, from a very small place, is where my community lies today.

The women who cannot read or write are the ones who haunt me here. They brought prison with them and now they are twice shackled. Some reach out for help and begin to grow. Too many do not. Sleep is their freedom. Sleep is their amusement. Sleep, a bottle of fingernail polish, and a hair curler are their world.

For others, the lucky ones, there are more options. They can be useful in small ways if they choose to and find satisfaction in the process. For them learning and reaching out to others can make the prison walls less ominous. We each bring our own world with us to prison. It is not so different outside. Others may never come to prison but create their own prisons wherever they are. We each live solitude in our own way. As for community, I read of beautiful pockets of it here and there, but the opportunity for far more of it is still waiting to be met. Perhaps some day there will even be a pocket of it for the women of Bedford when they enter the world again.

STANLEY HAUERWAS

Discipleship as a Craft, Church as a Disciplined Community

THE CHURCH SEEMS CAUGHT in an irresolvable tension today. Insofar as we are able to maintain any presence in modern society we do so by being communities of care. Pastors become primarily people who care. Any attempt to be a disciplined and disciplining community seems antithetical to being a community of care. As a result the care the church gives, while often quite impressive and compassionate, lacks the rationale to build the church as a community capable of standing against the powers we confront.

That the church has difficulty being a disciplined community, or even more cannot conceive what it would mean to be a disciplined community, is not surprising given the church's social position in developed economies. The church exists in a buyer's or consumer's market, so any suggestion that in order to be a member of a church you must be transformed by opening your life to certain kinds of discipline is almost impossible to maintain. The called church has become the voluntary church, whose primary characteristic is that the congregation is friendly. Of course, that is a kind of discipline, because you cannot belong to the church unless you are friendly, but it's very unclear how such friendliness contributes to the growth of God's church meant to witness to the kingdom of God.

In an attempt to respond to this set of circumstances, the primary strategy, at least for churches in the mainstream, has been to try to help people come to a better understanding of what it means to be a Christian. Such a strategy assumes that what makes a Christian a Christian is holding certain beliefs that help us better understand the human condition, to make sense of our experience. Of course, no one denies that those beliefs may have behavioral implications, but the assumption is that the beliefs must be in place in order for the behavior to be authentic. In this respect the individualism of modernity can be seen in quite a positive light. For the very fact that people are now free from the necessity of believing as Christians means that if they so decide to identify with Christianity, they can do so voluntarily.

In short, the great problem of modernity for the church is how we are to survive as disciplined communities in democratic societies. For the fundamental presumption behind democratic societies is that the consciousness of something called the *common citizen* is privileged no matter what kind of formation it may or may not have had. It is that presumption that has given rise to the very idea of ethics as an identifiable discipline within the modern university curriculum. Both Kant and the utilitarians assumed that the task of the ethicist was to explicate the presuppositions everyone shares. Ethics is the attempt to systematize what we all perhaps only inchoately know or which we have perhaps failed to make sufficiently explicit.

Such a view of ethics can appear quite anticonventional, but even the anticonventional stance gains its power by appeal to what anyone would think upon reflection. This can be nicely illustrated in terms of the recent movie, *The Dead Poets Society*. It is an entertaining, popular movie that appeals to our moral sensibilities. The movie depicts a young and creative teacher battling what appears to be the unthinking authoritarianism of the school as well as his students' (at first) uncomprehending resistance to his teaching method. The young teacher, whose subject is romantic poetry, which may or may not be all that important, takes as his primary pedagogical task helping his students think for themselves. We watch him slowly awaken one student after another to the possibility of their own talents and potential. At the end, even though he has been fired by the school, we are thrilled as his students find the ability to stand against authority, to think for themselves.

This movie seems to be a wonderful testimony to the independence of spirit that democracies putatively want to encourage. Yet I can think of no more conformist message in liberal societies than the idea that students should learn to think for themselves. What must be said is that most students in our society do not have minds well enough trained to think. A central pedagogical task is to tell students that their problem is that they do not have minds worth making up. That is why training is so important, because training involves the formation of the self through submission to authority that will provide people with the virtues necessary to make reasoned judgment.

The church's situation is not unlike the problems of what it means to be a teacher in a society shaped by an ethos that produces movies like *The Dead Poets Society*. Determined by past presuppositions about the importance of commitment for the living of the Christian life, we have underwritten a voluntaristic conception of the Christian faith, which presupposes that one can become a Christian without training. The difficulty is that once such a position has been established, any alternative cannot help appearing as an authoritarian imposition.

In this respect it is interesting to note how we—that is, those of us in mainstream traditions—tend to think about the loss of membership by mainstream churches and the growth of so-called conservative churches. Churches characterized by compassion and care no longer are able to retain membership, particularly that of their own children, whereas conservative churches that make moral conformity and/or discipline their primary focus continue to grow. Those of us in liberal churches tend to explain this development by noting that people cannot stand freedom, and therefore, in a confusing world devoid of community, seek authority. Conservative churches are growing, but their growth is only a sign of pathology.

Yet this very analysis of why conservative churches are growing assumes the presumptions of liberal social theory and practice that I am suggesting is the source of our difficulty. The very way we have learned to state the problem is the problem. The very fact that we let the issue be framed by terms such as *individual* and *community, freedom* and *authority, care* versus *discipline,* is an indication of our loss of coherence and the survival of fragments necessary for Christians to make our disciplines the way we care.

For example, one of the great problems facing liberal and conservative churches alike is that their membership has been schooled on the distinction between public and private morality. Liberal and conservative alike assume that they have a right generally to do pretty much what they want, as long as what they do does not entail undue harm to others. The fact that such a distinction is incoherent even in the wider political society does little to help us challenge an even more problematic character in relationship to the church. Yet if salvation is genuinely social, then there can be no place for a distinction that invites us to assume, for example, that we have ownership over our bodies and possessions in a way that is not under the discipline of the whole church. Recently I gave a lecture at a university that is identified with a very conservative Christian church. The administration was deeply concerned with the teaching of business ethics in the university's business school and had begun a lectureship to explore those issues. My lecture was called "Why Business Ethics Is a Bad Idea." I argued that business ethics was but a form of quandary ethics so characteristic of most so-called applied ethics. As a result, I suggested that business ethics could not help failing to raise the fundamental issues concerning why business was assumed to be a special area of moral analysis.

After I had finished, a person who taught in the business school asked, "But what can the church do given this situation?" I suggested to her that if the church was going to begin seriously to reflect on these matters, it should start by requiring all those currently in the church, as well as anyone who wished to join the church, to declare what they earn in public. This suggestion was greeted with disbelief, for it was simply assumed that no one should be required to expose their income in public. After all, nothing is more private in our lives than the amount we earn. Insofar as that is the case, we see how far the church is incapable of being a disciplined community.

However, one cannot help feeling the agony behind the questioner's concern. For if the analysis I have provided to this point is close to being right, then it seems we lack the conceptual resources to help us understand how the church can reclaim for itself what it means to be a community of care and discipline. Of course, "conceptual resources" is far too weak a phrase, for if actual practices of care and discipline are absent, then our imaginations will be equally impoverished. What I propose, therefore, is to provide an account of what it means to learn a craft, to learn—for example—how to lay brick, in the hope that we may be able to claim forms of care and discipline unnoticed but nonetheless present in the church.

To learn to lay brick, it is not sufficient for you to be told how to do it; you must learn to mix the mortar, build scaffolds, joint, and so on. Moreover, it is not enough to be told how to hold a trowel, how to spread mortar, or how to frog the mortar. In order to lay brick you must hour after hour, day after day, lay brick.

Of course, learning to lay brick involves learning not only myriad skills, but also a language that forms and is formed by those skills. Thus, for example, you have to become familiar with what a trowel is and how it is to be used, as well as mortar, which bricklayers usually call "mud." Thus "frogging mud" means creating a trench in the mortar so that when the brick is placed in the mortar, a vacuum is created that almost makes the brick lay itself. Such language is not just incidental to becoming a bricklayer but is intrinsic to the practice. You cannot learn to lay brick without learning to talk "right."

The language embodies the history of the craft of bricklaying. So when you learn to be a bricklayer you are not learning a craft *de novo* but rather being initiated into a history. For example, bricks have different names — klinkers, etc. — to denote different qualities that make a difference about how one lays them. These differences are often discovered by apprentices being confronted with new challenges, making mistakes, and then being taught how to do the work by the more experienced.

All of this indicates that to lay brick you must be initiated into the craft of bricklaying by a master craftsman. It is interesting in this respect to contrast this notion with modern democratic presuppositions. For as I noted above, the accounts of morality sponsored by democracy want to deny the necessity of a master. It is assumed that we each in and of ourselves have all we need to be moral. No master is necessary for us to become moral, for being moral is a condition that does not require initiation or training. That is why I often suggest that the most determinative moral formation most people have in our society is when they learn to play baseball, basketball, quilt, cook or learn to lay bricks. For such sports and crafts remain morally anti-democratic insofar as they require acknowledgment of authority based on a history of accomplishment.

Of course, it is by no means clear how long we can rely on the existence of crafts for such moral formation. For example, bricklayers who are genuinely masters of their craft have become quite scarce. Those who remain command good money for their services. Moreover, the material necessary for laying brick has become increasingly expensive. It has therefore become the tendency of builders to try as much as possible to design around the necessity of using brick in building. As a result, we get ugly glass buildings.

The highly functional glass building that has become so prevalent is the architectural equivalent of our understanding of morality. Such buildings should be cheap, easily built and efficient. They should be functional, which means they can have no purpose that might limit their multiple use. The more glass buildings we build, the fewer practitioners of crafts we have. The result is a self-fulfilling prophecy: the more buildings and/or morality we produce that eliminate the need for masters of crafts and/or morality, the less we are able to know that there is an alternative.

In his Gifford lectures, *Three Rival Versions of Moral Inquiry: Encyclopaedia, Genealogy, and Tradition,* Alasdair MacIntyre develops an extensive account of the craftlike nature of morality. In contrast to modernity, MacIntyre argues that the moral good is not available to any intelligent person no matter what his or her point of view. Rather, in order to be moral, to acquire knowledge about what is true and good, a person has to be made into a particular kind of person. Therefore transformation is required if one is to be moral at all. In short, no account of the moral life is intelligible that does not involve some account of conversion. This is particularly true in our context, because to appreciate this point requires a conversion from our liberal convictions.

This transformation is like that of making oneself an apprentice to a master of a craft. Through such an apprenticeship we seek to acquire the intelligence and virtues necessary to become skilled practitioners. Indeed, it is crucial to understand that intelligence and virtues cannot be separated, as they require one another. Classically this was embodied in the emphasis that the virtue of prudence cannot be acquired without the virtues of courage and temperance, and that courage and temperance require prudence. The circular or interdependent character of the relationship between prudence and courage suggests why it is impossible to become good without a master. We only learn how to be courageous, and thus how to judge what we must do, through imitation.

When the moral life is viewed through the analogy of the craft, we see why we need a teacher to actualize our potential. The teacher's authority must be accepted on the basis of a community of a craft, which embodies the intellectual and moral habits we must acquire and cultivate if we are to become effective and creative participants in the craft. Such standards can only be justified historically as they emerge from criticisms of their predecessors. That we hold a trowel this way or spread mortar on tile differently than on brick is justified from attempts to transcend or improve upon limitations of our predecessors.

Of course, the teachers themselves derive their authority from a conception of perfected work that serves as the telos of that craft. Therefore, often the best teachers in a craft do not necessarily produce the best work, but they help us understand what kind of work is best. What is actually produced as best judgments or actions or objects within crafts are judged so because they stand in some determinative relation to what the craft is about. What the craft is about is determined historically within the context of particularistic communities.

But what does all this have to do with the church? First it reminds us that Christianity is not beliefs about God plus behavior. We are Christians not because of what we believe, but because we have been called to be disciples of Jesus. To become a disciple is not a matter of a new or changed self-understanding, but rather to become part of a different community with a different set of practices.

For example, I am sometimes confronted by people who are not Christians but who say they want to know about Christianity. This is a particular occupational hazard for theologians around a university, because it is assumed that we are smart or at least have a Ph.D., so we must really know something about Christianity. After many years of vain attempts to "explain" God as trinity, I now say, "Well, to begin with we Christians have been taught to pray, 'Our father, who art in heaven . . .'" I then suggest that a good place to begin to understand what we Christians are about is to join me in that prayer.

For to learn to pray is no easy matter but requires much training, not unlike learning to lay brick. It does no one any good to believe in God, at least the God we find in Jesus of Nazareth, if they have not learned to pray. To learn to pray means we must acquire humility not as something we try to do, but as commensurate with the practice of prayer. In short, we do not believe in God, become humble and then learn to pray, but in learning to pray we humbly discover we cannot do other than believe in God.

But, of course, to learn to pray requires that we learn to pray with other Christians. It means we must learn the disciplines necessary to worship God. Worship, at least for

Christians, is the activity to which all our skills are ordered. That is why there can be no separation of Christian morality from Christian worship. As Christians, our worship is our morality, for it is in worship that we find ourselves engrafted into the story of God. It is in worship that we acquire the skills to acknowledge who we are – sinners.

This is but a reminder that we must be trained to be a sinner. To confess our sin, after all, is a theological and moral accomplishment. Perhaps nowhere is the contrast between the account of the Christian life I am trying to develop and most modern theology clearer than on this issue. In an odd manner Christian theologians in modernity, whether they are liberals or conservatives, have assumed that sin is a universal category available to anyone. People might not believe in God, but they will confess their sin. As a result, sin becomes an unavoidable aspect of the human condition. This is odd for a people who have been taught that we must confess our sin by being trained by a community that has learned how to name those aspects of our lives that stand in the way of our being Jesus' disciples.

For example, as Christians we cannot learn to confess our sins unless we are forgiven. Indeed, as has often been stressed, prior to forgiveness we cannot know we are sinners. For it is our tendency to want to be forgivers such that we remain basically in a power relation to those who we have forgiven. But it is the great message of the gospel that we will find our lives in that of Jesus only to the extent that we are capable of accepting forgiveness. But accepting forgiveness does not come easily, because it puts us out of control.

In like manner we must learn to be a creature. To confess that we are finite is not equivalent to the recognition that we are creatures. For creaturehood draws on a determinative narrative of God as creator that requires more significant knowledge of our humanity than simply that we are finite. For both the notions of creature and sinner require that we

find ourselves constituted by narratives that we did not create. As I indicated earlier, that is to put us at deep odds with
modernity. For the very notion that our lives can be recognized as lives only as we find ourselves constituted by a determinative narrative that has been given to us rather than
created by us, is antithetical to the very spirit of modernity.
But that is but an indication of why it is necessary that this
narrative be carried by a body of people who have the skills
to give them critical distance on the world.

In some ways all of this remains quite abstract because the
notions of sinner and creature still sound more like self-
understanding than characteristics of a craft. That is why
we cannot learn to be a sinner separate from concrete acts of
confession. Thus in the letter of James we are told, "Are any
among you sick? They should call for the elders of the
church and have them pray over them, anointing them with
oil in the name of the Lord. The prayer of faith will save the
sick and the Lord will raise them up; and anyone who has
committed sins will be forgiven. Therefore confess your
sins to one another, and pray for one another, so that you
may be healed. The prayer of the righteous is powerful and
effective" (5: 14–16). Such practice, I suspect, is no less important now than it was then. We cannot learn that we are
sinners unless we are forced to confess our sins to other
people in the church. Indeed, it is not possible to learn to be
a sinner without a confession and reconciliation. For it is
one thing to confess our sin in general, but it is quite another
to confess our sin to one in the church whom we may well
have wronged and to seek reconciliation. Without such con-
fessions, however, I suspect that we cannot be church at all.

For example, when Bill Moyers did his public broadcast
series on religion in America, the taping on fundamentalism was quite striking. He showed a fundamentalist pastor

in Boston discussing a pastoral problem with one of his parishioners. The parishioner's wife had committed adultery and had confessed it to the church. After much searching and discussion, the church had received her back after appropriate penitential discipline. However, her husband was not ready to be so forgiving and did not wish to receive her back.

The fundamentalist pastor said, "You do not have the right to reject her, for as a member of our church you too must hold out the same forgiveness that we as a church hold out. Therefore I'm not asking you to take her back, I am telling you to take her back."

I anticipate that such an example strikes fear in most of our liberal hearts, but it is also a paradigmatic form of what I take forgiveness to be about. In this instance one with authority spoke to another on behalf of the central skills of the church that draw their intelligibility from the gospel. There we have an example of congregational care and discipline that joins together for the upbuilding of the Christian community.

Of course, if the church lacks masters who have undergone the discipline of being forgiven, then indeed we cannot expect that such discipline will be intelligible. But I do not believe that we are so far gone as to lack such masters. Indeed, they are the ones who continue to carry the history to help us learn from our past so that our future will not be determined by the temptation to live unforgiven and thus unskillful lives.

PHIL CATALFO

America, Online

THIS WAS NOT FUNNY ANYMORE. Nearly five years ago, my wife and I were expecting our youngest child, and he was delaying his entry. The calendar marched days, then weeks, past the due date. It seemed we would be parents of The Baby Who Gestated Forever. Not surprisingly, Michelle's stamina (to say nothing of her patience) was wearing thin. I needed to be able to support, encourage, and reassure her, yet I too was running out of steam. I desperately needed to replenish my inner resources.

So I went to The WELL.

The Whole Earth 'Lectronic Link, better known by its acronym, The WELL, is a computer conferencing system—an electronic bulletin board that provides a forum for thousands of simultaneous online conversations covering just about everything under the sun. Its nerve center is a minicomputer housed in the Sausalito, California, offices of *Whole Earth Review* (publishers of the *Whole Earth Catalog*), but what makes it tick are the users—some 4,100 at last count, from all around the country—who plug in via their computer modems to read and comment on any of about 150 ongoing WELL colloquies, known as conferences.

Each conference offers a few dozen to several hundred

"topics"—discrete conversations on different subjects related to the conference theme. Those themes range from the self-explanatory—Sexuality, Spirituality, Politics, Current Events, Gardening, Books, Television, and so on—to slightly more obscure titles such as "Fringes of Reason," "Unclear," "Netweaver," and "Virtual Reality."

And then there is the conference called "Parenting," which is where I turned for help when we were sweating out our endless pregnancy. I had only recently gotten my first computer and had just begun to poke my nose into the mysteries of The WELL. Although I scarcely knew any of the dozens of people whose names and comments flashed before me—at the time, they seemed more like characters from my subconscious, or maybe a novel I was dreaming—they rallied to our cause like a host of electronic grandmothers knitting in a corner during labor. Relax, one cautioned. Try a gentle ride in a playground swing, another suggested. Apply some Evening Primrose Oil, a midwife offered. Don't worry, many counseled: The baby will come when he or she is ready.

Online computer services are generally heavy on the commerce side—data, mail order, stock prices, news services, and the like. But the freewheeling spirit of the grassroots computer subculture has also spawned something more profound: networks that are beginning to redefine personal relationships, political organizing, even democracy itself. And if current projections hold, this technology will, before long, be as pervasive as the telephone and television are today. Futurist Tom Mandel of the Menlo Park, California, consulting firm SRI International, estimates that presently some 1 to 1.5 million people in the United States engage at least occasionally in computer conferencing, and he expects that number to grow to between 5 and 10 million by the end of the decade. Other estimates are more robust. John Quarterman, networking consultant and author of *The Matrix* (perhaps the most exhaustive treatment of global computer networks to date), estimates that there are currently between 50 and 100 million active computer networkers worldwide. He says their number has been doubling annually since 1987 — a rate that, if sustained, means there could be well over a billion users before the decade is over. "Pretty soon this technology will be so widely distributed it will be hard to do without it," he says. "It's already getting to the point where, if you can't deal with this technology, you can't deal with society. Think about the telephone. Can you get along without one? Well, *sort of*. But when [computer conferencing] is as widely available as the telephone, it'll be even harder to get along without, because so much more is possible with it than is possible with the telephone." Those possibilities include electronic mail (or "e-mail," as it's more commonly called) and "many-to-many communication," in which large numbers of people can carry on coherent conversations from disparate locations (often oceans or continents apart) and can enter or leave the conversations at widely divergent times.

Of course, the basis of "many-to-many communication" is one-to-one contact. Enthusiasts see computer networking as the revival of a way of relating to strangers that seems to have all but disappeared from modern life. "It's like having the corner bar, complete with old buddies and delightful newcomers," says Howard Rheingold, an avid online networker and author of several books examining the farther reaches of the human/technology interface. "Except that instead of putting on my coat, shutting down the computer, and walking down to the corner, I just invoke my telecom program, and *voilà*: There they are." Janey Fritsche, a designer and producer of interactive multimedia, describes the atmosphere as "a community that disappeared with front porches." Media artist Ray Gallon, a New York University professor and regular visitor to ECHO (a lively WELL-like system based in New York City) describes the attraction this way: "At a time when New York is crumbling into detritus before our eyes, here's one thing that's in New York and oriented to New York that's growing, positive, and fosters human contact instead of pushing it away."

Over time, the proliferating conversations on a system such as ECHO coalesce into a kind of nonphysical community or, as WELL marketing director John Coate puts it, "a bundle of communities of interest." And often these "virtual" communities, as they're referred to in the computer world, become physical communities as well. ECHO participants gather for parties; scores of users from all over the San Francisco Bay Area likewise attend monthly WELL events. Imagine: a host of formerly spectral beings taking form before your dazzled eyes.

That this electronic intimacy takes place at all will surprise many who believe that computer networking is undertaken solely by lonely, isolated people with shirt pockets full of mechanical pencils, intent on swapping rocket trajectory formulae. But, in fact, it has become a part of online life for many thousands of diverse enthusiasts.

Some even meet their mates online. Last fall a Michigan bridegroom named Jay Libove, flush with joy, posted a delightful account on USENET (a worldwide network mainly linking universities and research sites) telling how he and his bride had met through an online network. Enrolled in schools more than seven hundred miles apart (he was in Pittsburgh, she in Iowa), they corresponded electronically and became fast friends. Although they did speak over the phone, they didn't meet face-to-face until two years later. Libove attributes the growth of their relationship largely to the fact that it began on the network: "We found that we learned as much about each other via the computer network, electronic mail, and telephone calls as we had about almost any of our in-person friends in the past," he said. "We found that a calm, reasonable, cautious approach to networking and to people whom you can't see can really lead to true knowledge of these remote, seemingly unreal beings."

A similar process led to the marriage of The WELL's Greta and Bob Bickford. "We met online about six months before we met face-to-face," says Greta. "We were able to find out a lot about one another – what the other thought, his or her philosophy of life, and so on – before we ever set eyes on each other. I credit The WELL not only as the meeting place, but also as a definite force in bringing us together, since we were able to establish common ideas and dreams by reading each other's postings."

Computer networkers help one another through rough times, as well. Jay Allison, a Massachusetts-based public radio producer, logged onto The WELL's Parenting conference a year ago during a string of sleepless nights caused by his two-year-old daughter's serious illness. "I found it full of twenty-four-hour compassionate ears and souls," he recalls. "They not only listened, they talked back. They helped. I found myself keeping a kind of online journal in the company of these people I'd never laid eyes on. It seemed kind of miraculous, really, this communion late at night in front of the screen."

When San Francisco physician "Flash" Gordon was hospitalized for an angioplasty after suffering a heart attack, his WELL friends mobilized to cheer him up. One even brought him a portable computer so he could log in from his hospital bed. "It kept me sane. It prevented cabin fever," Gordon says. "The WELL is the source of much of my human discourse; I'd be unwell without The WELL."

Lisa Carlson, CEO of Metasystems Design Group in Arlington, Virginia, discovered the potential for fostering emotional support via computer through a five-year online experiment in group dynamics with some friends. Based on the "T-group" model (of sensitivity-training fame), the group, called an "N-group" (short for "network"), was created solely for interpersonal exploration. The advantage of doing this sort of exploration via computer network instead of in person, says Carlson, is that when it's online, "the group doesn't just take place on Wednesday nights or end when the weekend's over. It's available all the time."

Carlson recalls a remarkable experience involving one member's long struggle with cancer. The man was an academic who, Carlson says, "had a hard time dealing with personal stuff." According to Carlson, the group gave him a forum to deal with his pent-up feelings. "He credited the group with opening him up," she recalls, and when he became ill, "we were able to support him, as well as process our feelings about his illness and death with each other." After he died, his widow joined the group. "She really appreciated the group because we allowed her to deal with her feelings about his death long after the fact"—an opportunity that can be hard to find in the outside world.

Along similar lines, ECHO offers its members (for an extra fee) group therapy, in an online conference called "Group" moderated by psychologist Josiane Caggiano. ECHO founder Stacy Horn reports that at one point a software feature called "chat," which allows a group to interact simultaneously and anonymously, proved helpful when things got particularly tense. "A number of the participants went online and used chat to do some old-fashioned role playing," says Horn. "They played each other, and apparently it worked very well. It broke the tension. People enjoyed it immensely, and they were able to go on with the group therapy."

One of the most dramatic examples of an online community grappling with real, life-and-death issues occurred last summer when one of The WELL's more vocal (and controversial) citizens took his own life. Blair Newman was a high-tech visionary and entrepreneur; his brilliant, sometimes abrasive, always thought-provoking comments could be found in every electronic nook and cranny of The WELL. Although he engendered a multiplicity of reactions from his fellow WELLers, he had come to be so much a part of the networking fabric that when he quietly left the system last spring – after erasing nearly all his innumerable postings – he continued to provoke responses. A month or so later it was announced, online, that he'd been found dead by his own hand, and the shock waves reverberated through the system for many weeks. Then an unexpected, unforgettable thing happened: The WELL held an impromptu online memorial service. Nearly three hundred comments were recorded in two weeks.

Ironically, Grateful Dead lyricist John Barlow, a friend of Blair's and a WELL habitué, had remarked to a radio reporter only a few days earlier (during an interview on "small towns, real and virtual") that "cyberspace villages like The WELL would never become real communities until they could address sex and death in ritual terms. Marriages and funerals are the binding ceremonies in real towns," he had commented, "but they have a hard time happening among the disembodied." Here, The WELL was breaking new ground, improvising a ritual to observe the passing of one of its least understood denizens.

In addition to nurturing interpersonal relationships and providing therapeutic support, the computer network is proving to be a flexible, relatively inexpensive, and lightning-quick medium for organizing real-world events and activities. Last May, for example, a yearlong exercise in global computer networking called KIDS-91 was launched. So far nearly three hundred ten- to fifteen-year-old students from five continents have been linked up for the purpose of sharing positive visions of the future and discussing ways of achieving those visions. Organizers aim to get as many children as possible involved in a global dialogue that will culminate in a worldwide online event on May 12, 1991. Teachers, students, and government agencies from several countries are signing up, and most of the organizing is taking place online via the Toronto-based system SciNet and on CompuServe, the largest commercial computer network.

One of the most promising online environments for organizing off-line activities can be found in a family of networks operated by the Institute for Global Communication (IGC). Based in San Francisco, IGC provides an umbrella for several overlapping networks: ConflictNet, devoted to conflict resolution; EcoNet, specializing in environmental news and political actions; and PeaceNet, focusing on social justice and peace issues. IGC also serves as the North American node of the Association for Progressive Communications (APC), another worldwide web of like-minded networks.

EcoNet's 1,700 users were active in both local and global preparations for last year's Earth Day activities. Earth Day headquarters in California would post their spokespersons' itineraries and other information on EcoNet, and local and regional groups accessed this information to enhance their own efforts.

The potential for effective organizing inherent in computer networking isn't limited to one-day events, however. Forest preservation groups in the Pacific Northwest tap into EcoNet to keep apprised of the ongoing work of similar outfits in, say, New Guinea or Brazil. A children's forest-preservation group in England uses London-based Green-

Net (another APC affiliate) to stay in touch with its adopted preservation group in Costa Rica. Lawyers from major environmental groups such as the National Resources Defense Council use EcoNet to provide help to smaller organizations such as the Trustees for Alaska. Through networking technology, groups large and small can draw upon resources otherwise unavailable to them.

Many observers point to a growing number of experiments in "electronic democracy" – the use of conferencing software as a tool for operating and improving the political system – as proof that this technology can be used to serve the body politic. There are already scores of systems in operation that enable citizens of various-sized towns and even statewide constituencies to interact, organize, and influence policy. In Montana, for example, Big Sky Telegraph links schoolteachers to their peers around the state and to educational resources worldwide. The privately administered system, Old Colorado City Communications, enables Colorado Springs residents to interact with each other and with civic officials.

But perhaps the most notable example is Santa Monica's Public Electronic Network (PEN). PEN is the only conferencing system actually owned and operated by a municipality for the express purpose of interacting with its constituency. The city provides free accounts to all residents and has "walk-up" terminals in libraries, recreation centers, and other public buildings for those who don't own computers.

Some 3,000 Santa Monicans use PEN. And though the *Wall Street Journal* dismissed this number as comprising barely 3 percent of the city's population of 95,000, the citizenry already has a track record of accomplishments using the potent new technology. Last year, for example, Santa Monicans organized themselves online to oppose a proposed beachfront luxury hotel development and emerged victorious at the polls in November.

PEN has also proved to be an innovative tool for serving the city's growing homeless population. Many of Santa Monica's homeless are avid PEN participants, making use of the system's walk-up terminals. In an ongoing discussion that began last winter, some commented online that they needed access to morning showers, clean clothes, and secure storage for their belongings in order to find and keep a job. The then-nascent PEN Action Group took up this issue as its first project. Group members decided to lobby the city to create a program that was dubbed SHWASHLOCK (for shower, washing machine, and locker). The city responded by allocating $150,000 for the addition of showers and lockers to an existing facility and by providing vouchers redeemable in local laundromats.

According to Ken Phillips, the director of information systems for Santa Monica, the network "really opens up government. More governments ought to consider doing it." One reason it's not done more often, he suggests, is that governments "see the people as the enemy, and are afraid of what they'll hear from their constituents." But far from being deluged with "crank complaints," the Santa Monica government has found that more than 50 percent of its incoming constituent messages contain, of all things, *praise.* Citizens feel a newfound sense of being integrally involved with their local government, and the government feels connected to the citizens. "A system like this really brings out the notion that we're here to serve the people, and not the other way around," says Phillips.

"Electronic democracy" advocates promote the use of computer conferencing because they say it is intrinsically democratic — all voices carry equal weight and everyone has equal access to the information on the system. It is inherently democracy-producing, as well: The very act of creating and maintaining self-directed discussions among a number of parties trains participants in the democratic process.

For these reasons, some electronic networkers are bullish when projecting the potential political impact the technology could have in the near future. Frank Burns, president of Metasystems Design Group, a company that is in the process of franchising conferencing systems to several Eastern European countries—including the Hungarian body charged with drafting that nation's new constitution—believes that the technology offers these nascent democracies their best hope for forming free-market economies and democratic institutions. People in countries such as Hungary are more vitally engaged in the democratic process than we are in this country, says Burns. With a tool enabling them to engage citizens from all segments of society in the drafting of their new constitutions, he says, these nations could actually eclipse the West in democratic evolution. "I believe they will more than catch up with us," he says. "I think they'll develop models for citizen-government interaction that exceed what we have in the U.S. Five years from now we'll be learning from Eastern European countries about democracy."

Of course, this medium does have limitations, and they can be more than a little unsettling. The lack of supplemental signals such as body language can make miscommunication easier. Some call this a problem of narrow "bandwidth." The term, borrowed from broadcast engineering, refers here to the ability of the medium to convey complex information without distortion. "We evolved as creatures who had to be able to evaluate what was going on around us," says Howard Rheingold. "We had to be able to recognize danger, or food, and so on. Our skill in face-to-face communication is the product of millions of years of evolution. You eliminate voice and visuals, and you narrow the bandwidth."

But for some critics, this argument—or "apology," they

might say – doesn't quite grasp how fundamental the technology's shortcomings are. Michael Phillips, producer of the weekly radio series "Social Thought" and author of *The Seven Laws of Money,* has participated in computer networks off and on since the early '70s. But he sees in them no panacea and is not willing to chalk up their limitations to bandwidth. "The implication of the bandwidth definition is that increasing it would solve the problem," he says. "Whereas TV, which has thousands of times the bandwidth of computer conferencing, has *worse* interpersonal communication. An increase in bandwidth won't solve it. What is the *human* bandwidth? It's not a matter of degree. This is like saying 'I can't fly because of a slight weight problem.'"

Other critics are even more skeptical. Jerry Mander, author of *Four Arguments for the Elimination of Television,* says that while computer conferencing probably offers some tangible benefits for those who participate in it, what he objects to is "its being sold as a substitute for real, grassroots, face-to-face organizing." He thinks the argument that computer networks can be used to build communities is preposterous. "We hear people say 'I'm never lonely anymore.' Well, they used to say that about TV. It's encouraging the use of technology as a surrogate community. But it's *not* a community, it's a reflection of the fact that there *is* none – that our real communities have broken down."

Chellis Glendinning, psychologist and author of *When Technology Wounds,* agrees. "We're living in an over-technologized world hungry for community," she says. "I can understand why people are striving for a sense of community, but a computer conference isn't it. A 'virtual community' doesn't feel real or embodied, the way community is supposed to."

I don't know if computer conferencing technology is lulling me into a false sense of community, or if it will restore a tribal cohesion that has been missing for centuries. I don't even know whether I was looking for community when I first logged onto The WELL. What I do know is that, ever since my first encounters with others online, computer networking has surprised me with its remarkable ability to connect people—not just screen to screen, but heart to heart. No doubt this sentiment stems from the warm reception my family was given as we fretted through that long June waiting for the birth of our baby.

Peter did eventually decide to exit the womb, but not before scores of WELL beings had organized a group mind-pull (dubbed "WELLBEAM") aimed in his direction. "Baby Catalfo, COME ON OUT! The water's fine!" exhorted a typical on-screen supporter. When baby finally did, I excitedly logged on to post a rapturous play-by-play account of his birth. He was promptly dubbed the first "WELLbaby." I had met not a single one of these people, but I felt as if I'd made a slew of lifelong friends. I had become part of a "virtual" community as strong or stronger than most any you can find in real life. The WELL's very name conjures up the image of people gathering on a central, common ground to share the prosaic and the profound, the small facts and large events that become landmarks in a community's life. And in the end, it is this spirit—the type of fundamental human regard that so often appears to be in short supply in the "real" world—that may prove to be the most exhilarating and empowering aspect of this evolving technology.

White Pelicans

Hundreds of white pelicans stand shoulder to shoulder on an asphalt spit that eventually disappears into Great Salt Lake. They do not look displaced as they engage in head-bobbing, bill-snapping, and panting; their large, orange gular sacs fanning back and forth act as a cooling device. Some preen. Some pump their wings. Others stand, take a few steps forward, tip their bodies down, and then slide into the water, popping up like corks. Their immaculate white forms with carrotlike bills render them surreal in a desert landscape.

Home to the American white pelicans of Great Salt Lake is Gunnison Island, one hundred sixty-four acres of bare-boned terrain. Located in the northwest arm of the lake, it is nearly one mile long and a half-mile wide, rising approximately two hundred seventy-eight feet above the water.

So far, the flooding of Great Salt Lake has favored pelicans. The railroad trestle connecting the southern tip of the Promontory peninsula with the eastern shore of the lake slowed the rate of salt water intrusion into Bear River Bay. The high levels of stream inflow help to keep much of Bear River Bay fresh, so fish populations are flourishing. So are the pelicans.

Like the California gulls, the pelicans of Gunnison Island must make daily pilgrimages to freshwater sites to forage on carp or chub. Many pelican colonies fly by day and forage by night, to take advantage of desert thermals. The isolation of Gunnison Island offers protection to young pelicans, because there are no predators aside from heat and relentless gulls. Bear River Bay remains their only feeding site on Great Salt Lake.

So are their social skills. White pelicans are gregarious. What one does, they all do. Take fishing for example: four, five, six, as many as a dozen or more forage as a group, forming a circle to corrall and then to herd fish, almost like a cattle drive, toward shallower water where they can more efficiently scoop them up in their pouches.

Cooperative fishing has advantages. It concentrates their food source, conserves their energy, and yields results: the pelicans eat. They return to Gunnison Island with fish in their bellies (not in their pouches) and invite their young to reach deep inside their throats as they regurgitate morsels of fish.

It's not a bad model, cooperation in the name of community. Brigham Young tried it. He called it the United Order.

The United Order was a heavenly scheme for a totally self-sufficient society based on the framework of the Mormon Church. It was a seed of socialism planted by a conservative people. So committed was this "American Moses" to the local production of every needful thing that he even initiated a silkworm industry to wean the Saints from their dependence on the Orient for fine cloth.

Brigham Young, the pragmatist, received his inspiration for the United Order not so much from God as from Lorenzo Snow, a Mormon apostle, who in 1864 established a mercantile cooperative in the northern Utah community named after the prophet. Brigham City became the model of people working on behalf of one another.

The town, situated on Box Elder Creek at the base of the Wasatch Mountains, sixty miles north of Salt Lake City, was founded in 1851. It consisted of some six families until 1854, when Lorenzo Snow moved to Brigham City with fifty additional families. He had been called by Brother Brigham to settle there and preside over the Latter-day Saints in that region.

The families that settled Brigham City were carefully chosen by the church leadership. Members included a schoolteacher, a mason, carpenter, blacksmith, shoemaker, and other skilled craftsmen and tradesmen who would ensure the economic and social vitality of the community.

Lorenzo Snow was creating a community based on an ecological model: cooperation among individuals within a set of defined interactions. Each person was operating within their own "ecological niche," strengthening and sustaining the overall structure or "ecosystem."

Apostle Snow, with a population of almost sixteen hundred inhabitants to provide for, organized a cooperative general store. Mormon historian Leonard J. Arrington explains, "It was his intention to use this mercantile cooperative as the basis for the organization of the entire economic life of the community and the development of the industries needed to make the community self-sufficient."

A tannery, a dairy, a woolen factory, sheep herds, and hogs were added to the Brigham City Cooperative. Other enterprises included a tin shop, rope factory, cooperage, greenhouse and nursery, brush factory, and a wagon and carriage repair shop. An education department supervised the school and seminary.

The community even made provisions for transients, declaring a "tramp department" which enlisted their labor for chopping wood in exchange for a good meal.

After the Brigham City Cooperative was incorporated into Brigham Young's United Order, members were told,

If brethren should be so unfortunate as to have any of their
property destroyed by fire, or otherwise, the United Order
will rebuild or replace such property for them. When these
brethren, or any other members of the United Order die, the
directors become the guardians of the family, caring for the
interests and inheritances of the deceased for the benefit and
maintenance of the wives and children, and when the sons
are married, giving them a house and stewardship, as the father would have done for them. Like care will be taken of
their interests if they are sent on missions or taken sick.

By 1874, the entire economic life of this community of four
hundred families was owned and directed by the cooperative association. There was no other store in town. Fifteen
departments (later to expand to forty) produced the goods
and services needed by the community; each household obtained its food, clothing, furniture, and other necessities
from these sources.

In 1877, the secretary of the association filed the total
capital stock as $191,000 held among 585 shareholders.
The total income paid by the various departments to some
340 employees was in excess of $260,000.

Brigham Young's ideal society where "all members would
be tending to their own specialty" appeared to be in full
bloom. The Brigham City Cooperative even caught the eye
of British social reformer, Brontier O'Brien. He noted that
the Mormons had "created a soul under the ribs of death."
Edward Bellamy spent a week in Brigham City researching
Looking Backward, a Utopian novel prophesying a new social
and economic order.

Home industry was proving to be solid economics.

But signs of inevitable decay began to show. A descendant
of a Brigham City man told Arrington that his grandfather
formed a partnership with another prominent Brigham
City citizen in the late 1860s. Their haberdashery was the
only place in town where material other than homespun

could be purchased. When they succeeded beyond their dreams, they were asked to join the association. They declined, and townfolk were immediately instructed not to trade with them. When some of the community persisted in trading with these men, despite orders from Church officials, members of the Church were placed at the door of the shop to record the names of all persons who did business inside, even though the men in partnership were Mormons in good standing. As a result of this tactic, the business soon failed and the men were forced to set up shop elsewhere.

The ecological model of the Brigham City Cooperative began to crumble. They were forgetting one critical component: diversity.

The United Order of Minutes, taken on July 20, 1880, states, "It was moved and carried unanimously that the council disapprove discountenance, and disfellowship all persons who would start an opposition store or who would assist to erect a building for that purpose."

History has shown us that exclusivity in the name of empire building eventually fails. Fear of discord undermines creativity. And creativity lies at the heart of adaptive evolution.

Lorenzo Snow's fears that the Brigham City Cooperative would not adapt and respond quickly enough to the needs of a growing population materialized. Fire, debt, taxes, and fines befell the Order. In 1885, Apostle Snow was indicted on a charge of unlawful cohabitation (polygamy). He served eleven months in the Utah State Penitentiary before his conviction was set aside by the United States Supreme Court. Finally, as a result of the 1890s depression, the cooperative store went bankrupt. By 1896, all that remained of Brigham City's hive of industry was the unused honey stored on the shelves of the new general store.

Fifteen years of United Order graced Brigham City, Utah. A model for community cooperation? In part. But there is an organic difference between a system of self-sufficiency and a self-sustaining system. One precludes diversity, the other necessitates it. Brigham Young's United Order wanted to be independent from the outside world. The Infinite Order of Pelicans suggests there is no such thing.

IV.

THE

ECOLOGICAL

MODEL

OF

COMMUNITY

THOMAS BERRY

Bioregions: The Context for Reinhabiting the Earth

THE UNIVERSE EXPRESSES ITSELF in the blazing radiance of the stars and in the vast reaches of the galactic systems. Its most intimate expression of itself, however, is in this tiny planet: a planet that could not exist in its present form except in a universe such as this one, in which it has emerged and from which it has received its life energies. The planet presents itself to us, not as a uniform global reality, but as a complex of highly differentiated regions caught up in the comprehensive unity of the planet itself. There are arctic and tropical, coastal and inland regions, mountains and plains, river valleys and deserts. Each of these regions has its distinctive geological formation, climatic conditions, and living forms. Together these constitute the wide variety of life communities that may be referred to as bioregions. Each is coherent within itself and intimately related to the others. Together they express the wonder and splendor of this garden planet of the universe.

The human species has emerged within this complex of life communities; it has survived and developed through participation in the functioning of these communities at their most basic level. Out of this interaction have come our distinctive human cultures. But while at an early period we were aware of our dependence on the integral functioning of these surrounding communities, this awareness faded as we learned, through our scientific and technological skills, to manipulate the community functioning to our own advantage. This manipulation has brought about a disruption of the entire complex of life systems. The florescence that distinguished these communities in the past is now severely diminished. A degradation of the natural world has taken place.

Even though humans as well as the other species are in a stressful situation, few of us are aware of the order of magnitude of what is happening. Fewer still have any adequate understanding of its causes or the capacity to initiate any effective program for the revitalization of these life systems upon which everything depends. Disruption of the life process has led to a severe disruption of the human community itself. If social turmoil and international rivalries have evoked significant concern, the disruption of earth's life systems remains only a vague awareness in the human mind. This is strange indeed when we consider that the disruption of our bioregional communities is leading to a poisoning of the air we breathe, the water we drink, the soil and the seas that provide our food. We seek to remedy our social ills with industrial processes that lead only to further ecological devastation. Indeed our sensitivity to human conflict over the sharing of earth's resources has distracted us from the imperiled condition of these resources themselves, a peril associated with the loss of topsoil, the destruction of forests, the desertification of fruitful areas, the elimination of wetlands and spawning areas, the exhaustion of aquifers, the salinization of irrigated areas, the damaging of coral reefs.

The urgency of a remedy for this situation is such that all social groups and all nations are called upon to reassess the human-earth situation. As was indicated by Edward Schumacher, we must rethink our industrial approach to "development." This rethinking involves appropriate technologies, but also appropriate lifestyles, and, beyond those, appropriate human-earth relations.

The most difficult transition to make is from an anthropocentric to a biocentric norm of progress. If there is to be any true progress, then the entire life community must progress. Any progress of the human at the expense of the larger life community must ultimately lead to a diminishment of human life itself. A degraded habitat will produce degraded humans. An enhanced habitat supports an elevated mode of the human. This is evident not only in the economic order, but also throughout the entire range of human affairs. The splendor of earth is in the variety of its land and its seas, its life-forms and its atmospheric phenomena; these constitute in color and sound and movement that great symphonic context which has inspired our sense of the divine, given us our emotional and imaginative powers, and evoked from us those entrancing insights that have governed our more sublime moments.

This context not only activates our interior faculties; it also provides our physical nourishment. The air and water and soil and seeds that provide our basic sustenance, the sunshine that pours its energies over the landscape – these are integral with the functioning of the fruitful earth. Physically and spiritually we are woven into this living process. As long as the integrity of the process is preserved, we have air to breathe and water to drink and nourishing food to eat.

The difficulty has come from our subversion of this integral life community, supposedly for our own advantage. In the process we have torn apart the life system itself. Our technologies do not function in harmony with earth technologies. With chemicals we force the soil to produce beyond its natural rhythms. Having lost our ability to invoke natural forces, we seek by violence to impose mechanistic patterns on life processes. In consequence of such actions, we now live in a world of declining fertility, a wasted world, a world in which its purity and life-giving qualities have been dissipated.

The solution is simply for us as humans to join the earth community as participating members, to foster the progress and prosperity of the bioregional communities to which we belong. A bioregion is an identifiable geographical area of interacting life systems that is relatively self-sustaining in the ever-renewing processes of nature. The full diversity of life functions is carried out, not as individuals or as species, or even as organic beings, but as a community that includes the physical as well as the organic components of the region. Such a bioregion is a self-propagating, self-nourishing, self-educating, self-governing, self-healing, and self-fulfilling community. Each of the component life systems must integrate its own functioning within this community to survive in any effective manner.

The first function, self-propagation, requires that we recognize the rights of each species to its habitat, to its migratory routes, to its place in the community. The bioregion is the domestic setting of the community just as the home is the domestic setting of the family. The community continues itself through successive generations precisely as a community. Both in terms of species and in terms of numbers, a certain balance must be maintained within the community. For humans to assume rights to occupy land by excluding other life-forms from their needed habitat is to offend the community in its deepest structure. Further, it is even to declare a state of warfare, which humans cannot win since they themselves are ultimately dependent on those very life-forms that they are destroying.

The second bioregional function, self-nourishment, requires that the members of the community sustain one another in the established patterns of the natural world for the well-being of the entire community and each of its members. Within this pattern the expansion of each species is limited by opposed life-forms or conditions so that no one life-form or group of life-forms should overwhelm the others. In this function of the community we include, for humans, the entire world of food gathering, of agriculture, of commerce, and of economics. The various bioregional communities of the natural world can be considered as commercial ventures as well as biological processes. Even in the natural world there is a constant interchange of values, the laying up of capital, the quest for more economic ways of doing things. The earth is our best model for any commercial venture. It carries out its operations with an economy and a productivity far beyond that of human institutions. It also runs its system with a minimum of entropy. There is in nature none of that sterile or toxic waste or nondecomposing litter such as is made by humans.

The third function of a bioregion is its self-education through physical, chemical, biological, and cultural patterning. Each of these requires the others for its existence and fulfillment. The entire evolutionary process can be considered as a most remarkable feat of self-education on the part of planet Earth and of its distinctive bioregional units. An important aspect of this self-educational process is the experiential mode of its procedures. The earth, and each of its bioregions, has performed unnumbered billions of experiments in designing the existing life system. Thus the self-educational processes observed in the natural world form a model for the human. There is presently no other way for humans to educate themselves for survival and fulfillment than through the instruction available through the natural world.

The fourth function of a bioregion is self-governance. An integral functional order exists within every regional life community. This order is not an extrinsic imposition, but an interior bonding of the community that enables each of its members to participate in the governance and to achieve that fullness of life expression that is proper to each. This governance is presided over in much of the world by the seasonal sequence of life expression. It provides the order in which florescence and exuberant renewal of life takes place. Humans have traditionally inserted themselves into this community process through their ritual celebrations. These are not simply human activities, but expressions of the entire participating community. In human deliberations each of the various members of the community should be represented.

The fifth function of the bioregional community is self-healing. The community carries within itself not only the nourishing energies that are needed by each member of the community; it also contains within itself the special powers of regeneration. This takes place, for example, when forests are damaged by the great storms or when periods of drought wither the fields or when locusts swarm over a region and leave it desolate. In all these instances the life community adjusts itself, reaches deeper into its recuperative powers, and brings about a healing. The healing occurs whether the damage is to a single individual or to an entire area of the community. Humans, too, find that their healing takes place through submission to the discipline of the community and acceptance of its nourishing and healing powers.

The sixth function of the bioregional community is found in its self-fulfilling activities. The community is fulfilled in each of its components: in the flowering fields, in the great oak trees, in the flight of the sparrow, in the surfacing whale, and in any of the other expressions of the natural world. Also there are the seasonal modes of community fulfillment, such as the mysterious springtime renewal. In conscious celebration of the numinous mystery of the universe expressed in the unique qualities of each regional community, the human fulfills its own special role. This is expressed in religious liturgies, in market festivals, in the solemnities of political assembly, in all manner of play, in music and dance, in all the visual and performing arts. From these come the cultural identity of the bioregion.

The future of the human lies in acceptance and fulfillment of the human role in all six of these community functions. The change indicated is the change from an exploitive anthropocentrism to a participative biocentrism. The change requires something beyond environmentalism, which remains anthropocentric while trying to limit the deleterious effects of human presence on the environment.

We have limited our discussion so far to the inner functioning of the regional communities because these provide the most immediate basis of survival. If these communities do not fulfill their most essential functions, then the larger complex of bioregions cannot fulfill its role. Each of these bioregions is, as we have noted, *relatively* self-sustaining. None is fully self-sustaining since air and water flow across the entire planet, across all its regions. So it is with the animals. Some of them range widely from one end of a continent to the other. Birds cross multiple bioregional, and even continental, boundaries. Eventually all bioregions are interdependent. This interdependence is presently accentuated by the toxic waste poured into the environment by our industrial society. Such toxic materials are borne across entire continents and even across the entire planet by water and air. Such an extensive continental problem would not exist, of course, if each of the various bioregions functioned properly within its own context.

The larger functioning of bioregions leads to a consideration that the earth be viewed primarily as an interrelated system of bioregions, and only secondarily as a community of nations. The massive bureaucratic nations of the world have lost their inner vitality because they can no longer respond to the particular functioning of the various bioregions within their borders. A second difficulty within these large nations is the exploitation of some bioregions for the advantage of others. A third difficulty is the threatened devastation of the entire planet by the conflict between bureaucratic nations, with their weaponry capable of continental, and even planetary, devastation. To break these nations down into their appropriate bioregional communities could be a possible way to peace.

The bioregional mode of thinking and acting is presently one of the most vigorous movements taking place on the North American continent. Its comprehensive concern is leading toward a reordering of all our existing establishments: political-legal, commercial-industrial, communications, educational, and religious. At present all of these establishments are involved in the devastating impact of the industrial society on the natural world. The human arrogance they manifest toward the other natural members of the life communities remains only slightly affected by the foreboding concerning the future expressed by professional biologists and by others who have recognized that the imminent peril to the planet is not exactly the nuclear bomb, but the plundering processes that are extinguishing those very life systems on which we depend.

Yet the numbers of those speaking and acting and leading others in programs of reinhabiting the earth in a more benign relationship with the other members of these natural communities are growing constantly. This movement, often referred to as the Green movement, is fostering an ecological or bioregional context for every aspect of life, for education, economics, government, healing, and religion. So far, the movement remains a pervasive and growing mode of consciousness that is groping toward a more precise articulation of its own ideals, its institutional form, and its most effective programs of action.

Of primary importance in North America is identifying the various bioregions. To do that requires a sensitivity akin to that of the shamanic personality of tribal peoples. While bioregions have certain geographic boundaries, they also have certain mythic and historical modes of self-identification. This identification depends on ourselves as we participate in this process, which only now we begin to understand or appreciate.

JAMES G. COWAN

Aboriginal Solitude

Pᴀᴜʟɪɴᴜs ᴏꜰ Nᴏʟᴀ, ᴡʀɪᴛɪɴɢ to his friend Ausonius in the fourth century, spoke of the solitary state in a way that has conditioned how we think of solitude and the hermit in Western monasticism ever since:

> Not that they be beggered in mind, or brutes,
> Because they have chosen to live in lonely places:
> Their eyes are turned to the high stars,
> The very stillness of truth.[1]

For the Australian Aborigine, as for most traditional people in other parts of the world, the idea of quitting the tribal community in order to seek out solitude is entirely alien. It is not that he is unaware of the psychological effects of aloneness, but that he sees such an act of solitude in terms of its social effect. To understand his behavior, one must first understand the complex metaphysical relationship an Aborigine has with the landscape, and how his Dreaming country conditions all his actions. For, in the sense that Paulinus of Nola meant it, an Aborigine cannot be alone in a desert place, unless he actually leaves his tribal country. Wherever he might happen to be in terms of tribal nomadic patterns, he will always find himself in close proximity to his ancestors, to his Dreaming cult-heroes, and to his totemic birthplace. In other words, an Aborigine, even when he is physically alone, lives in, and is sustained by, a metaphysical community.

The Aborigine relies on a small range of utensils and weapons to sustain himself. Living in the bush, he has been able to survive in this minimalist way for upwards of 50,000 years. Post Ice Age inundation may have periodically limited the arrival of new migrants to Australia from Asia, as well as new technological advances from which the Aborigine might draw benefit. But, it is doubtful whether he might have wished for any further improvements to his lifestyle, given that he had worked out a successful *modus vivendi* in keeping with his environment. His so-called backwardness was not the result of any intellectual incapacity, as was suggested by nineteenth-century ethnologists, but was instead indicative of his priorities: he had long ago decided that his spiritual life was more important to him than his physical life.

Since the ascetic principle does not exist for him as a separate reality, he need not withdraw from the tribal community in order to work out his salvation. This instead is taken care of in the context of tribal belief, custom, and law. The law of the community takes precedence over, and largely subsumes, any individual volition. The Aborigine sees himself as a member of a tribe first and foremost. This is not to say that his social identity eliminates all sense of individual persona – far from it. Aborigines have a singular presence, a sense of their totemic and matrilineal identity which makes each person unique in terms of his or her community relationships.

Like all traditional peoples, the Aborigine is deeply bonded to his tribal country by a set of beliefs and rituals. These take the form of his totemic identity, the songs and dances associ-

ated with his totem, the esoteric lore pertaining to his
Dreaming place (where he was conceived by way of his
spirit's "entry" into his mother's body, not as a result of any
physical liaison between his parents), and the cult-hero activity linked to the creation of the world at the time of the
Dreaming. For it is the timeless moment of the Dreaming,
when the world "was new," as one tribal Elder described it,
that prefigures all existence. This is no paradisiacal state,
nor is it a primordial condition, but a concept that embraces
continued ancestral existence *post mortem,* as well as the
moment when the world first became manifest. Various
cult-heroes are identified with this creation process, the
most important being the Rainbow Snake. His iconic presence is seen on cave walls throughout Australia, and features prominently in myth, story, and song.

Since the cult-heroes created the world – *i.e.,* the hills, the
watercourses, the valleys, individual stones, and unusual
landmarks – tribal territory becomes a complex grid of
mythic expression. An Aborigine can never escape the sacred history of his people. He is constantly in contact with a
metaphysical perspective which conditions his way of thinking and acting. Indeed Aboriginal activity is often fraught
with restrictions in the form of taboos, as tribal law figures
large in his scheme of things. In spite of the seeming end-
lessness of space and the idea of an unpeopled landscape
(which the early white settlers considered the continent to
represent), an Aborigine is conscious that wherever he
walks he confronts the remnants of mythic drama and its
concomitant prohibitions. A man does not walk free into a
desert landscape as the ancient Christian anchorites might
have seen themselves doing; instead he is forever living
within mythic territory created by ancestral heroes.

The concept of solitude as it is conventionally understood
does not exist for the Aborigine. His dialogue is not with

himself or with his Maker, but with the realm of hieratic activity – a realm governed by supra-mundane events. There is not identification between himself and a monotheistic god, nor does he recognize a personal relationship between himself and the otherness of the cult-hero. The cult-hero simply exists, or existed at the time of the Dreaming. The divine entity lives another life, a supernatural life, a life governed by celestial laws not pertaining to the human order. In other words, the Aborigine acknowledges two levels of reality which do not intersect, except during ritual activity when the channels of communication are deliberately opened. This means that man lives one sort of life, a mortal life, while the cult-hero lives another sort of life, a celestial life.

A state of solitude, therefore, can only exist for an Aborigine when the world of the cult-hero – that is, the world of the Dreaming – is denied him. Even when a young warrior is required to undergo tribal initiation and quit the tribe, sometimes for many months, his temporary exile does not mean that he is living beyond the frontier of culture. For he carries with him knowledge, limited perhaps (since he has not been fully initiated, and so certain esoteric information has been withheld), but nevertheless connected to the country over which he wanders. He is not set loose, so to speak, upon an alien landscape intellectually or spiritually blindfolded. He knows where he is going since he is familiar with the mythic symbols at his disposal.

Solitude, at least as we understand it, presupposes a rejection of all that we might consider as the "illusion of sensibility." Anchorites or solitaries set out to remove themselves from the web of ordinary reality in order to pursue a life of spiritual gnosis. In the process they often find themselves engaging in what Lorenzo Scupoli termed "unseen warfare" with demons and negative psychic phenomena. These in turn lead to a further desire to practice increasing austerities in the hope of purging the soul of its impurities. The physical appetites are finally pacified to the point where both mind and spirit are able to partake of a state of bliss. It is the ultimate objective for all ascetics, whether they are Christian, Buddhist, Hindu, or Moslem. The solitary life is intimately associated with the desire to transcend ordinary reality in the expectation of experiencing another order of reality altogether. It is the basis of much modern spiritual practice.

But for the Aborigine the idea of depriving himself of aspects of ordinary life in order to embrace a particular spiritual condition pertaining to another life does not figure largely in his scheme of things. This is not to say that he does not understand the benefits of ascetic activity: he does. Most initiatory ritual involves physical deprivation of some sort. Body scarring, tooth-knocking, circumcision, and other practices are designed to test a postulant so that he is able to resist pain. Physical pain is regarded as an important adjunct to the business of deepening one's awareness of manhood. Indeed an Aborigine often voluntarily subjects himself to mutilation at different times of his life so as to prove to himself, and to his tribal elders, what level of interiority he has attained as a man of knowledge, a "man of high degree."[2]

Ritual is the instrument by which he explores the otherworld, the Dreaming. He is the supreme liturgist, capable of devising ceremonies to embrace all aspects of cult-hero activity, whether they be real or imagined. Ritual is the material delineation of the metaphysical and imaginal[3] faculties. Embodying the immaterial in an action (dance) or a musical construct (song) gives physical credence to a range of numinous values and emotions. Similarly, since there is a natural link between ritual and various ascetic practices (circumci-

sion, blood-mingling as a method of signifying divine brotherhood) in major tribal ceremonies, such a nexus affirms
the invisible presence of the cult-heroes and so denotes the
consanguinity between man and spirit. Ascetic activity is
therefore rarely detached from ritual in the Aboriginal context. But the ideal of *self*-flagellation is entirely alien to him.
He does not want to attain to spiritual knowledge outside
the tribal forum. He is brother to his kind, and his spiritual
life is intimately associated with the collective spiritual life of
his community.

For the Aborigine, his landscape is also an extended
myth. He does not live "off" the land, but "in" a terranean
relationship with the otherworld, the Dreaming. His association with birds and animals also partakes of confraternity,
not separateness. These, after all, are a part of his totemic
life, which means that their existence is an echo of his own.
So a man can never be alone in a landscape when he knows
that he is living not only within proximity of myth (the cult-
hero), but also within physical proximity of his totem.

Physical solitude can only be realized when these conditions are absent. If a landscape becomes "dead" as a bearer
of sacred-history, or when the animals have departed (a
form of physical "deadness") because ritual life has abated,
then a tribal territory is in danger of becoming a metaphysical desert. A man walking out on such a landscape, not
knowing or no longer able to recall the Dreaming events associated with it, will find himself entering a state of existential solitude, the solitude brought on by metaphysical *angst*.

On my travels I have often met Aborigines who regret-
fully relate to me how the stories belonging to a particular
piece of country have been "forgotten," or that its custodian
("key-man") has died without passing on the stories related
to its Dreaming existence. Once this has happened, it is unlikely that the land will again be part of the community of
men. Often it becomes "rubbish country," a term Aborigi-

nes use to denote country devoid of its sacred history. It has become, literally, a mythical and metaphysical desert.

True exile for an Aborigine could not involve the abandonment of his birthright—that is, his Dreaming. Not only would such an event involve his spiritual death, but in many cases his physical death might ensue also. Roland Robinson relates a story told to him by a New South Wales Aborigine about a man who sold a mountain to the mayor of a local town. The mayor offered the tribal owner a few sovereigns and a bottle of rum as payment for the mountain, which was to be used as a quarry. The first charge of gelignite set under the mountain unleashed a stream of black water which took many weeks to dry up. During that time the tribal owner of the mountain fell sick and died. His Dreaming had been so damaged by the explosion that the man himself was mortally wounded. As Robinson's informant later remarked, the man had sold his birthright, his Dreaming.[4]

It is virtually impossible for an Aborigine to deny his relationship with the earth, with his Dreaming, with his totem. This triad conditions his intellectual and emotional outlook. It also conditions his attitude towards his community. Though he does recognize the need to retire from the community on ceremonial occasions, the sense of solitude he engenders at this time is carefully orchestrated by way of myth and ritual. He therefore is never "alone" as such. So complete and overreaching is the Dreaming that an Aborigine would find it difficult to break free and become "self-conscious" in the way we understand it, because his self cannot be detached from the web of relationships that he has with his mother, his father, his totemic kindred and the land which made him.

NOTES

1. Helen Waddell, *Medieval Latin Lyrics* (London: Penguin Classics, 1962).

2. See A.P. Elkin's book, *Aboriginal Men of High Degree* (Brisbane, Queensland, NSW: University of Queensland Press, 1977).

3. Corbin, Henry, "Towards a Chart of the Imaginal," *Temenos* 1, 1981. Corbin identifies the imaginal world as the "world of souls." An imaginal form is a mediation between the intellectual and sensible worlds. In this sense, it is above the merely "imaginative," which is often steeped in the sensible for its own sake. The imaginal form presupposes an encounter with Being and Knowledge, a theophany.

4. Roland Robinson, *The Man Who Sold His Dreaming* (Melbourne: Seal Books, 1965).

DAVID SUZUKI AND
PETER KNUDTSON

The Nature of Things

Waswanipi Cree, Canadian Subarctic

The ecological model is a model of internal relations. No
event first occurs and then relates to the world. The event
is a synthesis of relations to other events.... [Thus] the elements in the cell relate to one another and to the cell as a
whole more like the way the animal as a whole relates to its
environment.
—Charles Birch, biologist and John B. Cobb, Jr., theologian

IN THE WASWANIPI WORLD, the web of relationships
between the myriad beings and forces at play is not *mechanical*—as is the relationship between the whirling wheels and
gnashing metal gears that "animate" a ticking alarm clock. It
is not strictly *logical*—as is the cool, rational relationship between the lines of a computer program, unerringly encoded
in binary digits and computer languages, that "animates"
the screen of an office word processor. Nor is it primarily
abstract, intellectual, or *theoretical*—as are the abstract, lifeless,
mathematical and conceptual models constructed by population and systems ecologists as they strive to render more
intelligible the wondrous complexities and unities of entire
ecosystems—whole forests and seas, mountain slopes, and
grassy plans.

The relationships among the countless elements of the
Waswanipi cosmos—that breathe life, meaning, and sanc-

tity into it and that grant it lasting coherence – are more
fluid, more elusive, more steeped in symbolism than what
any of these potent but fragmentary Western images of the
natural world is capable of imparting. Traditional Waswanipi society tends to view the totality of nature through
the same lens through which the Waswanipi people view
themselves: the bonds of human kinship.

The diverse inhabitants, forces, and physical forms of the
Waswanipi universe are believed to be alive and imbued
with the same qualities of character and temperament as
human beings. Human beings, animal and plant species, local landforms, celestial bodies, winds and storms, and other
natural phenomena are instantly eligible for a very different kind of relationship from those of Western science's
more distant and disassociated images of nature. The diverse inhabitants of the natural world are seen an intimately
bound together by virtue not only of their common mythic
origins but their kindred "human" qualities, their capacity
of consciousness, their inherent and unquestioned "social"
worth. They are *thought of as being "like persons" in that they act
intelligently and have wills and idiosyncrasies, and understand and
are understood by men.* They are unabashedly embraced as
kindred relations.

Viewed through the same reverent lens of human kinship
through which Waswanipi people daily look upon their own
beloved mothers and fathers, uncles and aunts, children
and grandparents – what might seem overwhelmingly complex becomes infinitely more familiar and comprehensible.
No longer disturbing, alien, or aloof, all of nature is revealed as a community in the fullest sense of the word. It is a
vast, scintillating web of social memories, conversations,
and relationships – each potentially replete with the same
dimensions of pleasure and sorrow, misunderstandings
and mysteries as are ordinary human ties of blood kinship,
love, and camaraderie.

At the very heart of the differences between the traditional Waswanipi and the modern scientific perspectives on nature lie fundamentally different notions about the underlying causes of natural features and phenomena. Because Waswanipi ideas about causality are rooted in a blood- and bone-deep sense of kinship with nature's diverse forms and faces, they tend to be primarily *personal, not mechanical or [even] biological.* Just as the unfolding drama of human actions and reactions within a Waswanipi family might be partly illuminated by its past, the personal qualities of its members, and its surrounding influences, so might the wider community inhabiting the whole Waswanipi cosmos be illuminated by a grasp of the diverse personages animating the universe. Thus, when a traditional Waswanipi man or woman encounters a sudden winter snowstorm, the shimmering northern lights in the heavens, or some other vivid display of nature's extraordinary repertoire, he or she might understandably be more inclined to address the natural world by asking, *"Who did this?"* and *"Why?"* rather than *"How does that work?"*

This basic difference does not diminish the value of either worldview — Waswanipi or scientific. Canadian anthropologist Harvey Feit, in his perceptive studies of Waswanipi Cree society, suggests that modern Western ecology and traditional Waswanipi Cree thought may have much in common. Each in its own distinctive way sheds genuine light on the sense of awe-inspiring interconnectedness, the persistent resiliency, and the raw beauty that long, intimate contact with nature evokes in patient, sensitive human beings, regardless of their geographic, racial, or cultural pedigree. In fact, these two contemporary visions of the natural world are not only beautiful in their own right but are mutually enriching, each somehow supplying something that the other lacks.

Feit readily acknowledges that traditional Waswanipi con-

cepts of cause and effect in nature are infused by vibrant images of human character and kinship bonds that are utterly
foreign to the sensibilities of modern science. But many
broad *patterns* and processes of the natural world captured
in the Waswanipi map of the cosmos often coincide remarkably well with the broad *patterns* discerned by ecologists, as
in their studies of predator-prey relationships in Waswanipi
lands. Concludes Feit, *Despite the difference in world views, the
Waswanipi are recognizably concerned about what we would call
ecological relationships, and their views incorporate recognizable
ecological principles.*

Among the shared *ecological principles* that, in Feit's view
represent possible common ground between Waswanipi
and scientific notions is the idea that relationships between
human and prey populations are made up of a diversity of
dynamically interacting elements that, taken together, create a living, unified, harmonious whole. Thus, while *the causality that animates the Waswanipi ethno-ecosystem model is very
different from a scientific account, the structural relationships described are for the most part* [similar to] *those of a scientific account of the relationship of hunter animal population.*

Traditional Waswanipi nature-wisdom, rooted in and
evocative of concrete experience with life and land, tends to
follow the same contours of enlightened Western scientific
schemes for the long-term, sustainable management of
many natural resources. To the extent that Waswanipi ecological insights successfully infuse relationships between
human beings and the natural world with the visceral sensibilities and onerous burdens of human kinship, they are capable of elevating this shared land ethic from a lifeless theoretical abstraction to a passionate imperative.

TIM LUKE

Community and Ecology

Community, Class and Modernity

The populist critique of the New Class and its liberal agenda usually takes one of two lines of attack. The first, like MacIntyre's, "holds that liberal political theory accurately represents liberal social practice."[1] For populists to criticize liberal society, it is sufficient to take liberal theory on its own terms and accept the vision of subjectivity advocated by Locke, Smith or Bentham as true. That is, contemporary society is an aggregation of rational economic agents, existentially fragmented in an endless game of complex instrumental calculations. But, as Lasch points out, ordinary people do not want to live this way—a lifestyle they associate with New Class behavior.[2] Within that framework, there are no moral criteria to guide individual choice, except personal utility or the unstable interests of loosely aggregated voluntary associations. The inevitable result is a series of crises.

The second response, such as Bellah's, "holds that liberal theory radically misrepresents real life,"[3] In this view, most people live in a world of complex social ties lying beyond the scope of liberal theory. Atomized economic agents, set free to act instrumentally, will follow New Class ideals of upward social mobility and leave local communities.[4] Therefore, to criticize modern society, all one has to do is reject liberal theory on its own false terms, while attending to its surviving preliberal, nonliberal or postliberal attributes that make it work, since they are the only possible basis for building a viable social order.[5] Both these critiques contain an element of truth, but they do not go far enough. Any political discussion of community today must confront the fundamental question of ecology.[6]

Today, however, any evocation of "community" and "ecology" immediately comes under attack as a reactionary response to modernity and is associated with conservative images of "going back to nature"—a rejection of modernity's unilinear and irreversible character. Despite what sociological theory assumes, however, modernity is neither unilinear nor irreversible, going from primitive community to complex society. It is the result of critical choices made within particular historical conditions.[7] Earlier projects seeking alternative social arrangements providing for broader community autonomy can be reactivated to challenge increasing New Class domination. By interposing between production and consumption technical expertise and complex hierarchical organization centered in massive state bureaucracies and transnational corporations, the New Class systematically disempowers all other social agents. In substituting non-renewable energy-intensive production techniques for organic, labor-intensive ones, it has severed what were once close ties of communities to their particular ecological settings. The ecological destruction wrought around the globe indicates how costly these economic and political trade-offs have become.

New Class ideological agitprop constantly celebrates the unlimited abundance that hi-tech industry and scientific research will make possible. These promises of universal abundance and a more egalitarian distribution of its many benefits have not and cannot be kept.[8] It is physically impossible to produce enough wealth to bring everyone up to New Class "throw-away" standards of living, because the earth's already severely strained ecosystems simply cannot carry this load.

Generally speaking, the New Class designates the professional-technical intelligentsia or the knowledge-manipulating social strata which articulate and apply their expertise in both state bureaucracies and corporate enterprises.[9] Internally divided, the ranks of this New Class encompass both the adversary culture and the technical elites, liberal reformers and conservative technocrats, bureaucratic *apparatchiks* and cybernetic entrepreneurs. Nonetheless, their collective commitment to knowledge-driven projects of technological development and economic growth embroils them in elaborate schemes that disempower ordinary people and reduces nature to an alien entity that needs to be dominated. These attitudes lead to the destruction of nature and mystify the actual brutality and irresponsibility of New Class power by associating it with the plethora of material goods, cultural benefits, and social services that the presently unsustainable rates of exploiting nature now provides only for the few. These self-destructive dynamics need to be reexamined against a backdrop of concrete alternatives.

Community and Populism

Within this New Class framework, community tends to decay into the most "minimal" features with very little popular content. Composed of clients and consumers, communities today are not much more than an aggregation of atomized individuals organized into discrete geographic-legal units. Community becomes so thin because workplace and residence, production and consumption, identity and interests, administration and allocation are so divided in the New Class project of an advanced industrial society predicated primarily on geographic and social mobility. This division of interests, loss of common historical consciousness, weakening of shared beliefs, and lessening of ecological responsibility is what necessitates alternative approaches to understanding community.

Social theory, New Class ideology *par excellence,* interprets communities entirely in terms of modernization. Allegedly, with the spread of national and international networks of capitalist exchange, the close ties of organic local community (*Gemeinschaft*) crumbled into rubble as formalized social relations (*Gesselschaft*) buried it under the better organized and rational practices of modernity.[10] According to this logic, "community" is depicted as the warm, close, past-and-present social condition within an oversimplified conceptual dichotomy which opposes it to the cold, distant, present-and future social condition of "society."[11] Thus sociological analyses have interpreted community and its "premodern" institutions as a primitivism to be eliminated by the rational progress made possible by modernity's state bureaucracies and global markets. The alleged stasis of premodern communities provides a legitimating writ for imposing more fluid, mobile, and variable forms of everyday life, such as those manufactured by New Class experts.

Once community is framed in these categories, its meaning becomes even more problematic because New Class assumptions guard against "thicker" populist understandings. Social theory deals with alternative visions of community in three equally distorted ways. First, it interprets any emphasis on community as *conservatism,* or an effort by privileged interests to defend traditional practices. This approach, however, undermines New Class accounts of the irreversibility of the evolution from community to society embedded in modern social theory. It implicitly acknowl-

edges that some community-tradition-folk practices do survive and coexist with society-modernity-secular practices.
It stigmatizes concerns for surviving traditions as "conservative," because accepting traditional continuities implies
an endorsement of organic hierarchies rooted in age-old
prejudices, inequality, and oppression. As the architect
and guardian of modern thin communities, the New Class
takes great pains to argue that attempts to reconstitute traditional thick communities *necessarily* lead to perpetuating
premodern evils.

The second New Class criticism of community casts concerns with its "thick" reconstitution as *romanticism* or a wish
to return to long-lost but not forgotten sets of primitive relations. This reaction also undercuts the vision of community
inexorably evolving into society by acknowledging the
moral emptiness of modern society and admitting that the
closeness of traditional community returns as an unfulfilled
utopian image. The New Class sanctions any engagement
with notions such as "voluntary simplicity" or "small is beautiful" as nostalgia. Rather than embracing the unsettling un-
certainty of market exchange, this romanticism would turn
back the clock to recapture communal solidarity. Yet the
New Class also argues that such forms of communal life
never really existed and, even if they did, it would be impossible and undesirable to revitalize them. The teleological
role of an idealized past to help shape new projects of social
reconstruction thus flatten out within the New Class dogma
of "the end of history," reducing all future developments to
the mere extension of instrumental rationality and ever-
growing consumption.

The third approach sees longing for "thick" communities
as *collectivism,* or an impatience with the divisions, instability
and mobility of capitalist society. The New Class has closely
policed these aspirations for maximal community because
collectivist alternatives are but another form of New Class

domination – as can be seen from recent East European experiences, within which the very concept of the New Class
originally arose. Radical visions of a future condition of rational collectivist control threaten more modest advances in
the present. Instead of dealing with present problems of
minimal community on their own terms, such radical collectivism would rush the clock forward into some technologically defined maximal communitarianism constituting a
perfect rational utopia. The New Class may eventually gain
these powers, but prematurely calling for their realization
only exposes the fragility of power and sparks fears of the
despotic collectivist nightmares of "really existing socialism."

Talking about communal life, then, is hazardous. None
of these dangers in maximal populist community are necessarily guaranteed to occur, but New Class ideology continues to issue its iron-clad warranties. Unless one accepts the
thinnest, most minimal constructions of society, New Class
interests feel threatened. Any program to reconstruct
today's thin/minimal communities as new forms of thicker/
maximal community draws stern disciplinary indictments.
Because of their allegedly *conservative, romantic* or *collectivist*
aspirations, populist projects continue to be hassled by New
Class "concept cops" eager to defend against ordinary
people seeking to shape their lives and determine their destinies.

"Environmentalism" As New Class Ideology

In the US today, calling for greater ecological responsibility
has become politically imperative. While environmental
concerns are still associated with an all but vanished coun-
terculture, many New Class insiders have "gone green" by
integrating ecological concerns within bureaucratic corporate agendas. Thus the World Bank endorses "environmentalist" economic growth, transnational corporations claim

that every day is "Earth Day," and large government bureaucracies manage their office waste by buying "100% re-
cycled paper" file folders. Behind such mediagenic
window-dressing, however, lurk new projects of "environmental defense," "waste containment," or "worldwatching"
to legitimate expanding New Class interventionist power
and knowledge.

Ecological problems are global, borderless, and transnational. As the Cold War has faded, so has the concrete threat
of communist subversion which once justified state as well
as corporate projects of modernization. Yet the global economy and the interventionist state constructed as anti-
communist bulwarks remain, grow and continue to ravage
the environment. These New Class "worldwatchers" today
"think globally," but "act locally" to shore up their power by
defending the environment, containing waste, and watching the world in ways that insure their clients will remain
passive, dependent and powerless.

"Global thinking" has become the ideology of growth-
minded nation-states and transnational corporations. It demands uncritical acceptance of formal codes of instrumental rationality able to deal with elaborate statistical models
assumed to be identical to and exhaustive of the forms of
life captured within their disciplinary grids. It is reduction-
ist, instrumental, and destructive. Everything not disclosed
by its professional rules of statistical standard deviation or
mathematical multiple regression is crushed, ignored or
distorted to fit standardized uniform results on the pro-
jected slopes of statistical extrapolations.

The New Class empowers itself and disempowers local
communities all over the globe through a simple bargain. In
exchange for accepting their systems of knowledge and
power, the New Class promises that the short-term flow of
goods and services on a global scale will continue and grow
for a few more decades — even if only for the benefit of vari-

ous elites. To resist this project, the flow of goods and services may slow or stop, which could lead to major social and economic crises. The New Class is clearly transnational and highly homogenized. The elite professional spaces delimited within telecommunications links, jetports, hi-tech office complexes, upper-income neighborhoods, new science centers and powerful bureaucratic agencies all tend to reproduce the same sets of expectations. "Acting locally" while "thinking globally" means surfing in Maui and thinking about the next business deal in Manila, working at home but commuting cybernetically to the bond business pits in Tokyo, or contributing to the local PBS television station to pay its share of producing a documentary in London about saving elephants in Africa.

Beyond the New Class' environmentalist rhetoric, these increasingly borderless minimal "communities" remain ensnared in global exchange networks, living off millennia of slowly accumulated fossil fuels. Their major concern is with maximizing mobility rather than ensuring sustainability. Often none of their vital ecological support mechanisms are in the immediate environmental vicinity. Environmental inputs are not used on a sustainable scale appropriate to each bioregional setting. Instead, these supporting flows are sourced from around the larger nation-state or even the world, bound together by the wasteful expenditure of scarce non-renewable energy. Due to their location in the global network, some neighborhoods, cities, regions, and nation-states either enjoy exceptionally high rates of excess consumption or suffer from outrageously inadequate levels of basic goods and services.

The New Class is, first and foremost, grounded in transnational exchange and not embedded in a particular ecoregional setting. Being constantly on the move, it treats most places frivolously or disrespectfully. Any place is usually no better than any other. Indeed, every place is equally subject to potential destruction as a development site, economic raw material or fresh market to sustain the flow. Building a community in a particular location, accepting it on its own ecological terms, working to adapt a sustainable way of life, cherishing it for its unique differences are foreign notions to the New Class' operational logic. By "outsourcing" the material basis of everyday life or organizing production around importing incomplete segments or partial components of the total array of goods and services needed to survive, New Class state and corporate planners have broken many communal and organic ties to immediate ecoregional settings. By channeling communities toward "specializing" or exporting their small, limited stream of goods and services in sufficient volume to maintain a balance of trade with other communities in a global exchange network, New Class experts make them hostage to state and corporate bureaucracies. Profitable in an exchange-based accounting system drawn up for quarterly reports to New Class management, these cycles of global trade are ultimately unsustainable.

Resisting these New Class practices must take the form of acting and thinking ecologically. Unless and until most communities reconnect their economies with their immediate supporting ecoregions, they will be subject both to New Class domination and environmental collapse. Living in balance with the local bioregional surroundings while still tied to larger networks of information and expertise, communities can turn into sustainable commonwealths instead of predatory profiteers. More importantly, new kinds of knowledge, tied to the specificities of place and the particularities of local communities, would develop in creating a sustainable society. Such knowledge is not likely to suit the expectations of today's typical New Class expert. But it could develop openly once people and communities embed themselves ecologically in the immediate region. Knowledge of place should attend to the particularities of that ecoregion by suspending universal standards in favor of what is suitable to each community. Otherwise, inappropriate cultural codes, housing forms, dietary patterns, apparel styles, technical implements or energy systems unsuited to particular environments will give way to foreign disciplines of technological domination. These changes require demystification of New Class power and the reconstitution of communal concerns with local and regional commonwealths, because the limits of environmental sustainability have already been reached and in some settings are being exceeded.

Possibilities for Populist Resistance

The New Class myth of economic progress is becoming increasingly indefensible: the high standards of living it promises are not standard, have never been very high for most people, and do not guarantee a meaningful life. Communities may do better by determining their own ecologically appropriate ethos, redefining their own standards of life, and setting their own moral criteria. New Class ideology calls for communities and individuals to "think globally, act locally" to prop up the tottering political economy of advanced industrial society. An ecological populism needs communities and individuals which can "think locally" and "act globally."

For an ecological populism, nature must be brought back directly into everyday life in more subjective aesthetic or ethical forms. Rather than being only an alien entity from which to extract resources and into which to dump waste, nature must be treated as an equal vital presence. It should not remain the object of administration by New Class experts, but the most basic subjective site defining essential ends and basic values, such as responsibility, frugality, autonomy, sustainability and freedom. These ecological and populist notions of community must not be mistaken for utopian socialism or other long-discredited models promising organic reconciliation with nature. Returning to some idyllic past is neither likely nor necessary. An ecological populism would develop an alternative modernity by making different choices about community or forcing new popular relations of production.[12] An ecological populism must go well beyond bankrupt ecosocialist millenarianism.[13]

"Thinking locally" and "acting globally" means making several radical shifts towards some social forms conventionally regarded as "dead and gone." First, would be the creation of more complex, diverse, and skilled societies of small producers, owning real property and controlling a significant body of skills. Owning and controlling such assets at the local level tends to reunify production and consumption in the same population centers. This means changing who owns and controls as well as who uses and profits from land, capital and technology. Not only the benefits of consumption, but also the costs of production would then be immediately evident at the local level rather than only in distant environmental "sacrifice zones." A complex society of small-scale proprietors and regional producers, in turn, could nest their economies more ecologically in the particular sustainable ecoregion.[14]

Second, such a society would cultivate a new subjectivity grounded in new kinds of empowerment—technological, economic, political, and cultural. Since "the good life" would no longer be the endless consumption obsession of contemporary permissive individualism, it could be redefined in more demanding moral codes of hard work, frugality, ecological responsibility, humility, and skill perfection.[15] This, in turn, will generate new community institutions suited to the new context.[16] Here the real advances of secular rational civilization might counterbalance potential regres sions to a reactionary irrational culture. Racism, provincialism, xenophobia, sexism, and class hatreds need not be part of any populist society. Indeed, loyalty to community, ecoregion or place need not become lines of cultural conflict or group warfare.

Third, within such a context, centralized bureaucratic state control and standardized corporate penetration of local communities would be considerably curtailed, while individual responsibility would be greatly increased. Yet self-rule, self-ownership, and self-management are demanding social practices. Freedom entails the prospect of failures, reversals, and just having less at times without being automatically able to turn to centralized state powers for relief. While they are very likely to succeed at making a popular ecological community work, these communities may also collapse. This threat of failure makes their autonomy meaningful: if New Class big brothers are always standing in the background ready to pick them up, dust them off, and push them along their way, then there is little meaningful autonomy or real freedom for such populist commonwealths. The transnational character of the diminished but still very much functioning global economy with its time-and-space compressing communication and transportation systems will prevent most communities from withdrawing into isolationist self-sufficiency or collapsing after unforeseen natural disaster.

Finally, these shifts would involve reconstituting the fundamental writs of authority now underpinning public order. Propounding larger aggregates of these autonomous communities in the US would require real federal structures to protect and preserve such ecological commonwealths from outside interference and internal insecurity. A new debate about federalism must center on local autonomy without revitalizing traditional practices of racism or sexism, preservation of national and transnational ties without aggravating liberal practices of unrepresented rationalization, arbitrary decision-making and bureaucratic collective organization overriding popular consent.[17] By elaborating such unrealized possibilities, an ecological populism could shake many communities' traditional resistance to change as well as mount a political offensive against New Class domination.

NOTES

1. See Michael Walzer, "The Communitarian Critique of Liberalism," in *Political Theory*, Vol. 18, No. 1 (February 1990), p. 7. See also Alasdair MacIntyre, *After Virtue* (Notre Dame: University of Notre Dame Press, 1981).

2. See Christopher Lasch, *The True and Only Heaven: Progress and Its Critics* (New York: Norton, 1991), pp. 476–508.

3. Walzer, "Communitarian Critique," *op. cit.*, p. 9. Also see Robert Bellah *et. al.*, *Habits of the Heart* (Berkeley: University of California Press, 1985).

4. Lasch, *True Heaven, op. cit.*, pp. 509–32.

5. Cf. Gérard Raulet, "The New Utopia: Communication Technologies," in *Telos* 87 (Spring 1991), pp. 39–58.

6. Lasch vindicates populism as an alternative, but he ignores the American political traditions that have best approximated his ideal, i.e., those of ecological activism.

7. For a critique of this modernization model of progress, see Timothy W. Luke, *Social Theory and Modernity: Dissent, Critique and Revolution* (Newbury Park, CA: Sage, 1990), pp. 211–68. The most recent sociological analysis predicated on such modernization dynamics is to be found in Habermas. However, his framework of "system" and "lifeworld," which casts the system as an integrative force colonizing the lifeworld, represents system as society and lifeworld as community in essentially the same old unidirectional, irreversible and inexorable roles of modernization theory, even though the epicyclical construct of "civil society" can be interposed by between the two to make communication theory look like it mediates a serious struggle between system and lifeworld forces. See Jürgen Habermas, *The Theory of Communicative Action*, Vol. II, *Lifeworld and System: A Critique of Functionalist Reason*, trans. by Thomas McCarthy (Boston: Beacon Press, 1987).

8. This public relations blitz is the utopian literature of the present. For example, Rockwell International shows the technical breakthroughs that can be realized "Where Science Gets Down to Business." DuPont's timeless call to achieve "Better Living through Chemistry" is matched by today's General Electric pledging to "Bring Good Things to Light." AT&T empowers one "To Reach Out and Touch Someone," because "the System is the Solution" if you only make "The Right Choice." Toyota/Lexus promises "The Relentless Pursuit of Perfection," but Chevron unifies expert scientific producer and everyday energy consumer in its Zen-like "People Do." However, the tao of Dow Chemical perhaps surpasses them all as its corporate imagery shows soon-to-graduate, professional-technical students instructing their families, which are diversely shown as black ghetto-dwellers, comfortable white suburbans or hard-working farm folks, on how a New Class–based higher education will pay off technologically for them and humanity, while an unseen chorus of happy consumers jubilantly sings the musical score, "You Can Make a Difference in What Tomorrow Brings, Dow Lets You Do Great Things!"

9. In the US, inequality has grown since 1967 and has been increasing at a faster pace. See Kevin Phillips, *The Politics of Rich and Poor: Wealth and the American Electorate in the Reagan Aftermath* (New York: Random House, 1990), pp. 3–32; and Robert Reich, *The Work of Nations: Preparing America for the 21st Century* (New York: Times Books, 1991).

10. The original and problematic source in modern sociological theory for these notions is Ferdinand Toennies, Gemeinschaft und Gesellschaft (Leipzig: Reisland, 1987).

11. Although Rousseau, Smith, and Marx make similar arguments about modernization, these ideas gain their fullest professional-technical articulation only in modern social theory. See Henry Maine, *Ancient Law* (London: Murray, 1861); Emile Durkheim, *The Division of Labor in Society* (New York: MacMillan, 1933); Max Weber, *The Theory of Social and Economic Organization*, ed. by Talcott Parsons (New York: Free Press, 1947); Charles Horton Cooley, *Social Organization* (New York: Scribner, 1909); Ralph Linton, *The Study of Man* (New York: Appleton-Century, 1936); and Talcott Parsons, *The Social System* (Glencoe, IL: Free Press, 1952).

12. An ecological society should be an alternative modernity, not an antimodernity or post-modernity. See Murray Bookchin, *Toward an Ecological Society* (Montreal: Black Rose Books, 1980); and Timothy W. Luke, "Notes for a Deconstructionist Ecology," in *New Political Science* 11 (Spring 1983), pp. 21–32.

13. For outlines of these ecosocialist programs, see Martin Ryle, *Ecology and Socialism* (London: Radius, 1988); and Stuart Hall and Martin

Jacques, eds., *New Times: The Changing Face of Politics in the 1990s* (London: Lawrence and Wishart, 1989). An effective ecological populism must ask different questions to create an economy, society and polity beyond the romantic collectivism of such ecosocialist rhetorics. Today's ecosocialist programs read like agendas of re-empowerment for some kind of centralized statist collectivism, which looks to Maoist peasant work brigades or Cuban state farms for models of "a kinder, gentler socialism" serving green goals. Yet the collective mode of land holding, work organization and technological control of these models threatens a disappointing rerun of bureaucratic *nomenklatura* and *apparat* authoritarianism. The allure of appropriate technologies in ecosocialism also evokes new ill-considered infatuations. When viewed through the soft focus and warm glow of *Mother Earth News* or *The Whole Planet Earth Catalogue*, ecosocialism bizarrely parodies Lenin's declaration that "socialism equals electrification plus soviet power" with claims that "ecosocialism equals windmills, geodesic domes, and solar panels plus nonhierarchical decision-making." The technological enthusiasms of such "back to the land, here comes the sun" manifestos promise to exhaust their force in economic fragmentation, cultural frustration and political failure.

14. As Wendell Berry notes, some cities will never be sustainable, "New York City cannot be made sustainable, nor can Phoenix" (p. 63), but many others can and should be. See "Out of Your Car, Off Your Horse," in *Atlantic Monthly*, Vol. 267, No. 2 (February 1991), 60–63. Also see David Morris, *Self-Reliant Cities: Energy and the Transformation of Urban America* (San Francisco: Sierra Club Books, 1982); Richard Register, *Ecocity Berkeley: Building Cities for a Healthy Future* (Berkeley: North Atlantic Books, 1987); Wendell Berry, *Meeting the Expectations of the Land: Essays in Sustainable Agriculture and Stewardship* (San Francisco: North Point Press, 1984); and Wendell Berry, *The Unsettling of America: Culture and Agriculture* (San Francisco: Sierra Club Books, 1977).

15. See an initial consideration of these goals in Ken Anderson et. al., "Roundtable on Communitarianism," in *Telos* 76 (Summer 1988), pp. 2–32.

16. For more discussion, see Paul and Percival Goodman, *Communities: Means of Livelihood and Ways of Life* (New York: Random House, 1960).

17. For some preliminary considerations, see Murray Bookchin, *The Rise of Urbanization and the Decline of Citizenship* (San Francisco: Sierra Club Books, 1987).

V.

FINDING

THE

AMERICAN

TRIBE

LEWIS H. LAPHAM

Who and What is American?

> There may not be an American character, but there is the
> emotion of being American. It has many resemblances to the
> emotion of being Russian – that feeling of nostalgia for some
> undetermined future when man will have improved himself
> beyond recognition and when all will be well. – V.S. Pritchett

WERE I TO BELIEVE what I read in the papers, I would
find it easy to think that I no longer can identify myself simply as an American. The noun apparently means nothing
unless it is dressed up with at least one modifying adjective.
As a plain American I have neither voice nor authentic
proofs of existence. I acquire a presence only as an old
American, a female American, a white American, a rich
American, a black American, a gay American, a poor American, a native American, a dead American. The subordina-
tion of the noun to the adjectives makes a mockery of both
the American premise and the democratic spirit, but it
serves the purposes of the politicians as well as the news media, and throughout the rest of this election year I expect
the political campaigns to pitch their tents and slogans on
the frontiers of race and class. For every benign us, the candidates will find a malignant them; for every neighboring
we (no matter how eccentric or small in number), a distant
and devouring they. The strategies of division sell newspapers and summon votes, and to the man who would be king
(or president or governor) the popular hatred of govern-

ment matters less than the atmosphere of resentment in which the people fear and distrust one another.

Democratic politics trades in only two markets – the market in expectation and the market in blame. A collapse in the former engenders a boom in the latter. Something goes wrong in the news – a bank swindle of genuinely spectacular size, a series of killings in Milwaukee, another disastrous assessment of the nation's schools – and suddenly the air is loud with questions about the paradox of the American character or the Puritan subtexts of the American soul. The questions arise from every quarter of the political compass – from English professors and political consultants as well as from actors, corporate vice presidents, and advertising salesmen – and the conversation is seldom polite. Too many of the people present no longer can pay the bills, and a stray remark about acid rain or a third-grade textbook can escalate within a matter of minutes into an exchange of insults. Somebody calls Jesse Helms a fascist, and somebody else says that he is sick and tired of paying ransom money to a lot of welfare criminals. People drink too much and stay too late, their voices choked with anecdote and rage, their lexicons of historical reference so passionately confused that both Jefferson and Lincoln find themselves doing thirty-second commercials for racial quotas, a capital gains tax, and the Persian Gulf War.

The failures in the nation's economy have marked up the prices for obvious villains, and if I had a talent for merchandising I would go into the business of making dolls (black dolls, white dolls, red-necked dolls, feminist dolls, congressional dolls) that each of the candidates could distribute at fund-raising events with a supply of color-coordinated pins. Trying out their invective in the pre-season campaigns, the politicians as early as last October were attributing the cause of all our sorrows to any faction, interest, or minority that could excite in their audiences the passions of a beloved prejudice. David Duke in Louisiana denounced the subsidized beggars (i.e., black people) who had robbed the state of its birthright. At a partisan theatrical staged by the Democratic Party in New Hampshire, Senator Tom Harkin reviled the conspiracy of Republican money. President Bush went to Houston, Texas, to point a trembling and petulant finger at the United States Congress. If the country's domestic affairs had been left to him, the President said, everybody would be as prosperous and smug as Senator Phil Gramm, but the liberals in Congress (blind as mollusks and selfish as eels) had wrecked the voyage of boundless opportunity.

The politicians follow the trends, and apparently they have been told by their handlers to practice the arts of the demagogue. Certainly I cannot remember an election year in which the political discourse – among newspaper editorialists and the single-issue lobbies as well as the candidates – relied so unashamedly on pitting rich against poor, black against white, male against female, city against suburb, young against old. Every public event in New York City – whether academic appointment, traffic delay, or homicide – lends itself to both a black and a white interpretation of the news. The arguments in the arenas of cultural opinion echo the same bitter refrain. The ceaseless quarrels about the canon of preferred texts (about Columbus the Bad and Columbus the Good, about the chosen company of the politically correct, about the ice people and the sun people) pick at the scab of the same questions. Who and what is an American? How and where do we find an identity that is something other than a fright mask? When using the collective national pronoun ("we the people," "we happy few," etc.) whom do we invite into the club of the we?

Maybe the confusion is a corollary to the end of the Cold War. The image of the Soviet Union as monolithic evil held in place the image of the United States as monolithic virtue. Break the circuit of energy transferred between negative and positive poles, and the two empires dissolve into the waving of sectional or nationalist flags. Lacking the reassurance of a foreign demon, we search our own neighborhoods for fiends of convincing malevolence and size.

The search is a boon for the bearers of false witness and the builders of prisons. Because it's so easy to dwell on our differences, even a child of nine can write a Sunday newspaper sermon about the centrifugal forces that drive the society apart. The more difficult and urgent questions have to do with the centripetal forces that bind us together. What traits of character or temperament do we hold in common? Why is it that I can meet a black man in a street or a Hispanic woman on a train and imagine that he and I, or she and I, share an allied hope and a joint purpose? That last question is as American as it is rhetorical, and a Belgian would think it the work of a dreaming imbecile.

What we share is a unified field of emotion, but if we mistake the sources of our energy and courage (i.e., if we think that our uniqueness as Americans rests with the adjectives instead of the noun) then we can be rounded up in categories and sold the slogan of the week for the fear of the month. Political campaigns deal in the commodity of votes, and from now until November I expect that all of them will divide the American promise into its lesser but more marketable properties. For reasons of their own convenience, the sponsors of political campaigns (Democratic, environmental, racial, Republican, sexual, or military-industrial) promote more or less the same false constructions of the American purpose and identity. As follows:

That the American achieves visible and specific meaning only by reason of his or her association with the political guilds of race, gender, age, ancestry, or social class.

The assumption is as elitist as the view that only a woman endowed with an income of $1 million a year can truly appreciate the beauty of money and the music of Cole Porter. Comparable theories of grace encourage the belief that only black people can know or teach black history, that no white man can play jazz piano, that blonds have a better time, and that Jews can't play basketball.

America was founded on precisely the opposite premise. We were always about becoming, not being; about the prospects for the future, not about the inheritance of the past. The man who rests his case on his color, like the woman who defines herself as a bright cloud of sensibility beyond the understanding of merely mortal men, makes a claim to special privilege not unlike the divine right of kings. The pretensions might buttress the cathedrals of our self-esteem, but they run counter to the lessons of our history.

We are a nation of parvenus, all bound to the hopes of tomorrow, or next week, or next year. John Quincy Adams put it plainly in a letter to a German correspondent in the 1820s who had written on behalf of several prospective émigrés to ask about the requirements for their success in the New World. "They must cast off the European skin, never to resume it," Adams said. "They must look forward to their posterity rather than backward to their ancestors."

We were always a mixed and piebald company, even on the seventeenth-century colonial seaboard, and we accepted our racial or cultural differences as the odds that we were obliged to overcome or correct. When John Charles Frémont (a.k.a. The Pathfinder) first descended into California from the East in 1843, he remarked on the polyglot character of the expedition accompanying him south into the San Joaquin Valley:

"Our cavalcade made a strange and grotesque appearance, and it was impossible to avoid reflecting upon our position and composition in this remote solitude . . . still forced on south by a desert on one hand and a mountain range on the other; guided by a civilized Indian, attended by two wild ones from the Sierra; a Chinook from the Columbia;

and our own mixture of American, French, German – all armed; four or five languages heard at once; about a hundred horses and mules, half-wild; American, Spanish and Indian dresses and equipments intermingled – such was our composition."

The theme of metamorphosis recurs throughout the whole chronicle of American biography. Men and women start out in one place and end up in another, never quite knowing how they got there, perpetually expecting the unexpected, drifting across the ocean or the plains until they lodge against a marriage, a land deal, a public office, or a jail. Speaking to the improvised character of the American experience, Daniel Boorstin, the historian and former Librarian of Congress, also summed up the case against the arithmetic of the political pollster's zip codes: "No prudent man dared to be too certain of exactly who he was or what he was about; everyone had to be prepared to become someone else. To be ready for such perilous transmigrations was to become an American."

That the American people aspire to become more nearly alike.

The hope is that of the ad salesman and the prison warden, but it has become depressingly familiar among the managers of political campaigns. Apparently they think that no matter how different the native songs and dances in different parts of the country, all the tribes and factions want the same beads, the same trinkets, the same prizes. As I listen to operatives from Washington talk about their prospects in the Iowa or New Hampshire primary, I understand that they have in mind the figure of a perfect or ideal American whom everybody in the country would wish to resemble if only everybody could afford to dress like the dummies in the windows of Bloomingdale's or Saks Fifth Avenue. The public opinion polls frame questions in the alphabet of name recognitions and standard brands. The simplicity of the results supports the belief that the American citizen or the American family can be construed as a product, and that with only a little more time and a little more money for research and development all of us will conform to the preferred images seen in a commercial for Miller beer.

The apologists for the theory of the uniform American success sometimes present the example of Abraham Lincoln, and as I listen to their sentimental after-dinner speeches about the poor country grown to greatness, I often wonder what they would say if they had met the man instead of the statue. Throughout most of his life Lincoln displayed the character of a man destined for failure – a man who drank too much and told too many jokes (most of them in bad taste), who was habitually late for meetings and always borrowing money, who never seized a business opportunity and missed his own wedding.

The spirit of liberty is never far from anarchy, and the ur-American is apt to look a good deal more like one of the contestants on *Let's Make a Deal* (i.e., somebody dressed like Madonna, or Wyatt Earp, or a giant iguana) than any of the yachtsmen standing around on the dock of Kennebunkport. If America is about nothing else, it is about the invention of the self. Because we have little use for history, and because we refuse the comforts of a society established on the blueprint of class privilege, we find ourselves set adrift at birth in an existential void, inheriting nothing except the obligation to construct a plausible self, to build a raft of identity on which (with a few grains of luck and a cheap bank loan) maybe we can float south to Memphis or the imaginary islands of the blessed. We set ourselves the tasks of making and remaking our destinies with whatever lumber we happen to find lying around on the banks of the Snake or Pecos River.

Who else is the American hero if not a wandering pilgrim who goes forth on a perpetual quest? Melville sent Ahab across the world's oceans in search of a fabulous beast, and Thoreau followed the unicorn of his conscience into the silence of the Maine woods. Between them they marked out the trail of American literature as well as the lines of speculation in American real estate. To a greater or a lesser extent, we are all confidence men, actors playing the characters of our own invention and hoping that the audience — fortunately consisting of impostors as fanciful or synthetic as ourselves — will accept the performance at par value and suspend the judgments of ridicule.

The settled peoples of the earth seldom recognize the American as both a chronic revolutionary and a born pilgrim. The American is always on the way to someplace else (i.e., toward some undetermined future in which all will be well), and when he meets a stranger on the road he begins at once to recite the summary of the story so far — his youth and early sorrows, the sequence of his exits and entrances, his last divorce and his next marriage, the point of his financial departure and the estimated time of his spiritual arrival, the bad news noted and accounted for, the good news still to come. Invariably it is a pilgrim's tale, and the narrator, being American, assumes that he is addressing a fellow pilgrim. He means to exchange notes and compare maps. His newfound companion might be bound toward a completely different dream of Eden (a boat marina in Naples, Florida, instead of a garden in Vermont; a career as a Broadway dancer as opposed to the vice presidency of the Wells Fargo bank), but the destination doesn't matter as much as the common hope of coming safely home to the land of the heart's desire. For the time being, and until something better turns up, we find ourselves embarked on the same voyage, gazing west into the same blue distance.

That the American people share a common code of moral behavior and subscribe to identical theories of the true, the good, and the beautiful.

Senator Jesse Helms would like to think so, and so would the enforcers of ideological discipline on the vocabulary of the doctrinaire left. The country swarms with people making rules about what we can say or read or study or smoke, and they imagine that we should be grateful for the moral guidelines (market-tested and government-inspected) imposed (for our own good) by a centralized bureau of temporal health and spiritual safety. The would-be reformers of the national character confuse the American sense of equality with the rule of conformity that governs a police state. It isn't that we believe that every American is as perceptive or as accomplished as any other, but we insist on the preservation of a decent and mutual respect across the lines of age, race, gender, and social class. No citizen is allowed to use another citizen as if he or she were a means to an end; no master can treat his servant as if he or she were only a servant; no government can deal with the governed as if they were nothing more than a mob of votes. The American loathing for the arrogant or self-important man follows from the belief that all present have bet their fortunes (some of them bigger than others, and some of them counterfeit or stolen) on the same hypothesis.

The American premise is an existential one, and our moral code is political, its object being to allow for the widest horizons of sight and the broadest range of expression. We protect the other person's liberty in the interest of protecting our own and our virtues conform to the terms and conditions of an arduous and speculative journey. If we look into even so coarse a mirror as the one held up to us by the situation comedies on prime-time television, we see that we value the companionable virtues – helpfulness, forgiveness, kindliness, and, above all, tolerance.

The passenger standing next to me at the rail might be balancing a parrot on his head, but that doesn't mean that he has invented a theory of the self any less implausible than the one I ordered from a department-store catalogue or assembled with the tag lines of a two-year college course on the great books of Western civilization. If the traveler at the port rail can balance a parrot on his head, then I can continue my discussion with Madame Bovary and Mr. Pickwick, and the two gentlemen standing aft of the rum barrels can get on with the business of rigging the price of rifles or barbed wire. The American equation rests on the habit of holding our fellow citizens in thoughtful regard not because they are exceptional (or famous, or beautiful, or rich) but simply because they are our fellow citizens. If we abandon the sense of mutual respect, we abandon the premise as well as the machinery of the American enterprise.

That the triumph of America corresponds to its prowess as a nation-state.

The pretension serves the purposes of the people who talk about "the national security" and "the vital interest of the American people" when what they mean is the power and privilege of government. The oligarchy resident in Washington assumes that all Americans own the same property instead of taking part in the same idea, that we share a joint geopolitical program instead of a common temperament and habit of mind. Even so faithful a servant of the monied interests as Daniel Webster understood the distinction: "The public happiness is to be the aggregate of individuals. Our system begins with the individual man."

The Constitution was made for the uses of the individual (an implement on the order of a plow, an ax, or a surveyor's plumb line), and the institutions of American government were meant to support the liberties of the people, not the ambitions of the state. Given any ambiguity about the order of priority or precedence, it was the law that had to give way to the citizen's freedom of thought and action, not the citizen's freedom of thought and action that had to give way to the law. The Bill of Rights stresses the distinction in the two final amendments, the ninth ("The enumeration in the Constitution, of certain rights, shall not be construed to deny or disparage others retained by the people") and the tenth ("The powers not delegated to the United States by the Constitution, nor prohibited by it to the States, are reserved to the States, respectively, or to the people").

What joins the Americans one to another is not a common nationality, language, race, or ancestry (all of which testify to the burdens of the past) but rather their complicity in a shared work of the imagination. My love of country follows from my love of its freedoms, not from my pride in its fleets or its armies or its gross national product. Construed as a means and not an end, the Constitution stands as the premise for a narrative rather than a plan for an invasion or a monument. The narrative was always plural. Not one story but many stories.

That it is easy to be an American.

I can understand why the politicians like to pretend that America is mostly about going shopping, but I never know why anybody believes the ad copy. Grant the existential terms and conditions of the American enterprise (i.e., that we are all bound to invent ourselves), and the position is both solitary and probably lost. I know a good many people who would rather be British or Nigerian or Swiss.

Lately I've been reading the accounts of the nineteenth-century adventurers and pioneers who traveled west from

Missouri under circumstances almost always adverse. Most of them didn't find whatever it was they expected to find behind the next range of mountains or around the next bend in the river. They were looking for a garden in a country that was mostly desert, and the record of their passage is largely one of sorrow and failure. Travelers making their way across the Great Plains in the 1850s reported great numbers of dead horses and abandoned wagons on the trail, the echo of the hopes that so recently preceded them lingering in an empty chair or in the scent of flowers on a new grave.

Reading the diaries and letters, especially those of the women in the caravans, I think of the would-be settlers lost in an immense wilderness, looking into the mirrors of their loneliness and measuring their capacity for self-knowledge against the vastness of the wide and indifferent sky.

Too often we forget the proofs of our courage. If we wish to live in the state of freedom that allows us to make and think and build, then we must accustom ourselves to the shadows on the walls and the wind in trees. The climate of anxiety is the cost of doing business. Just as a monarchy places far fewer burdens on its subjects than a democracy places on its citizens, so also bigotry is easier than tolerance. When something goes wrong with the currency or the schools, it's always comforting to know that the faults can be easily found in something as obvious as a color, or a number, or the sound of a strange language. The multiple adjectives qualifying the American noun enrich the vocabulary of blame, and if the election year continues as it has begun I expect that by next summer we will discover that it is not only middle-aged Protestant males who have been making a wreck of the culture but also (operating secretly and sometimes in disguise) adolescent, sallow, Buddhist females.

Among all the American political virtues, candor is probably the one most necessary to the success of our mutual enterprise. Unless we try to tell each other the truth about what we know and think and see (i.e., the story so far as it appears to the travelers on the voyage out) we might as well amuse ourselves (for as long as somebody else allows us to do so) with fairy tales. The vitality of the American democracy always has rested on the capacity of its citizens to speak and think without cant. As long ago as 1838, addressing the topic of *The American Democrat,* James Fenimore Cooper argued that the word "American" was synonymous with the habit of telling the truth: "By candor we are not to understand trifling and uncalled for expositions of truth; but a sentiment that proves a conviction of the necessity of speaking truth, when speaking at all; a contempt for all designing evasions of our real opinions.

"In all the general concerns, the public has a right to be treated with candor. Without this manly and truly republican quality . . . the institutions are converted into a stupendous fraud."

If we indulge ourselves with evasions and the pleasure of telling lies, we speak to our fears and our weaknesses instead of to our courage and our strength. We can speak plainly about our differences only if we know and value what we hold in common. Like the weather and third-rate journalism, bigotry in all its declensions is likely to be with us for a long time (certainly as long as the next hundred years), but unless we can draw distinctions and make jokes about our racial or cultural baggage, the work of our shared imagination must vanish in the mist of lies. The lies might win elections (or sell newspapers and economic theories) but they bind us to the theaters of wish and dream. If I must like or admire a fellow citizen for his or her costume of modifying adjectives (because he or she is black or gay or rich), then I might as well believe that the lost continent of Atlantis will rise next summer from the sea and that the Japanese will continue to make the payments — now and forever, world without end — on all our mortgages and battleships.

Among all the nations of the earth, America is the one that has come most triumphantly to terms with the mixtures of blood and caste, and maybe it is another of history's ironic jokes that we should wish to repudiate our talent for assimilation at precisely the moment in time when so many other nations in the world (in Africa and Western Europe as well as the Soviet Union) look to the promise of the American example. The jumble of confused or mistaken identities that was the story of nineteenth-century America has become the story of a late-twentieth-century world defined by a vast migration of peoples across seven continents and as many oceans. Why, then, do we lose confidence in ourselves and grow fearful of our mongrel freedoms?

The politician who would lift us to a more courageous understanding of ourselves might begin by saying that we are all, each and every one of us, as much at fault as anybody else, that no matter whom we blame for our troubles (whether George Bush, or Al Sharpton, or David Duke) or how pleasant the invective (racist, sexist, imperialist pig), we still have to rebuild our cities and revise our laws. We can do the work together, or we can stand around making strong statements about each other's clothes.

SANYIKA SHAKUR,
AKA MONSTER KODY SCOTT

Can't Stop, Won't Stop

The Education of a Crip Warlord

I PROUDLY STRODE ACROSS the waxed hardwood stage of the auditorium at the Fifty-fourth Street school under the beaming stares of my mother, aunt, and Uncle Clarence. Taking my assigned place next to Joe Johnson, I felt different – older, more "attached" than any of my fellow classmates. This feeling made me stand more erect, made me seem more important than any of my peers onstage – even Joe Johnson, who was "king of the school."

It's quite amusing to rerun the day of my sixth-grade graduation, June 15, 1975, over in my mind and remember vividly how proud I was and how superior I felt next to Joe Johnson. I had first sensed my radical departure from childhood when I was suspended a month before this day, driven home by Mr. Smotherman, the principal, and not allowed to go on the grad-class outing because I had flashed a gang sign on the school panorama picture.

Mr. Smotherman was appalled and accused me of destroying a totally good picture, not to mention that I was, he said, "starting to show signs of moral decay." Actually, half of the things Mr. Smotherman told me I didn't catch because I wasn't listening, and besides, my mind had been made up weeks earlier. How I expected to get away with flashing on a photograph is beyond me! But it points up my serious intent even then, at age eleven. For I was completely sold on becoming a gang member.

As our graduation activities wore on, my disinterest and my annoyance at its silliness escalated. I was eager to get home to the 'hood and meet my moral obligation to a new set of friends who made Joe Johnson look weak. After the seemingly yearlong ceremonies, my mom, aunt, and Uncle Clarence congratulated me with lunch at Bob's Big Boy. While returning home I sat transfixed at the side window, looking out at the streets but not seeing anything in particular, just wishing Uncle Clarence would drive faster.

Tonight was to be my initiation, and I didn't want to miss out on any activities that would occur during my first night on duty. Bending the corner to our block in my uncle's Monte Carlo, I sank down into the backseat to avoid being seen in my white knit suit and tie. Peeping to make sure the coast was clear, I bolted past Moms into the house, down the hall, and into my room for a quick change.

"What's your damn problem, boy?" bellowed Moms from the hallway. "I know you don't think you going out anywhere until you have cleaned up that funky room, taken out this trash, and . . . "

I never heard the rest. I was out the window, steaming toward my destiny and the only thing in this life that has ever held my attention for any serious length of time—the streets. Stopping around the block to collect my coolness, I met up with Tray Ball, who had accepted my membership and agreed to sponsor me.

"What's up, Cuz?" Tray Ball extended his very dark, muscular, veined hand.

"Ain't nothin'," I responded, trying to hide my utter admiration for this cat, who was quickly becoming a Ghetto Star. (A Ghetto Star is a neighborhood celebrity known for gangbanging, drug dealing, et cetera.) "So what's up for tonight, am I still on or what?"

"Yeah, you on."

As we walked to the shack in silence, I took full advantage of the stares we were getting from onlookers who couldn't seem to make the connection between me and Tray Ball, the neighborhood hoodlum. I took their stares as signs of recognition and respect. At the shack, which was behind Tray Ball's house, I met Huckabuck, who was dark, athletic, very physical, and an awesome fighter. He came to Cali from New York — accent included. For the most part he was quiet. Leprechaun, whom we called Lep, was there. I had known him previously, as he went to school with my older brother. Lep had a missing front tooth and a slight build. Fiercely loyal to Tray Ball, Lep stood to be second in command. Then there was Fly, who dressed cool and with an air of style. Light-complected and handsome, he was a ladies' man and not necessarily vicious, but he was gaining a reputation by the company he kept. Next was GC, which stood for Gangster Cool. GC was possibly the most well-off member present, meaning he "had things." Things our parents could not afford to give us. He gangbanged in Stacy Adam shoes.

"What's your name, homeboy?" Huckabuck asked through a cloud of marijuana smoke from across the room.

"Kody, my name is Kody."

"Kody? There's already somebody named Kody from the nineties."

I already knew this from hearing his name. "Yeah, but my real name is Kody; my mother named me that."

Everyone looked at me hard and I squirmed under their stares, but I held my ground. To flinch now would possibly mean expulsion.

"What?" Huck said with disbelief. "Your mother named you Kody?"

"Yeah, no shit," I replied.

"Righteous, fuck it, then we'll back you. But you gotta put work in ["put work in" means a military mission] to hold it, 'cause that's a helluva name."

GC, who was dressed like a gas-station attendant in blue khakis with a matching shirt, and I started out to steal a car. All eyes were on me tonight, but I felt no nervousness and there was no hesitation in any of my actions. This was my rite of passage to manhood, and I took each order as seriously as any African would in an initiation ritual to pass from childhood to manhood.

GC was the expert car thief among the set. He learned his technique from Marilyn, our older homegirl, who kept at least two stolen cars on hand a week. Tonight we were out to get an ordinary car, possibly a '65 Mustang or '68 Cougar that could be hot-wired from the engine with as little as a clothes hanger touched on the alternator and then the battery.

We found a Mustang – blue and very sturdy. GC worked to get the hood up, and I kept point with a .38 revolver. I was instructed to fire upon any light in the house and anyone attempting to stop us from getting this car. I was quite prepared to empty six rounds into any house or at any person. Actually, I had fired a real gun only once, and that was into the air.

Under the cloak of darkness I heard GC grunt once and then lift the hood. It took him longer to lift the hood than to start the car. The engine turned once, then twice, and finally it caught and roared to life.

"It's on," GC said with as much pride as any brand-new father looking at his newborn child for the first time. We slapped hands and jumped in. Pulling out of the driveway, I noticed a light turn on. I reached for the door handle with every intent to shoot into the house, but GC grabbed my arm and said, "Don't sweat it, we got the car now."

On the way back to the shack I practiced my mad-dog stares at occupants of cars beside us at stoplights. I guess I wasn't too convincing because on more than a few occasions I was laughed at, and I also got a couple of smiles in return. This was definitely an area to be worked on.

At the shack we smoked pot and drank beer and geared up for the mission—which still had not been disclosed to me. But I was confident in my ability to pull it off. I have never, ever felt as secure as I did then in the presence of these cats, who were growing fonder of me, it seemed, with each successive level of drunkenness they reached.

"Cuz, you gonna be down, watch," Lep announced as if speaking to a son in law school. He stood over me and continued. "I remember your li'l ass used to ride dirt bikes and skateboards, actin' crazy an' shit. Now you want to be a gangster, huh? You wanna hang with real muthafuckas and tear shit up, huh?"

His tone was probing but approving.

"Get you li'l ass up. How old is you now, anyway?"

"Eleven, but I'll be twelve in November." Damn, I'd never thought about being too young.

I stood up in front of Lep and never saw Huck's blow to my head. Bam! And I was on all fours, struggling for equilibrium. Kicked in the stomach, I was on my back. Grabbed by the collar, I was made to stand again. A solid blow to my chest. Bam! Another, then another. Blows rained on me from every direction. I felt perfect solidarity with a pinball. I knew now that if I went down again, I'd be kicked. And from the way that last boot felt, I was almost certain that GC had kicked me with his pointed Stacy Adams.

Up to this point not a word had been spoken. I had heard about being courted in ("courted in" means to be accepted through a barrage of tests, usually physical, though it can include shooting people) or jumped in, but somehow in my still-childish mind I had envisioned it to be a noble gathering, paper work and arguments about my worth and ability in regard to valor. In the heat of desperation I struck out, hitting Fly full in the chest and knocking him back. Then I just started swinging with no style or finesse, just anger and the instinct to survive.

Of course this did little to help my situation, but it showed the others that I had a will to live. And this in turn reflected well on my ability to represent the set in hand-to-hand combat. The blows stopped abruptly and breathing filled the air. My ear was bleeding, and my neck and face were deep red, but I was still standing. Actually, when I think about it now, I realize that it wasn't necessarily my strength that kept me on my feet but the ways in which I was hit. Before I could sag or slump, I was hit and lifted back up.

Tray Ball came in and immediately recognized what had taken place. Looking hard at me, then at the others, he said, "It's time to handle this shit, they out there."

In a flash Lep was under the couch retrieving weapons—guns I never knew were there. Two .12-gauge shotguns, both sawed off—one a pump-action, the other a single-shot, a 4-10 shotgun, also single-shot, and a .44 Magnum that had no trigger guard and broke open to load.

"Give Kody the pump." Tray Ball's voice echoed over the clanging of steel chambers opening and closing, cylinders turning, and the low hum of music in the background. "Check this out." Tray Ball spoke with the calm of a football coach. "Kody, you got eight shots; you don't come back to the car unless they all are gone."

"Righteous," I said, eager to show my worth.

"These fools have been hangin' out for four days now. Hittin' people up ["hittin' people up" means asking where they're from—i.e., which gang are they down with], flaggin' and disrespectin' every Crip in the world."

I sat straight-backed and hung on Tray Ball's every word.

"Tonight we gonna rock they world."

Hand slaps were passed around the room, and then Lep spoke up. "If anybody get caught for this, ride the beef, 'cause ain't no snitchin' here."

We piled into the Mustang, Tray Ball driving—and without a gun. Lep sat next to Tray Ball with the old, ugly .44. Huck, directly behind Lep, held the 4-10 between his legs.

Fly, next to him, had the single-shot .12-gauge. I sat next to him with the pump, and GC was on my left with his .38. In silence we drove block after block, north into enemy territory.

"There they go!" Lep said, spotting a gathering of about fifteen people. "Damn, they deep too—look at them fools!"

I looked at my enemy and remember thinking, *Tonight is the night, and I'll never stop until I've killed them all.*

Driving down another block, we stopped and got out. Each checking his weapon (mine being the most complicated), we started out on foot, creeping up stealthily. Tray Ball sat idle in the car and was to meet us halfway after we had worked over the enemy. Hanging close to buildings, houses, and bushes, we made our way, one after another, to within spitting distance of the Bloods.

Huck and Fly stepped from the shadows simultaneously and were never noticed until it was too late. Boom! Boom! Heavy bodies hitting the ground, confusion, yells of dismay, running, and then the second wave of gunfire. By my sixth shot I had advanced past the first fallen bodies and into the street in pursuit of those hiding behind cars and trees.

One Blood who had seemingly gotten away tried to make one last dash from the safe area of a car to, I think, a porch. I remember raising my weapon and him looking back—for a split second it was as if we communicated on another level and I understood who he was—then I pulled the trigger and laid him down. With one shot left I jogged back to the initial site of contact. Knowing fully that I had explicit orders not to return with any rounds in my weapon, I turned and fired on the house in front of which they had originally stood. Not twenty paces later, Tray Ball sped to a stop and we all piled in, frightfully amped from the climax of battle.

Back in the shack we smoked more pot and drank more beer. I was the center of attention for my acts of aggression.

"Man, did you see this little muthafucka out there?" Fly

said to Huck with an air of disbelief.

"Yeah, I saw him. I knew he was gonna be down, I knew it and as—"

"Shut up, man, just shut the fuck up, 'cause he can still tell on all of us." Silence rang heavy in my ears, and I knew I had to respond to Lep's reaction.

"If I get caught, I'll ride the beef. I ain't no snitch."

Although my little statement lessened the tension, Lep's words had a most sobering effect. Tray Ball announced my full membership, and congratulations were given from all. It was the proudest moment in my life up until that time. Tray Ball told me to stay after the others had left. I milled around, still high from battle.

"Check this out," Tray Ball said. "You got potential, 'cause you eager to learn. Bangin' ain't no part-time thang—it's full-time, it's a career. It's bein' down when ain't nobody else down with you. It's gettin' caught and not tellin'. Killin' and not carin', and dyin' without fear. It's love for your set and hate for the enemy. You hear what I'm sayin'?"

"Yeah, yeah, I hear you," I said. And I had heard him and never forgot nothing he said from that point on.

Tray Ball became my mentor, friend, confidant, and closest comrade. He allowed me to engage in acts of aggression that made my name soar—with alarming effects.

The seriousness of what I had done that evening did not dawn on me until I was alone at home that night. My heart had slowed to its normal pace and the alcohol and pot had worn off. I was left then with just myself and the awesome flashes of light that lit up my mind to reveal bodies in grotesque shapes, twisting and bending in arcs that defied bone structure. The actual impact was on my return back past the bodies of the first fallen, my first real look at bodies torn to shreds. It did little to me then, because it was all about survival. But as I lay wide awake in my bed, safe, alive, I felt guilty and ashamed of myself. Upon further contemplation, I felt that they were too easy to kill. Why had they been out there? I tried every conceivable alibi within the

realm of reason to justify my actions. There was none. I slept very
little that night.
    I've never told anyone of these feelings before.

In the neighborhood, respect was forthcoming. In 1977, when I was thirteen, I turned my head while robbing a man and was hit in the face. The man then tried to run but was tripped by Tray Ball, who then held him for me. I stomped him for twenty minutes before leaving him unconscious in an alley. Later that night I learned that the man had lapsed into a coma and was disfigured from my stomping. The police told bystanders that the person responsible for this was "a monster." The name stuck, and I took it as a moniker.

As Monster, I consistently had to be more vicious to live up to the name. Tray Ball was there for me at every level, but he was at least four years older. Still, we could relate. In 1978, he was captured for knocking a guy out in front of the police, who were questioning the guy about being robbed. I was left with Fly, Lep, Huck, and GC, who lost their will to "get busy" when Tray Ball was locked up. So I went in search of a road dog (i.e., "best friend").

I had been seeing the name Crazy Dee written on walls for some time and had a pretty good idea who he was. While walking up the alley one day, I ran into Crazy Dee. We formally introduced ourselves, and I asked him if he wanted to kick it with us. Although he was already from the set, he kicked it with other people. A jovial cat of my age with happy eyes and a Hollywood smile, Dee became my road dog.

From this point on, Dee and I were inseparable. The set was still relatively small; everyone knew one another. (When I say "small" here, I mean approximately seventy-five to eighty people; that's a small set. Today it's not unusual for sets to be one thousand deep.) Though there were various sides and sections, we all met up at meetings in our park, though this usually occurred only when someone had been killed or some serious infraction had been committed. I continued to see and associate with GC, Lep, and the others, but it wasn't the same with Tray Ball missing. He was the glue that bound us.

I had escalated from "little homie" to "homie" and was putting in much work and dropping many bodies. In fact, some shied away from me because I took things "too serious." But Crazy Dee understood me and my thirst for reputation – the purpose of all gang members. I had learned that there were three stages to go through before the title OG – Original Gangster – applied righteously:

1) You must build the reputation of your name.

2) You must build your name in association with your set so that when your name is spoken, your set is also spoken of in the same breath, for they are synonymous.

3) You must establish yourself as a promoter of Crip or Blood, depending on which side of the color bar you live on.

In '78 I was fourteen and still working on the first stage. But I had as much ambition, vitality, and ruthlessness to succeed as did any corporate executive planning a hostile takeover; a merger, needless to say, was always out of the question. Gangbanging in the '70s was totally different from what's going on today. The gang community on both sides was relatively small, contained in certain areas, and sustained by a few who kept the faith.

By now, of course, I had acquired my own weapon – a blue steel .44 Bulldog. It was small and fit into my pocket. I kept it on me at all times.

My little brother and his friend Frank were eating chili dogs at Art's one afternoon when Frank's chili-dog wrapper blew to the ground. Eric, who had been hired by Art not just as a cook but as a watchdog, was a hothead and needed little provoking to act a complete fool. He told my brother to pick up the paper. When my brother explained that it was not his paper, Eric became angry and collared him and ripped his shirt. Upset and confused, my little brother went home and got my mother, older brother, and sister.

I was out on a ten-speed, patrolling the 'hood with, of course, my .44. I was sitting on the corner across from Art's when I saw my mother's car with everyone in it pull to a stop at the light. Here I was, waiting for some action and it pulled right up – fate, I guess. My older brother signaled for me, so I followed them on over to Art's. No one knew I was strapped. As I rode up, my older brother was standing there arguing with Eric. My brother hit Eric in the face and they began to fight. I immediately dismounted and rushed up on Eric's flank to get a hit in, but he was swift and struck me in the ear, knocking me backward. All the while my mother was frantically shouting for us to stop, stop the fighting. Mad now, and insulted, I drew my weapon, aimed, and pulled the trigger. Click.

Damn, I remember thinking, *I only got three bullets,* and I didn't know where in the cylinder they were! The click stopped everything – and then everybody seemed to move at once. Eric ran toward the chili stand, and my brother rushed toward me. Before I could aim and fire, my brother and I were wrestling over the gun.

"Give me the gun, I'll shoot him," my brother exclaimed.

"No, let me shoot him," I shouted.

The gun was now pointing at my mother's chest. Click.

My mother jumped. I was momentarily paralyzed with fright. I let go of the gun and my brother turned and fired into the chili stand. Boom! The .44 sounded like a cannon.

Click. Another empty chamber.

Eric by now had retrieved his shotgun and was on his way out after us. Seeing him coming, both my brother and I turned and ran. We had barely turned the first corner when the report from the shotgun echoed behind us. He chased us through several yards, firing and tearing up people's property. He fired a total of eight times, but we escaped un scathed – except for our pride. My mother, sister, and little brother also escaped unharmed, though in great fear for us because they didn't know our fate.

After meeting back at home, my mother wanted to send us all out to my uncle's house in West Covina. We protested and stayed. The next morning however, while standing at the bus stop waiting to go to school, Eric pulled up and mad-dogged me. "What you lookin' at, punk?" he shouted.

"You muthafucka!" I responded, though scared because he may have had a gun and I couldn't get mine out of the house; after the episode the day before, Moms was search-ing me. There were three young ladies standing there as well, so my pride and integrity were also involved, not to mention my reputation. I had to stand my ground.

Eric leaped from the car, circled from the front, walked up, and hit me in the mouth – bam! I faltered and became indecisive. But in an instant I knew I needed an equalizer, because he lifted his shirt to reveal the butt of a pistol in his waistband. I turned and bolted. Running at top speed with tears streaming down my face, I made my way back home, went right in, got my gun, and trotted back to the bus stop. I was hoping the bus hadn't come, because I wanted the three girls who saw me get hit to watch me kill him.

Art's chili-dog stand has been on Florence and Nor-mandie since the Forties, and up till that time it still had its original decor – open and primarily wood, with big win-dows facing out onto Florence Avenue. The bus stop was across Florence on Normandie. Turning the corner on Sev-enty-first at a steady trot, I was relieved to find the three girls still there, almost as if they were waiting for me. Passing them up, I heard one say to the other, "That boy is crazy!"

Taking no chances this time, I had six rounds and stood in the street in front of Art's. Traffic was moderate, so I waited for the light to turn red. Once I saw that I could safely break back across Florence and then to a backyard, I

opened fire on Art's. Boom! Boom! Loud echoes of bari-
tone cracked the morning stillness as chunks of wood and
shreds of glass flew off Art's with magical quickness. Cord-
ite filled my nostrils and revenge filled my heart. Boom!
Boom! Boom! Boom! I emptied six shots into the tiny dwell-
ing, hoping to kill Eric, who had just opened up for business.

No such luck. I was captured the next day and given sixty
days in juvenile hall but actually only served nineteen due to
overcrowding. Once I was out, my reputation was stronger
than ever. Even Eric gave me my due, if grudgingly.

The week after my release, Dee, myself, and Stone and
Snoopy, of the Rollin' Sixties Crips (later the Sixties and my
set – the Eight Trays – would become mortal enemies), were
on our way to Rosecrans Skating Rink, which was where everybody who was somebody in the gang world went. Walking up Manchester Avenue, we passed Pearl's Gym and the
Best Yet hair salon. Still within the boundaries of my set, we
came to a halt at the corner of Manchester and Gramercy
Place, waiting for the light to change so we could trek onto
Van Ness, where our bus was to depart. We heard two reports from what sounded like a .38. The sound came from
the direction of Duke's hamburger stand. Duke's had recently become contested territory, as the Inglewood Family
Bloods had begun to frequent it in hopes of establishing it as
theirs.

As our attention turned to the sound, we saw Fly and
Tracc breaking out of Duke's and coming toward us across
the street. Tracc appeared to have a big, long-barrel .38 revolver in his left hand. Running past us, one of them exclaimed, "Y'all bail, we just busted on some Families!"

We hadn't done anything, so we kept on our way. Not a
minute later, a white Camaro came screeching out of Duke's

parking lot. "There they go," we heard an almost hysterical voice yell from the car. A second car, a huge orange Chrysler, came barreling out of the parking lot on the bumper of the Camaro, which was now coming directly at us. We scattered.

Dee and I darted right into an adjacent alley behind Best Yet, and I don't know where Stone and Snoopy went. The chase was on. Hopping a fence in the alley, Dee and I hid ourselves in the back of Pearl's Gym. The Camaro and the Chrysler roared up and down the alley as we lay in dense shrubbery. I hoped the Blood who had been shot would die.

There were no Crip-on-Crip wars raging in these times. The worst enemies were Crip and Blood sets. Today Crips are the number-one killers of Crips. In fact, Crips have killed more Crips in the past twelve years than the Bloods have killed in the entire twenty-two-year conflict. And sets in the Crip and Blood communities have increased twenty-fold — now there is literally a gang on every street. There are the huge conglomerate sets spanning hundreds of city blocks, extending into other cities and counties. It's not at all unusual for one of these huge conglomerates to be policed by five separate divisions of the L.A.P.D. and the sheriff's department.

After an hour or so we emerged from hiding and walked east. Stopping at Western Avenue and Manchester, we found Snoopy and Stone. We devised a new strategy, as we were well aware that the Families were now out en masse looking for revenge. Just then the orange Chrysler hit the corner of Eighty-fifth Street packed with Bloods. We had two choices: run into the street and try to make it across Western and farther into the interior of our 'hood and possible safety or run into the surplus store behind us and hope they wouldn't follow us into such a big civilian crowd. Quickly we chose the second option.

Dee broke first, with me, Snoopy, and Stone heavy on his heels. Looking back, I immediately understood that we had made a terrible decision, for the Bloods were bailing out of the huge Chrysler like beans from a bag and chasing us straight up into the store! I remember taking one last look back after I had jumped the turnstile, and I knew then that we were trapped.

The surplus kept a huge green trash can by the door that was full of ax handles of heavy oakwood; each Blood grabbed one as he entered. Alarmed and not knowing if this was a gang raid on his store, the manager locked the door once the last Blood had come in. I thought we'd be beaten to death.

Snoopy and Stone went one way, and Dee and I went another. I followed Dee up some stairs that led to an attic supply room and further entrapment. Four Bloods followed us up, swearing to kill us. One guy was shouting about the victim being his brother. *Damn, how in the hell had we gotten into this?*

Running up into the small attic area, I seriously thought about death for the first time in my life, and for the slightest second I wanted to turn and tell the Bloods, "Hey, all right, I quit. I'm only fourteen, can't we talk?" Diplomacy was as foreign as Chinese to us all, but it's a trip that when you're under pressure, clear thoughts seem to abound.

Stopping and crouching – they had momentarily lost my tail among the rows and aisles of stocked clothing – I heard Dee trying to explain that they had made a mistake. "Hold it, man, it wasn't us." Dee's voice resounded in a cracking tone of sincerity and terror.

"You a muthafuckin' lie, we saw you, blood!"

Crack! "Ahh!" Crack! "All right, man, all..." Crack! "Ahh!"

Terrified, I crouched lower and closed my eyes, hoping they wouldn't kill Dee, who was now on the ground and silent. But the beating continued. I felt completely helpless.

"Here go another one!" Crack! Across the top of my head the heavy ax handle came down. *Swoosh!* A miss, and in an instant I was on my feet. Crack! One to the back, as I tried to get past another Blood in the semidarkness.

"Wait, wait!"

"Fuck that shit, fool, you didn't wait when you shot Mike!" Crack! "Ohh." Crack! "Ahh . . . " Blackness.

When I came to I was on my stomach, handcuffed. Next to me was Dee. Both of us were bloody and swollen. Craning my neck to the left, I saw Snoopy and Stone. They, too, looked whipped and soiled.

"Which one of you did the shootin'?" a police asked from somewhere behind me.

"Him, the one in the blue overalls and sweat jacket."

That was me! "What?" I managed to say through fog and loose teeth. "Who, me?"

"Yeah, you, you little crab-ass punk!" ("Crab" is a disrespectful term used by Bloods against Crips—defacing the enemy.)

For the first time I noticed her—a girl. Looking up, I brought her into focus. Never seen her in my life.

"You a lie, bitch . . ." I blurted out, and was abruptly cut short by a police boot on the back of my neck.

"Shut up, asshole. Are you sure this is the shooter, ma'am?"

"Yes. Yes, I'm sure, officer."

I was transported to the Seventy-seventh Division and booked for attempted murder. Now I was hoping Mike, the Blood, wouldn't die. I was the only one who had been arrested. At the station I was asked a series of questions of which I answered none. I was taken to Los Padrinos Juvenile Hall to await court, no doubt facing a term for the attempted murder, which I hadn't even committed. The strict code of the street held me, though, and I didn't say a word to anyone about who had really shot the Blood.

I went to trial three months later. The gang turnout was surprising. Along with my family, at least fifteen of my homeboys came. All were in full gear ("gear" is gang clothes, colors and hats – actually uniforms). On the other side, the Bloods came in force in full gear. Tension ran thick through the courtroom as stares of hate were passed back and forth.

After the first day I was told that a shoving and shouting match took place in the hallway outside the courtroom. My homeboys had to serve as bodyguards for my family. On my next court date, I was released into the custody of my mother, pending trial proceedings.

The atmosphere was tight with rage. I couldn't believe how personal these Bloods were taking this. After all, their homie had been shot "legally" – that is, within the known guidelines of gang warfare. He had been fired on in a contested free-fire zone. We had gotten numerous reports of Blood sightings and he just happened to be the first caught.

And now here they were, taking the war off the streets and into the courtroom, where neither of us had the experience to win. Blood after Blood testified to my shooting of their homeboy Mike. The final witness was the victim himself. Thin and wearing cornrowed braids, he would seal my fate with his testimony. After the prosecutor asked Mike to convey the events of that day, he asked if he saw the person in court who had shot him. Silence. And then . . .

"No, he ain't the one who shot me."

"What?" the D.A. couldn't believe his ears.

Murmurs filled the court as his homies whispered their disbelief at his honesty. Snickers and taunts came from our side. I sat still and just looked at Mike, who stared back without a semblance of hate but with a sort of remorse for having put me through this.

The judge's gavel struck wood. "Case dismissed."

I stood, still looking at Mike, who was dismounting the witness stand.

"Tell Tracc," Mike whispered as he passed me, "that I'll see him at another time."

I said nothing, and fell into step with my crew. That night

I led an initiation party into Family 'hood and dropped two bodies. No one was captured.

My relationship with my mother continued to sour as I was drawn deeper and deeper into the streets and further away from home and school. My sixth-grade graduation had been my first and last. Actually, it was the last time I ever seriously attended school for academic purposes. My home-boys became my family; the older ones were father figures. They congratulated me each time I shot someone, each time I recruited a combat soldier, each time I put another gun on the set. When I went home I was cursed for not emptying the trash. Trash? Didn't Moms understand who I was?

Dee and I continued to campaign hard, but we couldn't transcend that first stage of reputation. On February 14, 1979, when I was fifteen, I was captured for assault and auto theft. I took a car from a man by striking him over the head. Too drunk to drive, I hit every car on the block in my attempt to flee the area. The last and final car I struck was a Cadillac. The bumpers must have got caught, because the car I was in would not go into reverse. As I left the vehicle, I was surprised to find practically the whole block chasing me. Actually, it turned out to be just the owners of the cars I had hit. They had sticks and baseball bats and were running together in a tight group. But as I accelerated, their group dwindled to two.

Both men were quite intent on catching me. I continued to run, however, at top speed. Falling farther and farther behind, I heard them cursing and swearing to kill me. I struggled on. Rounding the corner on my block, I was elated to see that my pursuers were at least four houses be-hind. I darted down the drive of our next-door neighbor and hopped the fence into our backyard. I then staggered heavily into the house and literally collapsed on my mother's bed. Pulling myself up, I began to discard my clothing, pulling on fresh pants, socks, and sneakers. I deliberately omitted a shirt to look as at-home as possible.

Not ten minutes later, I heard the police helicopter hovering above my house. It felt good at least to know that my mother was, as usual, at work. Five minutes after I heard the first hum of the helicopter, I heard voices coming from the front room. I quickly hid in my mother's closet, but to no avail. I was violently pulled from the closet and promptly arrested. I later found out that it was a crazy cat named Theapolis who had snitched me off to my pursuers, who in turn had summoned the police.

During the trial on assault and grand-theft-auto charges, my sister, Kendis, tried to save me from a jail term but was not convincing enough against the thirteen witnesses who had originally given chase. I was convicted and sentenced to nine months in Camp Munz. (Camp is the third in a series of tests to register one's ability. The streets, of course, being the first; juvenile hall being the second. With each successive level—the Hall, Camp, Youth Authority, Prison—comes longer, harder time.)

Nine months later I was released from Camp Munz and dropped off in the initial stages of a war that would forever change the politics of Cripping and the internal gang relations in South-Central. Although my camp term lent prestige to my name, it did little to help me break through to the second level of recognition. Crazy Dee, I learned, was not yet out, so I just did "odd jobs"—i.e., wrote on walls, advertised, collected guns, and maintained visibility.

It was during my stay in camp that my younger brother chose to follow me into banging and allied himself with the Eight Trays. It was '79, the year of the Li'ls, the year of the third generation of Eight Tray gangsters. All those who were of the second resurrection—beginning in 1975 and ending in 1977—acquired little homies bearing their names. For example, there was Li'l Monster, Li'l Crazy Dee, Li'l Spike, et cetera. The set doubled within a nine-month period.

Meanwhile, the war between us and the Rollin' Sixties was beginning to heat up. The first casualty was on their side. Tyrone, the brother of an OG Sixty, was gunned down during a routine fistfight by a new recruit who called himself Dog. The OG whose brother had been killed wanted us to produce the shooter before a full-scale war broke out. The shooter, whom few knew, as he was new, immediately went into hiding, so we couldn't produce him. As a result, our relationship with the Sixties soured dramatically.

Until then only one of our homies had been killed, and his death was attributed to the Inglewood Families. Threats of revenge grew loud, as did rumors of a war. In the midst of these imminent warnings, our homeboy Lucky was ambushed on his porch and shot six times in the face. Witnesses reported seeing "a man in a brown jogging suit flee the area immediately after shots rang out." The night Lucky was murdered, Mumpy, a member of the Sixties, was seen at Rosecrans Skating Rink in a brown jogging suit. It had been further noted that Mumpy was heard telling Lucky that "since one of my homeboys died, one of yours gotta die." A fight ensued and was subsequently broken up by members of both sides.

After Lucky's death, tension ran high. We wanted the shooters to fall under the weight of our wrath. A meeting of both sets was called by the OGs in a last effort to curtail a war, which would no doubt have grave consequences. The most damaging thing was that we knew where the other set stayed—not more than six months earlier, we had been the best of friends. The meeting was a dismal failure, erupting into an all-out gang fight reminiscent of the old rumbles. Diplomatic ties were broken and war was ceremoniously declared. They quickly suffered another casualty when their homeboy Pimp was ambushed and killed. Several others were wounded.

In the interim, Dee was released. After relaying to him the drastic events of recent times, we both chose to give 100 percent to the war effort. And perhaps, we concurred, this was a conflict that would carry us both over into the second realm of recognition on our climb to OG status.

In retaliation for Pimp's death, our homie Tit Tit was shot, and while he lay in the street mortally wounded, the gunmen came back around the corner in a white van. Before we could retrieve Tit Tit, they ran over his head and continued on. The occupants in the van had also shot two other people, both civilians. This was the second homie to die in a matter of months. Shit was getting major.

Although we had been engaged in a war with the Families, it had always somehow been confined to fistfights and flesh wounds, with the exception of Shannon—who, to this day, we contend, died at the hands of the Families. This escalation was new and quite alarming. For Crips tend to display a vicious knack for violence against other Crips. Seemingly, every Crip set erupted into savage wars, one against the other, culminating in today's Beirut type of atmosphere.

The recent news-catching items of violence are a result of clashes between Crips and Crips and not, as the media suggests, between Crips and Bloods. Once bodies began to drop, people who were less than serious about banging began to fall by the wayside. There were lots of excuses of having to "be home by dark" and having to "go out of town."

Dee and I held fast and seized the time. China, a very pretty but slightly plump homegirl, became my steady. She and I would often dress alike to further show off our union.

One afternoon she lent me her eight-track tape player. As Dee and I were walking with China's radio, we drew fire from a passing car—no doubt filled with Sixties. Unscathed but very angry, Dee and I climbed from the bushes.

"Check this out," Dee said with barely controlled anger. "Kody, we gotta put a stop to these muthafuckas shootin' at us and shit."

He was looking at me hard in search of some signs of understanding. I said, "You right homie, I'm wit' it."

"You serious?" Dee asked with a sinister smile. "All right, then," he continued, "let's make a pact right now to never stop until we have killed all of our enemies. This means wherever we catch 'em, it's on!"

"All right, I'm serious, Dee," I remember saying as I pledged my life to the Sixties' total destruction, or mine—whichever came first.

With that, I spun and threw China's radio high into the air. The radio seemed to tumble in slow motion, twisting and twirling, as my gang life until that time flashed across my mental screen. From graduation to this—*blam!* The radio hit the ground, shattered into a hundred pieces, and the screen in my mind went blank.

There was Dee with his hand extended. I grabbed and shook it with vigor. From that point on, the medium of exchange in my life has been gunfire.

GARY SNYDER

Coming in to the Watershed

watershed: 2. The whole region or area contributing
to the supply of a river or lake; drainage area.
— *Webster's New Collegiate Dictionary*

In February of 1992 Jeff Lustig asked me to give the keynote
talk for the annual conference of the Center for California
Studies based at Sacramento State University. The theme of
the conference was "dancing on the edge" — of ecological
breakdown, social confrontations, and versions of history. I
wanted to look again at the question of engagement with
place, and speak of bioregional and watershed organizing as
ways to get down, get on the ground, and make "biodiversity"
and public lands issues walk, not just talk. Although framed
in terms of California, the same points can be made for the
whole country. The possibility of Watershed Councils becoming the building blocks of a continent-wide bioregional/
ecosystem governance has broad relevance. Recovering wilderness in North America must start with grassroots (tree
roots, sagebrush roots ...) people and their communities.

Biological and Cultural Diversity in our
California Habitat

THE QUESTION OF "place" is curiously cogent to our
present political, social, and environmental condition. Eco-
nomically we're in misery, politically we are hopelessly stag-
nant, educationally we're a disgrace, and socially we are

watching the emergence of a multi-racial multi-ethnic population that will radically shape the future direction of the
culture of our country. We are also seeing the reemergence
of a crude racism and chauvinism that may destroy us all. As
for the land itself we see fine agricultural soils and orchards
being steadily converted by real estate development. The
publicly owned forests of the West are being overcut, and
the long-range effects of erosion and air pollution raise the
very real possibility of their gradual slide from productive
forest lands to steady-state brushfields. There's a parallel
deterioration of grasslands and semi-desert. Yet, at the
same time it looks as though non-indigenous North Americans are on the verge of discovering—for the first time—
their place. People are slowly coming to the realization that
they can become members of the deep old biological communities of the land in a different kind of citizenship.

In February my son Gen and I were visiting friends in Arcata and Crescent City on the north coast of California. We
drove north from Marysville—through that soulful winter
depth of pearly tule fog—paralleling the Feather and then
crossing the Sacramento at Red Bluff. From Red Bluff
north the fog began to break, and by Redding we had left it
behind. As we crossed the mountains westward from Redding on 299 we paid special attention to the transformations
of the landscape and trees, watching to see where the natural boundaries could be roughly ascertained. From the
great valley with its tules, grasses, valley oak and blue oak,
we swiftly climbed into the steep and dissected Klamath
range with its ponderosa pine, black oak, and manzanita
fields. Somewhere past Burnt Ranch we were in the redwood and doug-fir forests—soon it was the coastal range.
Then we descended past Blue Lake to come out at Arcata.

We drove on north. Just ten or fifteen miles from Arcata,
around Trinidad Head, the feel of the landscape subtly
changed again—much the same trees, but no open mead-

ows, and a different light. At Crescent City and again Manila we asked friends Jim Dodge (the novelist) and poet Jerry Martien just what the change between Arcata and Crescent City was. They both said (to distill a long discussion), "You leave 'California.' Right around Trinidad Head you cross into the maritime Pacific Northwest." Even though the political boundary is many miles yet to the north.

So we had gone in that one afternoon's drive from the Mediterranean-type Sacramento Valley climate, with its many plant alliances toward the Mexican south, over the interior range with its dry pine forest hills, into a uniquely Californian set of redwood forests, and on into the maritime Pacific Northwest: the edges of four major areas. These boundaries are not hard and clear, though. They are porous, permeable, arguable. They are boundaries of climates, plant-communities, soil-types, styles of life. They change over the millennia, moving a few hundred miles this way or that. A thin line drawn on a map would not do them justice. Yet such are the markers of the natural nations of our planet, and they establish real territories with real differences, to which our economies and our clothing must adapt.

On the way back we stopped at Trinidad Head for a hike and a little birding. Although we knew they wouldn't be there until April, we walked out to look at the cliffs on the Head, where tufted puffins nest. This is virtually the southernmost end of the tufted puffins' range. Their more usual nesting ground is from Southeast Alaska through the Bering Sea and down to northern Japan. In winter they are far out in the open seas of the North Pacific. At this spot, Trinidad, we could not help but feel that we touched on the life-realm of the whole North Pacific and Alaska. We spent that whole weekend enjoying "liminality" and dancing on the brink of the continent.

I have taken to watching the subtle changes of plants and climates as I travel over the West. This vast area called "California" is large enough to be beyond any one individual's ability to travel it and take it all into imagination clearly enough to see the whole picture. Michael Barbour, a botanist at UC Davis, is bringing out a book to be called *California's Changing Landscapes*. He writes of the complexity of California: "of the world's 10 major soils, California has all 10. . . . As many as 375 distinctive natural communities have been recognized in the state. . . . California has more than 5,000 kinds of native ferns, conifers, and flowering plants. Japan has far fewer species with a similar area. Even with four times California's area, Alaska does not match California's plant diversity, and neither does all of the central and northeastern United States and adjacent Canada combined. Moreover about 30% of California's native plants are found nowhere else in the world."

But all this talk of the diversity of California is a trifle misleading. Of what place are we speaking? What is this "California?" It is, after all, a recent human invention with straight-line boundaries that were drawn with a ruler on a map and rushed off to an office in DC. This is another illustration of Robert Frost's lines, "The land was ours before we were the land's." The political boundaries of the Western states were established in haste and ignorance. Landscapes have their own shapes and structures, centers and edges, which must be respected. If a relationship to a place is like a marriage, then the Yankee establishment of jurisdiction called California was like a shotgun wedding with six sisters taken as one wife.

California is made up of what I take to be about six regions. (The numbers could be argued, but the main outlines of agreement will remain.) They are of respectable size and native beauty, each with its own makeup, its own mix of bird calls and plant smells. Each of these proposes a slightly

different life style to the human beings who live there. Each
led to different sorts of rural economies – for the regional
differences translate into things like raisin grapes, wet rice,
timber, and cattle pasture.

The central coast with its little river-valleys, beach dunes
and marshes, and oak-grass-pine mountains is one region.
The Great Central Valley is a second, once dominated by
swamps and wide shallow lakes and sweeps of valley oaks
following the streams. The long mountain ranges of the Sierra Nevada are a third. From a sort of Sonoran chaparral
they rise to arctic tundra. In the middle elevations they have
some of the finest mixed conifer forests in the world. The
Modoc plateau and volcano country – with its sagebrush
and juniper – makes a fourth. Some of the Sacramento
waters rise here. The fifth is the northern coast with its deep
interior mountains – the Klamath region – reaching (on
the coast) as far north as Trinidad Head. The sixth of these
six sisters is the coastal valleys and mountains south of
the Tehachapis, with natural connections on into Baja. Although today it supports a huge population with water
drawn from the Colorado River, the Owens Valley, and the
Great Central Valley, it is naturally almost a desert.

One might ask what about the rest? Where are the White
Mountains, the Mojave Desert, the Warner Range? They
are splendid places, but they do not belong with California.
Their watersheds and biological communities belong to the
Great Basin or the lower Colorado drainage, and we should
let them return to their own families. Almost all of core California has a summer-dry Mediterranean climate, with (usually) fairly abundant winter rain. More than anything else,
this rather special type of climate is what gives our place its
fragrance of oily aromatic herbs, its olive-green drouth-
resistant shrubs, and its patterns of rolling grass and dark
forest.

I am not arguing that we should instantly re-draw the

boundaries of the social construction called California, although that could happen some far day. We are becoming aware of certain long-range realities, and this thinking leads toward the next step in the evolution of human citizenship on the North American continent. The usual focus of attention for most Americans is the human society itself with its problems and it successes, its icons and symbols. With the exception of most Native Americans and a few non-natives who have given their hearts to the place, the land we all live on is simply taken for granted – and proper relation to it is not taken as part of "citizenship." But after two centuries of national history, people are beginning to wake up and notice that the United States is located on a landscape with a severe, spectacular, spacey, wildly demanding, and ecstatic narrative to be learned. Its natural communities are each unique, and each of us, whether we like it or not – in the city or countryside – live in one of them. When enough people get that picture, our political life will begin to change, and it will be the beginning of the next phase of American life, coming to live on "Turtle Island."

Those who work in resource management are accustomed to looking at various maps of the West, each of which addresses a rich set of meanings. Land ownership categories give us (in addition to private land) Bureau of Land Management lands, National Forests, National Parks, State Parks, military reserves, and a host of other public holdings. The idea of public domain is descended from the historic institution of the Commons in Europe. These lands host much of the water, forest, and wildlife that is left to us. Although they are in the care of all the people, they have been too often managed for special interests.

Conservationists have been working since the 1930s for the preservation of key blocks of public land as wilderness.

There has been some splendid success in this effort, and we are all indebted to the single-minded (and often unpaid) dedication of the people who are behind every present-day Wilderness Area that we and our children walk into, take heart in. Our growing understanding of how natural systems work brought us the realization that an exclusive emphasis on disparate parcels of land ignored the insouciant freeness of wild creatures. Although individual islands of wild land serving as biological refuges are invaluable, they cannot of themselves guarantee the maintenance of natural variety. As biologists, public land managers, and the involved public have all agreed, we need to know more about how natural systems work at larger scales, and find "on the ground" ways to connect wild zone to wild zone wherever possible. Thus the notion of biological corridors or connectors. The Greater Yellowstone Ecosystem concept came out of this sort of recognition. Our understanding of nature and our practice in regard to it has been radically altered by systems theory. Specifically, systems theory as it comes through the science of Ecology, and in particular the very cogent sub-disciplines called Island Biogeography and Landscape Ecology. They provide some extraordinary detail to fill out the broader generalization that comes both from John Muir and the 8th century AD Chinese Buddhist philosophers, "Everything is connected."

No single group or agency could keep track of or take care of grizzly bears, which do not care about park or ranch boundaries and have ancient territories of their own. A recognition that habitat flows across private and public land is needed to provide the framework for the "management" of bears, owls, or redwoods. A definition of place unencumbered by the illogical boundaries of states and counties is essential. Such a territory would have its own functional and structural coherence. It often might contain or be a watershed system. It would usually be larger than a county, but smaller than a western U.S. state. One of the names of such a space is "bioregion." The concept is basic and sensible, that of the simple fact of naturally observable regions.

Colors of the Land, Colors of the Skin

The word "bioregion" has thus begun to be common vocabulary in California, but in a context of some dubiousness. A group of California-based federal and state land managers trying to work together on biodiversity problems saw that it must be done in terms of natural regions. Their "memorandum of understanding" calls for us to "move beyond existing efforts focused on the conservation of individual sites, species, and resources . . . to also protect and manage ecosystems, biological communities, and landscapes." The memorandum goes on to say that "public agencies and private groups must coordinate resource management and environmental protection activities, emphasizing regional solutions to regional issues and needs." The group identified 11 or so such working bioregions within California, making the San Francisco Bay/Delta into one, and dividing both the Sierra and the Valley into northern and southern portions. There are lumpers and there are splitters. It is entirely appropriate that the heads of the BLM, the Forest Service, Fish and Wildlife Service, California Department of Fish and Game, California Department of Forestry, and such should take these issues on: almost 50% of California is public domain.

Hearing about this agreement, some county government people, elected officials, and timber and business interests in the mountain counties went into a severe paranoid spasm, fearing—they said—new regulations and more centralized government. An anonymous circular made its way around towns and campuses in northern California under the title "Biodiversity or New Paganism?" It says that "California Resource Secretary Doug Wheeler and his self-appointed bioregional soldiers are out to devalue human life by placing greater emphasis on rocks, trees, fish, plants, and wildlife." It quotes me as having written that "Those of us who are now promoting a bioregional consciousness would, as an ultimate and long-range goal, like to see this continent more sensitively redefined, and the natural regions of North America—Turtle Island—gradually begin to shape the political-entities within which we work. It would be a small step toward the deconstruction of America as a super power into seven or eight natural nations—none of which have a budget big enough to support missiles." I'm pleased to say I did write that. I'd think it was clear that my stateme: s not promoting more centralized government, but these gents want both their small-town autonomy and the Military-Industrial State at the same time. Many a would-be Westerner is a "libertarian" in name only, and will scream up a storm if taken too far from the government tit. The real intent of the circular seems to be—as it urges people to write the state Governor—to resist long-range sustainability and the support of biodiversity, and to hold out for maximum resource extraction.

As far as I can see, the intelligent but so far toothless California "bioregional proposal" is simply a basis for further thinking and some degree of cooperation between agencies. The most original part is the call for the formation of "bioregional councils" that would have some stake in decision-making. Who would be on the bioregional councils is not spelled out. Even closer to the roots, the memorandum that started all this furor suggests that "watershed councils" be formed, which would be the truly local bodies that could help design agreements for the preservation of natural variety. Like, let's say, helping to preserve the spawning grounds of the wild salmon that still come (amazingly) into the lower Yuba River gravel wastelands. This effort would have to involve a number of groups and agencies, and would have to include the blessing of the usually development-minded Yuba County Water Agency.

The term "bioregion" was adopted by the signers to the Memorandum on Biological Diversity as a technical term from the field of biogeography. I'm sure they couldn't have known that there were already groups of people around the United States and Canada talking in terms of bioregionally-oriented societies. They could not have known about the first North American Bioregional Congress held in Kansas in the late 80s, and subsequent gatherings right down to a "Shasta Nation" (northern California) gathering held last September in the Napa Valley. (Continent-wide gatherings have dropped the name North America and refer to our larger place as "Turtle Island," after the Native American creation myth.) They had no idea of the twenty-year history of community and ecology-minded dwellers-in-the-land living in places called "Ish" (Puget Sound and lower British Columbia) or "Columbiana" (upper Columbia River) or "Mesechabe" (lower Mississippi), or "Shasta" (northern California), all of whom had periodicals, field trips, gatherings, and were active in local politics.

That "bioregion" was an idea already in circulation was the bad, or good, luck of the biodiversity agreement people, depending on how you look at it. As it happens, the bioregional people are also finding "watershed councils" to be the building blocks of a long-range strategy for social and environmental sustainability.

A watershed is a marvelous thing to consider: This process of rain falling, streams flowing, and oceans evaporating causes every molecule of water on Earth to make the complete trip once every two million years. The surface is carved into watersheds—a kind of familial branching, a chart of relationship, and a definition of place. The watershed is the first and last nation, whose boundaries, though subtly shifting, are unarguable. Races of birds, subspecies of trees, and types of hats or rain gear go by the watershed. The watershed gives us a home, and a place to go upstream, downstream, or across in.

For the watershed, cities and dams are ephemeral, and of no more account than a boulder that falls in the river, or a landslide that temporarily alters the channel. The water will always be there, and it will always find its way down. As constrained and polluted as it is at the moment, it can also be said that in the larger picture the Los Angeles River is alive and well under the city streets, running in giant culverts. It is possibly amused by such diversions. But we who live in terms of centuries rather than millions of years, must hold the watershed and its communities together, that our children might enjoy the clear water and fresh life of this landscape we have chosen. From the tiniest rivulet at the crest of a ridge, to the main trunk of a river approaching the lowlands, the river is all one place, and all one land.

The water cycle is our springs and wells, our Sierra snowpack, our irrigation canals, our carwash, and the spring salmon run. It's the spring peeper in the pond and the acorn woodpecker chattering in a snag. It's where our friends live, it *is* our friends. The watershed is beyond the dichotomies of orderly/disorderly, for its forms are free, but somehow inevitable. And the life that comes to flourish within it constitutes the first kind of community.

The agenda of a watershed council starts in a modest way: like saying "Let's try and rehabilitate our river to the point that wild salmon can successfully spawn here again." In pursuit of this local agenda, a community might find itself combating clearcut timber sales upstream, water-selling grabs downstream, Taiwanese drift-net practices out in the North Pacific, and a host of other national and international threats to the health of salmon. A small but significant number of watershed councils are already in existence, fully awake and conscious, with some strong views about what should be done. These include the Friends of the Los Angeles River, the Putah Creek Council, the Yuba Watershed Institute, The Greenwood Watershed Association, The Redwood Coast Watersheds Alliance, and the Mattole Restoration Council.

They are ready and willing to play ball with the California BLM, the State, the Pacific Southwest Region office of the Forest Service, and the others who signed the 1991 Agreement for a "coordinated regional strategy for saving biological diversity in California." If a wide range of people join this effort—people from timber and tourism, settled ranchers and farmers, fly-fishing retirees, the businesses and the forest-dwelling new settlers—something might come of it. But if this joint agreement is implemented as a top-down prescription it will go nowhere. Only a grassroots engagement with long-term land issues can provide the political and social stability needed to keep the biological richness of California's regions intact.

All public land ownership is ultimately written in sand. The boundaries and the management-categories were created by Congress, and Congress can take them away. The only "jurisdiction" that will last in the world of nature is the watershed, and even that changes over time. If public lands come under greater and greater pressure to be opened for exploitation and use in the 21st century, the local people, the watershed people, will prove to be the last and possibly most effective line of defense. Let us hope it never comes to that.

The mandate of the public land managers and the Fish and Wildlife people inevitably directs them to resource concerns. They are proposing to do what could be called "ecological bioregionalism." The other movement could be called "cultural bioregionalism." I would like to turn my attention now to cultural bioregionalism and to what practical promise these ideas hold for *fin de millennium* America.

Living in a place. The notion has been around for decades, and has usually been dismissed as provincial, backward, dull, and possibly reactionary. But new dynamics are at work. The mobility that has charactered American life is coming to a close. As Americans begin to stay put, it may give us the first opening in over a century to give participatory democracy another try.

Daniel Kemmis, the mayor of Missoula, Montana, has written a fine little book called *Community and the Politics of Place*. Mr. Kemmis points out that in the 18th century the word *republican* meant a politics of community engagement. Early republican thought was set against the federalist theories which would govern by balancing competing interests, devise sets of legalistic procedures, maintain checks and balances (leading to hearings held before putative experts) in place of direct discussion between adversarial parties.

Kemmis quotes Rousseau: "Keeping citizens apart has become the first maxim of modern politics." So what organizing principle will get citizens back together? There are many and each in its way has its use. People have organized themselves by ethnic background, religion, race, class, employment, gender, language, and age. In a highly mobile society where few people stay put, thematic organizing is entirely understandable. But place, that oldest of organizing principles (next to kinship), is a novel idea in the United States.

" . . . what holds people together long enough to discover their power as citizens is their common inhabiting of a single place," Kemmis argues. Being so placed, people will volunteer for community projects, join school boards, and accept nominations and appointments. Good minds, which are often forced by company or agency policy to keep moving, will make notable contributions to the neighborhood if allowed to stay put. And since local elections deal with immediate issues, more people will turn out to vote. There will be a return of civic life.

This will not be "nationalism" with all its dangers as long as sense of *place* is not entirely conflated with the idea of a nation. Bioregional concerns go beyond those of any ephemeral (and often brutal and dangerous) politically designated space. They give us the imagination of "citizenship" in a place called (for example) the Great Central Valley, which has valley oaks and migratory waterfowl as well as humans among its members. A place (with a climate, with bugs) as Kemmis says, "develops practices, creates culture."

Another fruit of the enlarged sense of nature that systems ecology and bioregional thought have given us is the realization that cities and suburbs are parts of the system. Unlike the ecological bioregionalists, the cultural practice of urban bioregionalism ("Green Cities") has made a good start in San Francisco. One can learn and live deeply in regards to wild systems in any sort of neighborhood – from the urban to a big sugarbeet farm. The birds are migrating, the wild plants are looking for a way to slip in, the insects live an untrammeled life, the raccoons are padding through the crosswalks at 2 AM, and the nursery trees are trying to figure out who they are. These are exciting, convivial, and somewhat radical knowledges.

An economics of scale can be seen in the watershed/bioregion/city-state model. Imagine a Renaissance-style city-state facing out on the Pacific, with its bioregional hinterland reaching to the headwaters of all the streams that flow through its bay. The San Francisco/Valley rivers/Shasta headwaters bio-city-region! I take some ideas along these lines from Jane Jacob's tantalizing book, *The Wealth of Cities*, in which she argues that the city, not the nation-state, is the proper locus of an economy, and then that the city is always to be understood as being one with the hinterland.

Such a non-nationalistic idea of community, in which

commitment to pure place is paramount, cannot be ethnic or racist. Here is perhaps the most delicious turn that comes out of thinking about politics from the standpoint of place: anyone of any race, language, religion, or origin is welcome, as long as they live well on the land. The Great Central Valley region does not prefer English over Spanish or Japanese or Hmong. If it had any preferences at all, it might best like the languages it heard for thousands of years such as Maidu or Miwok. Mythically speaking the region will welcome whoever chooses to observe the etiquette, express the gratitude, grasp the tools, and learn the songs that it takes to live there.

This sort of future culture is available to whoever makes the choice, regardless of background. It need not require that a person drop his or her Buddhist, Voudun, Jewish, or Lutheran beliefs, but simply add to his or her faith or philosophy a sincere nod in the direction of the deep value of the natural world, and the subjecthood of non-human beings. A culture of place will be created that will include the "United States," and go beyond that to an affirmation of the continent, the land itself, Turtle Island. We could be showing Cambodian and Vietnamese newcomers the patterns of the rivers, the distant hills, saying "It is not only that you are now living in the United States. You are living in this great landscape. Please get to know these rivers and mountains, and be welcome here." Euro-Americans, Asian Americans, African Americans, can—if they wish—become "born-again" natives of Turtle Island. In doing so we also might even (eventually) win some respect from our Native American predecessors, who are still here and still trying to teach us where we are.

Watershed consciousness and bioregionalism is not just environmentalism, not just a means toward resolution of social and economic problems, but a move toward a profound citizenship in both the natural and the social worlds. If the ground can be our common ground, we can begin to talk to each other (human and non-human) once again.

> California is gold-tan grasses, silver gray tule fog,
> olive-green redwood, blue-gray chaparral,
> silver-hue serpentine hills.
> Blinding white granite,
> blue-black rock sea cliffs.
> – blue summer sky, chestnut brown slough water,
> steep purple city streets – hot cream towns.
> *Many colors of the land, many colors of the skin.*

DANIEL KEMMIS

The Last Best Place: How Hardship and Limits Build Community

WHILE THE SPIRIT OF democracy sweeps eastward across Europe, over the Urals, whistling through the cracks in the Great Wall, America stands bemused, with no hint of any awareness, at least in official policy, of what all this might mean. Schiller's words and Beethoven's music resound in Berlin and will again, I believe, in Beijing. But in Boston or Boise a self-satisfied smugness resembling a hypnotic slumber holds the world spirit at bay.

Watching all of this, I can't help but recall certain words of Hegel, whose articulation of the idea of a spirit of history seems indispensable to capturing what is happening to the world. In 1820 Hegel set out to write his *Philosophy of History*, seeking to identify those forces that had made and would make real human history. Hegel paused for a moment at the starting gate to dispose of one nagging question, namely whether America had any prospect of contributing anything worthwhile to the history of human civilization. His answer, delivered without hesitation, was "no." His reason speaks still to America, and especially to the American West.

In a nutshell, Hegel predicted that America would not begin to contribute to civilization until it had confronted its own limits. Specifically, he argued that the safety valve of the frontier had prevented and would continue to prevent the development of a truly civil society. In making his case, Hegel took a position diametrically the opposite of Jefferson's. Jefferson had argued that civic culture was essentially rooted in agriculture and threatened by the growth of cities. He therefore assigned to the Western frontier a crucial and at the same time foredoomed role, which he repeated over and over in a standard Jeffersonian formula that went like this: Civic culture would remain strong in America as long as agriculture expanded faster than cities grew, which would happen as long as there was "vacant" Western land into which agriculture could expand. That this pattern could not recur indefinitely—that there had to be an end, sometime, to the filling in of what white Americans called vacant land—was a reality that Jefferson chose to suppress. In doing so, he contributed very substantially to the Myth of the West—specifically, to the myth that it was somehow a place without limits.

Hegel, as I have said, argued that civic culture, far from depending on the existence of the frontier, could only be achieved once the frontier was closed. More specifically, he turned Jefferson on his head by assuming that civic culture was an essentially urban phenomenon—something that really only occurred when significant numbers of people were forced to stop farming and to gather in cities. He agreed with Jefferson that the Western frontier allowed agriculture to outpace urbanization. His conclusion was simply the exact opposite of Jefferson's; he wrote that until Americans began facing each other in cities, they would not become a truly civil society and would not make a substantial contribution to the history of civilization.

Now, one hundred years after the 1890 census, which led the Census Bureau and then Frederick Jackson Turner to declare the frontier closed, we stand, here in the West, at a cross-wiring of historical currents that almost forces us to ask who we are and where we are going. We mark the centennial of the closing of the frontier just as world history turns Karl Marx on his head, which presumably might mean that Hegel has again landed on his feet. If Hegel were here at this conference, along with Thomas Jefferson, what would he say now about the West and about the possibility of its contributing to the history of civilization?

I'm going to use the challenge of this occasion to propose an answer to that question. I believe the world spirit is alive in Western valleys and to the leeward side of Western cutbanks where people claimed by this landscape have gathered to carry out the business of living well in hard country. I believe that there is, native to this soil, a politics of truly human proportions. It is a politics that we have not yet been bold enough to propose to ourselves. But the hour of its being proposed is drawing near. When that proposition is articulated in a genuinely Western voice, the West will respond, and its response will make its mark on the course of history.

Now, predictions like these deserve to be subjected to a variety of tests, the chief one being, of course, the test of time. Beyond that, anyone making such predictions might be asked to warrant in some way his or her standing to make predictions. In America, we can always make the grand claim of citizenship; we can remind our listeners that it is, after all, a free country, and I can predict anything I want to. Since I hope to deal with a more meaningful form of citizenship, I had better pass up that way of backing my claim. Others can warrant predictions by their training in the discipline of history, but while I deeply admire the discipline, I am certainly not trained in it. It is, rather, as a politician that I make my predictions about the near future of the West. And I think that is fitting enough, since my predictions are about the political future of the region.

I have long believed that places select people. Portland selects people who like rain. Having grown up in Montana in a pioneer family that settled four generations ago in eastern Montana, I have observed over the years how frequently recurring the pattern of my own ancestors was in the settlement of the high plains of the state. My great-grandparents tried Oregon in the early 1880s, but the rain and the overcrowding finally drove them away, and they moved east, back across the Rockies, to the open country that could be cursed in an almost infinite variety of ways but could never be accused of being too wet. Over time, the place of my upbringing came to be peopled by folks whose words were as sparse as rain and whose humor was as dry as the hills out of which they eked a living.

The shaping of a people by the land they inhabit takes time, and in America it has taken longer, simply because we have never been quite sure that we were here to stay. Wendell Berry begins his book *The Unsettling of America* by observing that Americans have never quite intended to be where they were—that they have always thought more in terms of where they would go, rather than of where they actually were. But Berry also identifies a second strain in the pattern of settlement—what he calls a tendency to stay put, to say, "No further—this is the place." One peculiarity of the settlement of the West is that it attracted—it selected—people who were more given than others to escape settlement. Only they would be willing to put up with the harshness, the inhospitality of the land, which grew more inhospitable the nearer they came to inhabiting the last of the frontier.

So the West drew to itself more than its share of unsettlers, of people whose essential relation to place was the denial of place. And yet the places that they came to, being the last place to go, finally took hold of them, drew them down into their flinty soil, rooted them, claimed them, shaped them the way they shaped sagebrush. Over the gen-

erations, these people increasingly came to recognize themselves and to recognize their neighbors in the forms the land
produced. And the selection process did not stop at some
point; it goes on still. People still are drawn here not just in
spite of but because of the hardness of the land.

Gradually, a culture grew out of the land, a group of sto-
rytellers and imagemakers capable of holding this people
up to itself. In Montana we relied on people like Joseph Kin-
sey Howard and K. Ross Toole to show us who we were, and
in each locality there were similar voices. But there have
been regional voices as well, not least that of Wallace Steg-
ner, and now a new generation including voices like Bill Kit-
tredge's. Bill and Annick Smith have proven, dramatically,
how deep and powerful the common culture of place is by
producing for Montana's centennial an exceptional and exceptionally popular collection of voices entitled *The Last Best
Place*.

Let me touch now for just a moment on democracy—
about what, at least from the perspective of a practicing politician, democracy is or might be. There is an unsettling pre-
monition, as we watch East Berliners pouring through the
breached wall to go shopping in West Berlin, that democracy may in the end not reach very far beyond some notion
of equal access to all good things, especially blue jeans and
cheeseburgers. As a politician, I have had my fair share of
exposure to the behavior, and the fundamental insatiability,
of the citizen as consumer. I am convinced that democracy is
steadily diminished, just as the earth's capital is steadily
diminished, by this version of democracy. It is a democracy
that cannot endure, and all true democrats must warn
against its dangers.

In the age of fast food and pervasive fingertip convenience, we have come to believe that democracy is a birthright that is as easy to practice as a precooked microwave
dinner is to heat and serve. But it has never been so, and it

will not be so for the coming generation of world democrats. Here, at least, Frederick Jackson Turner still speaks in a voice of Jeffersonian democracy to which we need to attend if we are to understand what makes democracy possible. Turner speaks of how the frontier created democrats; he writes that the rigors of the frontier instilled (and I would argue selected for) what Turner called a "competency" – a capacity to get done what needed doing – which translated into a truly democratic confidence. Hard country breeds capable people – capable, among other things, of genuine democracy.

But let's take a little closer look at this competence. It is, has always been, and must necessarily be the competence, not simply of individuals, but of a *demos,* of a people. To have this kind of competence, a people must be bound to-gether in ways that enable them to work together. What the project of inhabiting hard country does, above all, is to cre-ate these bonds. And when I speak of bonds here, I do not mean to evoke anything particularly soft or mushy. These are practical bonds, although they do often lead to a kind of affection among those so bonded. But they are in the first instance practical. They are the kinds of bonds that made of barn-building and similar acts of cooperation something that must be understood as a culture. It is a culture bred of hard places, nurtured by the practice of inhabiting those places.

I want to draw attention to two words I have just used. The first is "practice" (and its derivative "practical"). The second is "inhabitation." These words are rooted – quite lit-erally rooted – in the same quite literal soil. Inhabitation depends upon habits; to inhabit is to dwell in a place in an habituated way. To do this requires practice. This practice revolves around certain practical necessities of living in hard country, necessities like a good barn. But to say a "good barn" is not to speak lightly, for not just any barn will do, and this is true of great range of such practical necessities. What was done must be done well or it would not survive — it would not enable survival. Thus, the practices that lie at the root of all true inhabitation — especially of the inhabitation of hard country — are always practices that carry within themselves demanding standards of excellence.

It is these standards of excellence, arising out of the soil itself, bodied forth in certain habituated and deeply shared patterns of behavior — it is these lived standards of excellence that alone give meaning to the concept of "value." Over the past decade or so, more and more people have engaged in a vague recognition of the fact that "values" are somehow an important political factor. This has been a rather astonishing realization for liberals, instructed as we all have been in the liberal dogma that values are private concerns, and no business of the state. But as politics has increasingly become a game of "values, values, who's got the values?" even liberals have had to pay lip service to this new political icon.

But we have not yet understood that values are not something that simply come out of a black box in the individual soul, as the liberal dogma would have it, or from a deep voice on a mountaintop, as the fundamentalists think. What makes values shared and what makes them politically powerful is that they arise out of the challenge of living well together in hard country. When people do that long enough to develop a pattern of shared values, those values acquire a political potency.

It is here that the West has the capacity to contribute something deep and important and lasting to the history of politics and civilization. Simply because we have for so many generations worked on the project of living together in hard country, we have, although we don't recognize it, developed among ourselves certain patterns of behavior, which amount to shared values. The question is whether we will recognize this Western fact of life. The question is whether those of us who call ourselves liberals and those of us who call ourselves conservatives, all of whom are inhabitants of the West, can begin to turn to each other and begin to recognize what it is we have built together in terms of shared patterns of inhabitation and therefore of shared values. That is the challenge of the West. If we can begin to understand how we have been shaped by this country, shaped in similar ways, not so that we think alike all the time, not so that we believe alike, but so that we in fact have developed some shared values that give us the capacity to do difficult and important work together, then on this basis we can begin to contribute to democracy and to the history of civilization.

I say this as a politician who is willing to bet his career on the fact that this is a possibility. I am absolutely convinced that people will respond to being appealed to as inhabitants of a common place. They are willing to respond to anyone who will speak to their weariness with the kind of deadlock that our politics all too often creates. They will respond to a politics that speaks directly to their deep desire to be respected and to be treated as people – people who are capable of treating other people with respect. They will respond to a politics that speaks to their commonly shaped patterns of doing good work, to a politics that says to people on the right and on the left, "You are one people; you understand each other better than you think you do and you are capable of treating each other as if you do understand each other." And finally, they will respond to a politics that addresses their sense of what a good city or a good community might be, and how we would have to treat each other if we were going to go about the task of creating it.

It is said of Athens that in spite of its deep social divisions, it sustained its experiment in democracy and developed an outstanding culture because, in the end, each of the contestants in each divisive issue cared more about Athens than they cared about winning. I am convinced that in communities across the West, a majority of the people care more about their communities than they care about winning. But they have not been given a politics that encourages them to behave in that way. They have been given a politics that only encourages them to care about winning.

Are we capable of real politics in the West? I believe we are if we are willing to face ourselves and our neighbors in a way that we have never done. We need to be willing in the first instance to face the implications of our historical unwillingness to face ourselves. Jefferson, democrat that he was, believer that he was in the idea that democracy could only exist when it was practiced on a small scale, was yet willing through the Louisiana Purchase to engage in the building of an empire. He did that because in the long run he believed that democracy could only survive if it was rooted on the farm and that it could be rooted on the farm only if agriculture could expand endlessly. So he bought into an empire, and our ancestors bought into an empire, and we, by inheritance, bought into an empire. Part of the reason for this is because we, like Jefferson, have been unwilling to image the possibility of a good city. Jefferson could not image a city being good. All too often, I think, we are guilty of the same way of thinking. Robinson Jeffers, in his poem "Shine Perishing Republic," talks about the republic "heavily thickening into empire," and he ends the poem by writing:

> But for my children, I would have them keep their distance
>   from the thickening center; corruption
> Never has been compulsory, when the cities lie at the
>   monster's feet, there are left the mountains.

That has been too much the Western attitude. We believed – we still believe – that we can somehow escape ourselves by slipping into the mountains, avoiding the hard task of facing up to ourselves in cities. Our mistake has always been that we have let empire shape our cities, rather than letting cities shape themselves and, above all, demanding of people that they shape their cities.

But the complicity goes beyond that. Once Thomas Jefferson bought the Louisiana Purchase, we had no choice but to buy both the military and the bureaucratic superstructure that went with it. We can take the attitude of saying all of that has been forced on the West. Or we can say that we have been complicit in it and that we have the capacity to do something about it. The way we will do something about it is to claim our homeland – to say this is our home, and to be able to say "our" and mean it, not only of the people that think and dress and behave like us, but of the other inhabitants of the region who are equally rooted here. When the West is ready to do that, then it will be ready for a real politics of inhabitation.

I will make one final prediction: that when that time comes, we will understand that, like every other region of the country, we are going to have to be in control of our homeland. That means that 90 percent of it can't be owned someplace else. The imperial presence would have to be removed from the ownership of Western lands. The West will not be ready for its own politics until it is ready to claim its own land. The real test of that will be whether we ever understand that the U.S. Senate was created in order that land-dominated regions like the West might assert their own land-based ways of life. When the time comes, when we are ready to develop a history and politics of the West, we will begin to elect a cadre of U.S. senators who will go to Washington to assert sovereignty over this country that we inhabit. Will we do it? Are we serious? Or are we just playing games?

In 1636 John Winthrop, soon to become governor of the Massachusetts Bay Colony, sailed with a shipload of Pilgrims from England toward the land to the west. As they sailed, he prepared for his shipmates a sermon on how they should expect to go about the task of inhabiting the fiercely inhospitable land that they hoped to make their home. He knew how hard it would be. And he knew how, out of that hardship, they might create what he called "the city on a hill." This is what he said to them: "We must delight in each other. We must labor together, suffer together, rejoice and mourn together, keeping always before our eyes our condition as members of one body."

In our time, Wendell Berry, in a poem called "Work Song," sought to capture once again the essence of the enterprise of winning a good living from a hard piece of land. "This is no paradisal dream," he wrote. But in a land-rooted voice of hope that is the true voice of the West, he concluded, "Its hardship is its possibility."

ABOUT THE AUTHORS

THOMAS BERRY has studied the languages and cultures of India and China and has participated in the educational program of the T'Boli tribes in Mindanao, the Philippines. He is currently the director of the Riverdale Center for Religious Research in New York.

PHIL CATALFO is a Contributing Editor of *New Age Journal* and a frequent contributor to *Parenting, Whole Earth Review,* and other publications. He is also a member of the Earthworks Group, creators of the book *50 Simple Things You Can Do to Save the Earth.*

JAMES G. COWAN is the author of a number of books on Aboriginal cosmology, including *Mysteries of the Dreamtime, Letters from a Wild State,* and more recently *Messengers of the Gods.* He is currently researching a Dream journey with a number of old Aborigines in the central desert region of Australia.

THOMAS FLEMING is the editor of *Chronicles: A Magazine of American Culture.* He has taught Greek and Latin at Miami University (Ohio) and the College of Charleston. His essays and reviews on literature and politics appear in a variety of publications.

JEAN HARRIS spent several decades as a teacher and administrator as well as headmistress of the Madeira School in McLean, Virginia. She was convicted of second degree murder in the death of Dr. Herman Tarnower and served a sentence at the Bedford Hills Correctional Facility, where she authored several books.

STANLEY HAUERWAS is professor of theology and ethics at the Divinity School at Duke University. He is the author of numerous books and articles, including *Against the Nations* (University of Notre Dame Press), *Naming the Silences* (Eerdmans), and *Character and Christian Life* (University of Notre Dame Press).

VÁCLAV HAVEL is an internationally renowned playwright and the author of many influential essays on totalitarianism and dissent. He was imprisoned in 1979 for his involvement in the Czech human rights movement, and after his release in 1989, he became his country's president.

DANIEL KEMMIS is the mayor of Missoula, Montana; senior fellow and project director for the Northern Lights Research and Education Institute; and a former Montana state legislator. He has worked, both theoretically and practically, on community building and is the author of *Community and the Politics of Place*.

PETER KNUDTSON is a Vancouver-based writer whose articles have appeared in *Natural History, Science 85,* and *Equinox*. He holds a master's degree in biology, specializing in animal behavior and ecology, and has written on a wide range of topics in science, medicine, and anthropology.

JANE KRAMER has been a writer at *The New Yorker* since 1963 and regularly writes its "Reporter in Europe" series. Her book *Unsettling Europe* won the American Book Award for Nonfiction in 1981.

LEWIS H. LAPHAM is the editor of *Harper's Magazine,* and he writes a monthly essay for that magazine under the rubric "Notebook." He has been a journalist since the late 1950s, and his many essays and articles have appeared in the *Saturday Evening Post, National Review, Life,* and the *New York Times,* among many other periodicals.

PETER LASLETT, of Trinity College, Cambridge, is co-founder and now Advisory Director of the Cambridge Group for the History of Population and Social Structure, and Director of the Rank Xerox Unit at the Cambridge Group.

JOHN LEO teaches literature, theory, and communications at the University of Rhode Island, where he is Associate Professor of English. He has published widely on media, theory, and American Studies.

TIM LUKE is Professor of Political Science at the Virginia Polytechnic Institute and State University. His articles have appeared in sociology and political journals nationwide, and he is the author of two books: *Screens of Power,* and *Social Theory and Modernity*.

KATHLEEN NORRIS is poet in residence with the North Dakota Arts Council in Fargo. She has published two collections of poetry, and has contributed to numerous anthologies and magazines including *WomanPoet, The West, The Nation,* and *Prairie Schooner.*

JUDITH ORTIZ COFER resides in Athens, Georgia. She is the author of two books of poems and the acclaimed novel, *The Line of the Sun. Silent Dancing* was awarded the 1991 PEN/Martha Albrand Special Citation for Nonfiction and was selected for The New York Public Library's 1991 Best Books for the Teen Age.

SANYIKA SHAKUR, aka Monster Kody Scott grew up in war-torn South Central Los Angeles. He became involved with the Crips combat branch when he left school after sixth grade. Ten years, several arrests and convictions later, he continued his education while in solitary confinement in San Quentin, and began writing about social issues at that time. His work now appears in *Crossroads.* He is currently serving seven years for assaulting a crack dealer.

ELIEZER SHORE is editor of *Bas Ayin,* a journal of Chassidic thought. He writes and teaches on topics of Jewish spirituality, and translates texts from the Hebrew.

GARY SNYDER is a Professor of English at the University of California at Davis. He has been publishing collections of poetry since the late 1950s and essays since the late 1970s.

DAVID SUZUKI is a Professor of Genetics at the University of British Columbia. He hosts the Discovery Channel series "The Nature of Things." Among the many science and the media awards he has received are the Order of Canada and *UNESCO*'s Kalinga Prize.

TERRY TEMPEST WILLIAMS is Naturalist-in-Residence at the Utah Museum of Natural History in Salt Lake City. Her first book, *Pieces of White Shell,* received the 1984 Southwest Book Award. She is also the author of *Coyote's Canyon,* as well as two children's books.